Seminaries, Theologates, and the Future of Church Ministry

An Analysis of Trends and Transitions

Katarina Schuth, O.S.F.

Contextual Introductions by

R. Scott Appleby
Victor Klimoski
James Walsh

A Michael Glazier Book
THE LITURGICAL PRESS
Collegeville, Minnesota

A Michael Glazier Book published by The Liturgical Press

Cover design by David Manahan, O.S.B. Photo: COREL Photos.

1   2   3   4   5   6   7   8

Library of Congress Cataloging-in-Publication Data

Schuth, Katarina.
    Seminaries, theologates, and the future of church ministry : an analysis of trends and transitions / Katarina Schuth.
        p.   cm.
    "A Michael Glazier book."
    Includes bibliographical references and index.
    ISBN 0-8146-5861-X (alk. paper)
    1. Catholic theological seminaries—United States.   2. Theology—Study and teaching—Catholic Church.   3. Theology—Study and teaching—United States.   I. Title.
    BX905.S39   1999
    230'.07'3273—dc21
                                                                98-47377
                                                                CIP

For My Father
whose enduring faith, love, and integrity,
sustains us, his family

Contents

■   ■   ■   ■   ■   ■   ■   ■   ■

Acknowledgments   vii

Preface   xi
Rev. Msgr. William Baumgaertner

Introduction   xv
   A. Background   xv
   B. Methodology   xvi
   C. Outline of the Study   xix

Part I. Context   1
   A. Surviving the Shaking of the Foundations: United States
      Catholicism in the Twenty-First Century   1
      Dr. R. Scott Appleby
   B. Reaping Harvests, Sowing Seeds: Vatican Influences and
      National Developments in United States Seminaries
      from the Mid-Nineteen Eighties to the Present   24
      Rev. James Walsh
   C. The Priest as Parish Leader: A Contextual Analysis   35
      Dr. Victor Klimoski

Part II. Mission and Members of Theologate Communities   54
   A. The Mission of Theologates   54
   B. Students and Their Backgrounds: Religious, Intellectual,
      and Human   66

C. Board Members, Administrators, and Faculties   94

Part III. Formation Programs   124
   A. Evolution and Development of Formation Programs   124
   B. Human and Spiritual Formation in Theologates   131
   C. Intellectual Formation   153
   D. Pastoral Field Education   192

Part IV. The Future   207
   A. Perceptions about Church and Ministry   207
   B. Perceptions about Priesthood   223

Conclusion   231

Appendix A: Theologate Ownership and Operation   245

Bibliography   249

Index   254

Acknowledgments

■   ■   ■   ■   ■   ■   ■   ■   ■

An undertaking as substantial as writing a book requires a choir of supporters. All during the research and writing I have been blessed by hundreds of people who assisted me with their wisdom, encouragement, and prayers. Members of the seminary and theologate communities—the subject of the study— constitute the first important group. The research required the cooperation of administrators, faculties, staffs, students, and trustees at all the American theologates. Without exception their response to my many requests for data and time were generously answered. They have trusted me with their stories—their life experiences, their hopes and expectations, and their questions and concerns relating to theological education. Although they are too numerous to mention by name, I am grateful to each of them for their candid views and insights, which form the basis of this book.

The National Advisory Committee provided valuable assistance in so many ways: developing survey instruments, analyzing findings, evaluating various sections of the book, and, above all, offering moral support throughout the project. The members of the committee and the positions they held at the time of their service were Rev. Gerald Brown, S.S., provincial, The Priests of Saint Sulpice; Rev. Msgr. Blase J. Cupich, rector, Pontifical College Josephinum (now bishop of Rapid City, S.D.); Mr. Fred Hofheinz, program director, Lilly Endowment Inc.; Most Rev. Gerald F. Kicanas, auxiliary bishop of Chicago; Rev. John O'Malley, S.J., faculty, Weston Jesuit School of Theology; Sr. Maria Pascuzzi, faculty, Seminary of the Immaculate Conception,

New York; Rev. Donald Senior, C.P., president, Catholic Theological Union; Rev. James Walsh, executive director, National Catholic Educational Association Seminary Department; and Rev. Msgr. Robert J. Wister, faculty, Immaculate Conception Seminary, Seton Hall University. I thank each of them for their time, interest, wise counsel, and friendship.

Several others contributed in specific and invaluable ways to the book. Dr. R. Scott Appleby, director of the Cushwa Center at the University of Notre Dame, took time from his extensive research agenda to write the introductory chapter describing the changing cultural context of Catholicism in the United States. I am honored to include his essay in the book. Rev. Msgr. William Baumgaertner, a mainstay in theological education for nearly fifty years—as rector of The Saint Paul Seminary, executive director of the NCEA Seminary Department, associate director of the Association of Theological Schools, and now professor emeritus and consultant—graciously agreed to write the preface. His name is recognized as a leader of the seminary community around the world. Dr. Victor Klimoski, academic dean at The Saint Paul Seminary School of Divinity, wrote the book's third chapter, which will be beneficial especially to parish staffs and parishioners. I am grateful to him for his clear and informative research, but even more because he is a colleague and friend. On a day-to-day basis, more than anyone else, he has offered encouragement and reassurance; he has shown indefatigable interest in even the most modest findings. That has made all the difference. Of all those who have assisted me, Rev. James Walsh has contributed the greatest share of work. He made numerous on site visits to interview dozens of individuals, he wrote chapter 2 on developments in the Church affecting seminaries, and he reviewed several drafts of my manuscript. His enthusiasm, thoughtfulness, and important insight have added immensely to the book.

Ten years ago three individuals played pivotal roles in helping me with my original book on theologates. The first of these is Elizabeth Burr, editor of this book and of my previous one. Through God's providence she moved to St. Paul in 1997 and for over a year has been a steadfast companion in bringing clarity of thought to my ideas. The value of her guidance and advice are surpassed only by her friendship. I have no way of thanking her adequately for the extraordinary skill and dedication that she has again brought to helping me give life to this book. John O'Malley, S.J., a colleague from my time at Weston Jesuit

School of Theology, has again improved my work with his intelligent questioning, clear understanding, and devoted caring. A decade ago and again now, the Lilly Endowment Inc. has funded my research on Roman Catholic theologates. I am grateful for their sponsorship and for their confidence in me. Mr. Fred Hofheinz, program director in the religion division at the Endowment, has been a consistent supporter and advocate. Without his understanding of and appreciation for my research, neither this book nor my career in theological education would exist.

So many others—lifelong companions, friends, and family— have stayed with me. For nearly forty years my Franciscan community of Rochester, Minnesota, has prayed for me and stood by me. My extended family has always given caring support and shown continual interest in my travels and research. My colleagues at the University of St. Thomas, and especially at The Saint Paul Seminary School of Divinity, provide intellectual stimulation and immeasurable personal and professional support. Numerous individuals, both within and beyond these institutions, have helped in meaningful ways—Ellen, Fred, Phil, Jean, Dennis, Jeanne, Jeff, David, Peter, Ron, Janet, Dan, Paul, Ed, Charlie, Vince, Mike, Barbara, Mary, Dominic, Gene, Colleen, Bob, Tom, Joanne, John, Doug, Carol, Paul Therese, Kevin, Christa, Pat, Bill, Jim, Jerome, Cathy, Chris, Jan, Dick, and many more whom I should mention by name. I attribute to them the joy that pervades my life. God has abundantly blessed me with faith, family, and friends. I am profoundly grateful.

July 31, 1998

Preface

■　　■　　■　　■　　■　　■　　■　　■　　■

Building on the research that yielded her first work on the status of Roman Catholic theologates, *Reason for the Hope* (1989), Katarina Schuth, O.S.F., has completed a second comprehensive study. Both studies involved site visits, personal interviews, questionnaires, and the evaluative assistance of a national advisory committee. The first study, which was extremely well received, offered support and direction for theologates. It analyzed the response over twenty years to the directives of Vatican II for seminaries. As someone who was in seminary administration during most of that period, I can say that the implications for programs of the Council's directives unfolded quite slowly. Our response was ready and willing but often hesitant. The direction was not always clear; we learned from our mistakes. Vatican II opened remarkably uncharted territory. Nonetheless, Sr. Schuth's earlier study concluded that there were indeed grounds for hope and confidence in the future. Looking forward to the results of her present study, we discover continued reason for hope but also growing challenges in new dimensions that we must understand and cannot afford to ignore.

The present study analyzes what has transpired in the decade since the first report. It commands even more careful attention, both from the immediate participants in theological education for ministry and from the broader Church constituency, since it relates the mission and programs of theologates directly to the mission of the Church in the modern and postmodern worlds. This book is the mature work of a mature and dedicated scholar. The author's doctorate in cultural geography and her advanced degrees in theology, together with her teaching experience at several theologates, offer a unique perspective on the scope, the challenges, and the possibilities for theological education in the future. We are grateful and fortunate that her present position at The Saint Paul Seminary School of Divinity of the University of St. Thomas provides a base for further teaching and further research. Her commitment in faith to theological education is reflected in the sensitivity and enthusiasm that she brings to her work.

Just as the author's original study benefited from the perspective provided by the historical essay prepared by Dr. Joseph White, so the present volume is significantly richer for the three perceptive and pointed essays that help define various aspects of the present context of theological education: recent societal trends; the influence of major Church statements and directives; and a contextual analysis of pastoral leadership in parish life today. If in the past we have rarely taken time to evaluate the influence of the context of theological education or the success of our programs, the present volume opens the door in that direction by using social analysis to help us interpret the significance of the extensive data contained in the chapters. Thus with careful attention to the concrete experience of the schools, Sr. Schuth gives us insight into the creative teaching methods used by faculty, the substantive improvements in pastoral education, and the ways in which Church directives have served to standardize many aspects of programs while initiating definite changes. We are confronted with a major challenge to Catholic identity from the ethnic, generational, and class diversity of our culture, together with the challenge to religious belief from a heavily consumerist society. St. Cyril of Jerusalem, writing in the fourth century in his great *Catechesis*, listed five classic aspects of the Church's catholicism. Perhaps we have to ask ourselves again what the word will mean for us in the near and distant future.

In a recent book, *Catholic Education at the Turn of the New Century* (1997), Joseph O'Keefe, S.J., reflects that Catholic colleges have gone through two phases of evolution and are entering a third phase. Each phase (Colonial times to 1960, 1960 to the present, and the third millennium) can be characterized by a broadening in the understanding of accountability to the Church in the college's mission. His thoughts move me to reflect on the somewhat parallel phases for Catholic theologates. The first phase, up to Vatican II, started with the founding (and failure) of many small seminaries in the early and mid-1800s. The founding of larger major seminaries followed in response to the Third Plenary Council of Baltimore in 1883. Later the 1918 *Code of Canon Law* contained detailed legislation for the conduct and staffing of seminaries, tying them very closely to Rome. The context was strictly controlled, quasi-monastic, and the dominant concept of priesthood in the first phase was that of the seventeenth-century reformer. In the second phase, the legislation of Vatican II altered the traditional context radically in directing that candidates for priesthood be educated in relation to the people they will serve. For three decades now theologates have worked diligently to interpret and implement these directives, thereby providing creditable programs at a graduate level with a deep sense of accountability to the Church for their quality and effectiveness. It becomes apparent that we are facing a third phase with the turn of the century, a challenge of accountability to the Church and her mission in the postmodern world with its emphasis on pluralism and otherness, and on the regional and local churches. The new context may be threatening, but it may also enable us to deepen our understanding of the gospel.

If the seminary reformers at the turn of the last century were working to move beyond the older supposition that the priest should have just enough formal learning to administer sacraments, current leaders now are asking questions about the impact of the rapidly changing cultural context on the preparation of both ordained and lay ministers for the Church. For this they will need to call on a variety of disciplines and on the resources not only of seminaries but also of our Catholic colleges, universities, and beyond. The needs are clear. How to define them and respond to them will demand discipline and prayer. I agree with those who say that the fundamental virtues for our time are courage and hope. We have to know how to "make the most of these times" and to meet the challenge of learning to serve future generations.

Rev. Msgr. William L. Baumgaertner
Professor Emeritus
The Saint Paul Seminary School of Divinity of
the University of St. Thomas

Introduction

.   .   .   .

A. Background

"Do you still have hope?" This question refers to the title of a parallel study that I conducted ten years ago, *Reason for the Hope: The Futures of Roman Catholic Theologates,* and it is the question most frequently asked by people who are aware of my current research. Resoundingly my answer to their question is "Yes, I do have hope" about the future of theologates in the United States, although the reasons for hope have altered somewhat and new problems now confront us. In this book I will elaborate on many hopeful signs and positive changes, such as enhanced faculty preparation, enriched program offerings, broader board of trustee participation, and improved financial accountability. I will also note some growing concerns, such as small enrollments, more diverse and sometimes minimally qualified students, overburdened faculty and administrators, and overcrowded programs. In essence, ten years later I believe that institutions are programmatically stronger and better managed, but low enrollments and time pressure prevent faculty and students from providing or acquiring the extensive formation needed for the Church's future ministry.

Since the beginning of this study in 1995, I have searched for a scriptural passage that would capture the spirit found in theologates today. While no single passage expresses it as succinctly as did 1 Pet 3:15 ("be ready to give the reason for the hope"), I am drawn to Ephesians. The theme of this letter is God's purpose in establishing and extending the Church of Jesus Christ. As is true for our time in history, members of the Church in its earliest days came from diverse backgrounds and nationalities, but all were called to redemption and forgiveness in Christ. As I review the results of this research, I find that the overriding motivation of faculty and administrators is, in fact, to fulfill God's purpose by preparing laborers—priests and laywomen and laymen—for the enduring mission of building up the body of Christ.

One phrase (Eph 5:16) from the letter's exhortation relates especially to this study. The author exhorts the disciples to "make the most of these times" by acting wisely, understanding the will of God, and giving thanks in the name of the Lord Jesus Christ. In the great tradition of training disciples as Paul did, theologates aim to help students become wise and worthy ministers through various programs of human and spiritual, academic and pastoral formation. Faculty and administrators are "making the most" of the present situation by encouraging promising directions in ministry and overcoming some of the undesirable trends that concern Church leaders. The goal of this book is to explore how and how well the schools are fulfilling their mission of preparing men and women for ministry in the twenty-first century.

With each passing decade the context of the Catholic Church in the United States has shifted perceptibly, and within the past decade perhaps even radically—with more cultural diversity, greater numbers, and fewer ordained and religious. Nowhere are the shifts more consequential than in the seminaries and theologates where men are preparing for priesthood, and women and men for other full-time ministerial service. Church members are concerned about how future ministers will transmit the faith to the next generation, how their own faith will be nurtured, and how they can become more involved in the mission of the Church. Those responsible for the education of future priests and lay ministers must read the external context accurately so that the preparation they provide corresponds to the evolving reality of the Church. Measures of the effectiveness of their work are presented in this book.

B. Methodology

The data for this research were drawn from several sources and apply to forty-four schools: forty-two of them enroll students who are studying for priesthood, and many of them also enroll laywomen and laymen; the remaining two schools, The

Institute of Pastoral Studies at Loyola University, Chicago, and the Institute of Catholic Theological Studies at Seattle University, offer master of divinity degrees but enroll only lay students. The generic terms "theologate" and "school" are used throughout the book to identify the forty-four institutions that enroll seminarians and/or lay students studying at the graduate level as they prepare for ministry. The two terms distinguish these schools from seminaries that operate at the high school and college levels.

The most extensive information for the study was collected during interviews conducted by myself or Father James Walsh, or by both of us. We visited thirty-eight of the forty-two theologates (major seminaries and schools of theology) currently in operation in addition, the Institute of Pastoral Studies at Loyola University, Chicago. I conducted site visits at thirty-four theologates and at Loyola, nine of them with Father Walsh; he visited four others by himself. I talked with several individual faculty members and administrators at the remaining four theologates, but did not make site visits.

At each school we held one-hour interviews with about fifteen to twenty people, typically five or six administrators, ten faculty, and four or five students. Almost all rectors/presidents, academic deans, formation directors, and field education directors were interviewed, as well as faculty representing various disciplines. Student interviewees selected from diverse cultural and educational backgrounds, included all age groups and levels of study. Altogether we interviewed just over 550 faculty, administrators, and students, almost all of them individually. We also talked informally with hundreds of other students during the two or three days of interviewing at a given school, and with dozens of board members at various meetings and conferences.

About three weeks in advance of the campus visit a letter was sent to each interviewee with an outline of the areas to be covered. Cooperation was exceptional; no one refused to be interviewed, though in several cases faculty were not available due to sabbaticals or off-campus engagements. For the sake of confidentiality, we agreed that individual responses would be anonymous unless the person specifically asked to be quoted. I would characterize almost all of the interviews as forthright and candid.

In reporting the overall results of the interviews, specific numbers have generally not been used, since everyone in every category was not in a position to respond to all the questions and many of the questions were open-ended, leading to qualitative rather than quantitative data. The categories of respondents are identified, and then the approximate proportion of those within the category who answered in a particular way is designated as "a few" meaning under 10 percent, "some" meaning 10 to 40 percent, "about half" meaning over 40 but under 60 percent, "many" meaning between 60 and 90 percent, and "almost all" meaning over 90 percent.

To supplement the field research, I gathered data from other sources as well. Of special importance were questionnaires sent to all rectors/presidents of the theologates. Of the forty-three to whom the survey was sent, forty-two responded, including one whose school closed in 1997–1998; the only one who did not respond felt that he was too new in his position to answer the questions. Rectors/presidents from every theologate also supplied documents such as catalogs, brochures, faculty and formation handbooks, and trustee materials. A second survey covered a random sample of faculty.[1] Statistical data were supplied primarily by the CARA seminary directories from 1966 to 1998. Vocation directors also answered a questionnaire in which they were asked about their methods of screening candidates for priesthood, the criteria they use in selecting theologates for their students, and any recommendations they had based on their interactions with theologates. A National Advisory Committee, named in the acknowledgments, assisted with developing survey instruments, analyzing findings, and evaluating various sections of the book.

Research of this kind, which includes interviews, surveys, and statistics, has both limitations and capabilities. Theologates are dynamic and vital institutions, always engaged in change and modification. Yet the findings represent just one moment in the life of these institutions, not their entire history. At the same time they also convey the generalized picture or the average situation, so that what is reported will not be entirely true or untrue for any individual school. Because any study involves interpretation, some readers may find this one too optimistic, believing that it glosses over serious problems; others may find the report too pessimistic, believing that such problems have

[1] This 1993 study, funded by the Lilly Endowment Inc., was part of the Project on the Future of Theological Faculty conducted at the Auburn Center for the Study of Theological Education by Barbara Wheeler and Katarina Schuth. A total of 216 faculty teaching in Roman Catholic theologates responded to the 1993 survey.

been overemphasized. My intention has been to offer a full and careful summary of what was said during interviews and what the data indicate according to my "reading." The usefulness of the research will ultimately be measured by how well it furthers the development of the institutions from which it is derived, or put another way how much preparation for ministry has been strengthened. Since this research is comprehensive, it enables each theologate to review its own status and circumstances in relation to all other theologates, and to plan and adapt accordingly. To the extent that the stronger, more viable aspects of schools are portrayed as models for improving the rest, this research will have made a worthy contribution.

C. Outline of the Study

Preparing for ministry in the Church in the United States is a complex undertaking. The entire society is undergoing tremendous transformation, the Catholic population is growing rapidly and becoming increasingly diverse, and Church personnel and structures are in the midst of massive evolution. Because theologate faculty and administrators are necessarily involved in these major happenings, the scope of the study is naturally broad. The three chapters of Part I provide an overview of the context in which the Catholic Church in the United States finds itself now. The remaining chapters describe how and analyze how well Roman Catholic theologates understand and are responding to that context as they prepare men and women for Church service.

The first chapter, by Dr. R. Scott Appleby, examines the effects of some contemporary societal trends on religion in general and the Church in particular. It focuses on themes such as the ethnic and racial makeup of the Catholic population, the decline in the number of priests and the rising number of lay ministers, and the ideological configuration of Catholics. Chapter 2, by Fr. James Walsh, takes note of developments in theologates resulting from Church documents on seminary formation.[2] It considers

---

[2] The two major documents are John Paul II, *Pastores dabo vobis: Postsynodal Apostolic Exhortation on the Formation of Priests in the Circumstances of the Present Day, Origins* 21 (16 April 1992) (hereafter *PDV*), and *Program of Priestly Formation*, 4th ed. (National Conference of Catholic Bishops), 1993 (hereafter *PPF*).

the effects of theologate visitations by bishops and assesses the impact of assemblies held for rectors/presidents and for bishops and religious superiors who sponsor theologates. Concluding Part I is a chapter by Dr. Victor Klimoski that presents a contextual analysis of pastoral leadership as it is exercised in today's parishes. This analysis leads to a model for interpreting the attitudes and behavior of parish members and their expectations of priests. The first two chapters delineate the societal and ecclesial contexts in which theologates prepare religious and diocesan priests, and lay women and men for ministry. The third chapter focuses on parochial ministry, which applies primarily to diocesan priests, but also to many lay ministers and to some religious priests.

Part II appraises the mission and goals of theologates, the students who attend them, the faculty who teach at them, and the administrators who manage and govern them. Since the primary mission of most of these forty or so schools is the formation of seminarians, considerable attention is given to their preparation. Many of the schools also educate women and men for other ministries; thus the initial chapter studies those programs and students as well. It examines how effectively the mission statements of theologates reflect recent trends in the larger Church, and so how well students are being prepared to meet the ministerial requirements of the present and future Church.

The second chapter of Part II evaluates the students who attend theologates, and the third chapter pertains to faculty, administrators, and governing boards. Based on interviews and surveys, a mosaic picture of students emerges revealing a range of educational and religious backgrounds, and of personal strengths and weaknesses. The statistical data about students also prove enlightening and show why most schools are struggling to increase their enrollment. The third chapter informs the reader about the academic and vocational status of faculty and administrators, their preparation for teaching and management, and their thoughts on all aspects of theologate life. The functioning of boards, along with review of their membership, is also covered.

Part III assesses the design of human and spiritual formation programs as well as academic and pastoral programs. Considering the many pressures and counterpressures that theologates experience from disparate quarters of the Church, faculty in dialogue with the broader Church have adapted programs both to changing external circumstances and to their students who are studying at them. The first chapter gives an account of why and how programs have changed in recent years, a description of the settings in which formation is provided, and an overview of the goals of the programs. The second chapter focuses on human and spiritual formation programs and personnel, the third chapter discusses intellectual formation, and the fourth deals with pastoral field education. Questions about the content of each area of formation are asked: Which elements of human and spiritual formation are stressed, and why have they received renewed emphasis? What is being taught about evangelization, ecumenism, the encounter with New Age religions and fundamentalism? How does one teach students to communicate with people in parishes through liturgy, faith development, and other forms of spiritual involvement?

Part IV, which concludes the study, elicits from a broad sample of students, faculty, and administrators images of Church, ministry, and priesthood. Relevant questions are, What is the nature of the local and universal mission of the Church in which people seek to serve these days? What is their vision of the Church's future? How must people be prepared to carry out their vision of the Church's ministry? What are their fears, hopes, and anxieties about ministry? What types of ministry are important for Church members today, and what structures if created would respond adequately to these requirements?

The conclusion sums up some of the major issues arising from the research and lays out the challenges that must be met if theologates are to be viable and effective institutions in the future. Where will we find students and faculty, in addition to financial and moral support, for these institutions? Will the schools survive by being flexible and creative, or will being cautious and holding steady be the prime measures of survival? In short, what kind of ministry can we expect in the twenty-first century, given what we have learned about our future ministers and the quality of their preparation for service in the Church?

Part I. Context

■   ■   ■   ■   ■   ■   ■   ■   ■

A. Surviving the Shaking of the Foundations: United States Catholicism in the Twenty-First Century
Dr. R. Scott Appleby, University of Notre Dame

What world awaits Roman Catholic priests and lay ministers over the near horizon of the twenty-first century?

In the United States it is not one "world" that awaits, but several brave new worlds. More than ever before, the hallmark of American Catholicism is diversity—in ethnic heritage, social class, family structure, educational level, spiritual formation, and theological orientation. Readers even casually acquainted with the history of the American Church will recognize the phrase "more than ever before" to be a significant, almost startling claim: Catholicism, which helped establish the nation's reputation as a "melting pot" of diverse peoples, has been *the* leading American "community of communities" since the mid-nineteenth century. A more mongrel church could scarcely be imagined.

Never before, however, have the pastoral challenges posed by the Church's ethnic, social, and cultural diversity been compounded by the proliferation of so many differing (and often competing) theologies, worldviews, and models of what the Church is and ought to become. No previous generation of American Catholics, it could be argued, inherited so little of the content and sensibility of the faith from their parents as have today's Catholic youth. At no point during the previous 150 years of Catholic life in America has a need for the widespread catechesis and reevangelization of broad segments of the Catholic community

1

coincided with so dire a shortage in the number of priests, religious, and seminarians.[1]

Both the challenges and the resources for meeting them come from the dizzying variety of peoples that constitute the Church. The Second Vatican Council (1962–1965) renewed the Church in its perennial task of adapting its liturgies, catechesis, and ministries to the disparate communities of Catholics and would-be Catholics around the world, and to their cultures— the encompassing sets of symbols and practices by which societies variously interpret and act upon the world.[2] The Dogmatic Constitution on the Church in the Modern World described the proper relationship between the Church and the cultures it seeks both to serve and to transform. In creative fidelity to the faith inherited from Christ and the apostles, the Church "fosters and takes to herself, in so far as they are good, the abilities, the resources and customs of the people," proclaims *Lumen gentium.* "In so taking them to herself [the Church] purifies, strengthens and elevates them."[3]

---

[1] Gone are the halcyon days when priests staffed every parish, sacramental theology made sense to most laity, and sisters in abundance educated and formed five million parochial school students. In 1960 United States Catholicism boasted the low-cost, labor-intensive dedication of 52,689 priests and 164,922 nuns. More than 30,000 young men filled diocesan and religious-order seminaries. In addition to the 10,000 Catholic elementary schools and 2,400 high schools, there were 223 Catholic "associations, movements, and societies" with an explicit educational purpose: Jay P. Dolan, *The American Catholic Experience* (New York: Doubleday, 1985), 388, 399, 437. Since 1960 the Catholic population has grown from 40 to approximately 55 million, but the number of priests (45,000 in 1994) and women religious (90,000) has declined as a result of resignations, retirements, and thinning ranks of new recruits. By 1994 the number of seminarians at all levels of study had dropped to about 5,100, hardly enough to replace the wave of retirements on the near horizon, much less to keep up with the increasing size of the laity. Communities of women religious—the sisters who built and sustained the United States Catholic infrastructure for decades— are also aging dramatically and face an uncertain future. See *The 1997 Catholic Almanac* (Huntington, Ind.: Our Sunday Visitor, 1997) 542.

[2] Also see Scott Appleby, "One Church, Many Cultures," *Church* 14, 2 (Summer 1998) 5–9.

[3] "Dogmatic Constitution on the Church," *Documents of Vatican II*, ed. Austin P. Flannery (Grand Rapids, Mich.: William B. Eerdmans, 1975) 364.

At the dawn of a new Christian millennium, several distinct communities and cultures coexist within the American Church, each needing "purifying and strengthening," each requiring its own specialized pastoral ministries and programs of theological education and spiritual formation. With their radically different historical experiences and patterns of assimilation and "Americanization," these various Hispanic, Asian, European, and African American communities face the new century from their separate social locations and at various degrees of cultural and psychological distance from their ancient homelands. Moreover, there is considerable diversity *within* each of the ethnic and "post-ethnic" Catholic communities, divided as they are into generations with differing levels of education, language, and differing attitudes toward the Asian, Latin American, or European country of origin.

The Hispanic "community" in the United States, for example, includes millions of native-born Americans as well as first-generation immigrant populations. Those called "Hispanic" or "Latino/a" hail from Cuba, Puerto Rico, Mexico, and elsewhere; they do not constitute a single Hispanic-American subculture in the United States. Nor do Asian Catholics, who began to arrive in the late nineteen-sixties from the Philippines, the Koreas, Cambodia, and Vietnam, constitute a unified Asian-American subculture. Yet through baptism, the Eucharist, the hierarchy, and other visible signs and means of Roman Catholic unity, all of these peoples belong to one Church.

If their calling to be active members of the body of Christ binds together these various American Catholics, another common experience threatens to pull them apart. Like all Americans of religious conviction, Catholics find their faith and morals put to the test by the secular ethos of mainstream United States society—its rampant materialism and hedonistic lifestyles. Thus the ministers of the Church, priests and laity alike, encounter not one but two major threats to Catholic identity: the threat to unity posed by ethnic, generational, and class diversity; and the threat to religious belief itself posed by a consumerist society that has attained unprecedented affluence for some while remaining mired in moral and material poverty.

The Euro-American Catholics:
A Tale of Three Generations

White middle- and upper-middle-class Catholics are "post-ethnic" Americans, to borrow the historian David Hollinger's phrase.[4] No longer segregated into coherent subcultures, these Americans of Irish, German, Italian, Polish, Lithuanian, or other European descent have formed multiple associations with one another and with non-Catholics in social locations far removed from the traditional formative triangle of home, church, and ethnic neighborhood. If the enclave has disappeared, however, another set of boundaries and barriers has taken its place in the widely differing religious sensibilities of the three adult generations comprising these forty million white American Catholics of European descent.

Only a dwindling minority were formed by "the old church"— the "church militant" of the preconciliar era (1920–1960), with its supernaturalist theology, liturgies, and architecture saturated by the smells, sounds, and images of the sacred, and its burgeoning subculture sustained by the thick associational and devotional bonds of the immigrant community. These Catholics, fifty and older in the nineteen-nineties, came of age late in the immigrant era. Unlike their children, they believe that the magisterium, not the individual, is the supreme moral judge in matters of personal and sexual morality such as abortion, homosexuality, and birth control. Approximately six out of ten pre-Vatican II Catholics polled in the 1996 survey *Laity: American and Catholic* said "the Church is important," whereas less than one-third of their children thought so. The older generation attended Mass twice as frequently as did their children, and were more familiar with Church teaching.[5] In addition, a larger proportion of preconciliar Catholics tended to think of the Roman Catholic Church as the privileged or exclusive vehicle of salvation.

Catholics formed during the Vatican II era (1960–1980), by contrast, were taught to think of themselves as "the people of God," a pilgrim people sinful and flawed but redeemed in Christ and joined by other peoples of different religious traditions in the journey of faith. Change came most powerfully for this generation through the trickle-down impact of the new theologies that emerged after the Council. In many Catholic colleges and

---

[4] David A. Hollinger, *Post-Ethnic America: Beyond Multiculturalism* (New York: Basic Books, 1995).

[5] James D. Davidson, Dean R. Hoge, and Ruth A. Wallace, *Laity: American and Catholic—Transforming the Church* (Kansas City, Mo.: Sheed and Ward, 1996).

universities and seminaries, Thomism was supplemented or supplanted by narrative, feminist, liberationist, and other inductive theologies grounded in the communal and personal experiences of the multicultural people of God. The pluralism of method and perspective that characterized postconciliar American Catholic theology eventually made its way into the theology and religion courses taught in Catholic high schools and Confraternity of Christian Doctrine (CCD) programs.[6] Lost to most American Catholics amidst these rapid developments was the sense of belonging to a Church whose unity was based on an underlying theological and liturgical homogeneity. No longer did the Tridentine Latin Mass and widespread popular devotion to the Holy Father and the Blessed Virgin (both powerful symbols of the universal Church centered in Rome) provide even the illusion of uniformity.

Indeed, the exercise of the Church's universal governance from Rome allowed and even seemed to encourage expressions of the integrity and (limited) autonomy of the national and local Catholic churches. These churches, in turn, participated more fully in the "inculturation" of the faith—the adaptation of Roman rites and understandings to local idioms along with indigenous cultural forms, languages, and symbol systems. Coinciding with a new wave of immigrants who came to the United States from Latin America and Asia, this process of inculturation and localization was accelerated by the growing availability of the new experience-based theologies and spiritualities. The result was the emergence of a United States Catholicism more complexly catholic than ever.

New theologies and spiritualities were not the only developments competing for the attention of the middle-class white Catholics born between 1946 and 1962. As members of the baby boomer generation, they enjoyed upward social mobility and access to public as well as Catholic institutions of higher education. Taking their cues from their professional colleagues, the

---

[6] The fragmentation was perhaps most evident in the effective collapse of an intellectual system—Thomism—that had been inspired in its earlier forms by a spirit of antimodernism. See Benedict M. Ashley, O.P., "The Loss of Theological Unity: Pluralism, Thomism and Catholic Morality," in *Being Right: Conservative Catholics in America*, ed. Mary Jo Weaver and R. Scott Appleby, (Bloomington, Ind.: Indiana University Press, 1995) 63–87.

marketplace, the law, the health-and-recreation industry, and other relatively autonomous zones of public life, they made their own way, constructing their identities at a greater distance from the institutional Church than did their parents. Adopting a de-institutionalized and democratic view of the Church, boomer Catholics reserved the right to make up their own minds on religious and moral as well as political and economic issues. The aforementioned 1996 sociological study reported that boomers placed a higher priority on being a good Christian than on being a good Catholic, and were more likely than their parents' generation to disagree with the Church's teachings, about which they were generally uninformed.[7]

Less religiously literate than their parents, boomer Catholics did a poorer job in handing on the faith to their own children, the so-called Generation X Catholics, who lack a recognizably Catholic moral and religious vocabulary. In fairness to the millions of boomer parents who sought to keep the faith, they were trying to raise Catholic children at a particularly difficult time in history for both Roman Catholics and Americans. As the first generation of American Catholics to enjoy the full benefits of cultural acceptability and economic prosperity, the boomers possessed the capacity to lose themselves in the seductions of a "culture of narcissism" that took American fondness for "rugged individualism" to solipsistic extremes. Some boomer Catholics were influenced by a personally expressive mode of religiosity, based in part on a consumerist model, that encouraged Ameri-

---

[7] Davidson, Hoge, and Wallace, *Laity: American and Catholic.* Pollsters funded by the Lilly Endowment reported in 1989 that 81 percent of Christians polled agreed that "one should arrive at his or her religious beliefs independent of a church or synagogue," and 78 percent agreed that "one can be a good Christian or Jew without attending a church or synagogue." Americans were split evenly between "family attenders" (of church or synagogue services) and "religious individualists." Forty-one percent of the religious individualists said that children should be allowed to make their own decisions about attending church; 73 percent of the religious individualists and 54 percent of the family attenders agreed with the statement, "Church is something freely chosen by each person rather than passed on from generation to generation." Cited in Wade Clark Roof and Lyn Gesch, "Boomers and the Culture of Choice," in *Work, Family and Religion in Contemporary Society,* ed. Nancy Tatom Ammerman and Wade Clark Roof (New York and London: Routledge, 1995) 61–78.

cans to create their own spiritual identities by picking and choosing, mixing and matching items from an eclectic menu of disembedded cultural practices and philosophies advertised as "self-help" or "New Age" religion. The sociologist Robert Bellah described this highly privatized style of religion as "Sheila-ism." He borrowed the term from Sheila Larson, a nurse who described her faith ("my own little voice") as a personal construct, an amalgam of her own religious backgrounds, spiritual experiences, and cultural preferences.[8]

Those boomer Catholics who turned instead to the institutional Church for guidance sometimes found priests and women religious preoccupied to varying degrees with their own personal and professional problems. Not least of these were the career and vocations crises provoked by the wholesale rethinking of the Catholic priesthood and religious life that actually preceded Vatican II but accelerated in its aftermath. The Council charted new directions in Catholic self-understanding and in the Church's relation to the world that were overwhelming in their cumulative impact. The bishops, priests, sisters, and newly laicized priests and religious of the conciliar era had little choice but to focus their energies on the daunting challenge of comprehending "the new Church" in order to reinvent their ministries around it.[9]

It took many years, in fact, for "professional Catholics" to work out the practical pastoral and institutional implications of Vatican II's people of God ecclesiology, its dramatic development of Catholic social teaching and defense of religious liberty, and its retrieval of Scripture as the primary source for Catholic theology. What, for example, were the limits of the Church's new openness to the sciences and secular knowledge in general? How should the hierarchy respond to the Vatican II-inspired call for a deeper involvement of the laity in the pastoral ministries and public witness of the Church? Which of the proposed

---

[8] Robert Bellah et al. *Habits of the Heart: Individualism and Commitment in American Life* (Berkeley, Calif.: University of California Press, 1985).

[9] For a discussion of the "professionalization" of priesthood and other postconciliar adjustments, see R. Scott Appleby, "Present to the People of God: The Transformation of the Roman Catholic Parish Priesthood," in *Transforming Parish Ministry: The Changing Roles of Catholic Clergy, Laity, and Women Religious,* Jay P. Dolan, R. Scott Appleby, Patricia Byrne, and Debra Campbell, (New York: Crossroad, 1989) 54–89.

liturgical reforms—and innovations—were to accompany the introduction of the *Novus Ordo* Mass in the vernacular?

Reformers and would-be reformers of Catholic religious education did not sit idly by while these and other fundamental questions were being raised and debated. Inevitably perhaps, the late nineteen-sixties and nineteen-seventies were a time of experimentation in parochial school and CCD curricula. With noble intentions but decidedly mixed results, textbook authors attempted to wed traditional Catholic doctrine to Sheila-like borrowings from pop psychology, secular values, and non-Catholic religious precepts. Adult education programs were overhauled, eventually for the better, but not before years of hit-or-miss experimentation. At every level fundamentals were ignored or subordinated to the instructor's "interpretations" of Church history; these sometimes radical revisions of the Catholic past were often drawn from the personal faith journey of the instructor rather than from a more objective study of the subject. Influential Catholic educators questioned the compatibility of "education" and "formation," concepts that preconciliar Catholics had understood to be intimately related. Some reformers downplayed content—that is, doctrine and morals—in favor of "independent" reasoning and formation of conscience, while others attacked the very concept of formation, preferring educational methods supposedly more in keeping with inductive secular models of learning and with the new Catholic emphasis on ecumenism.[10]

The Catholic Culture Wars

While priests, women religious, and laity were busy constructing and inhabiting new religious and political identities and revising the curricula and pedagogy of Catholic religious education, they did not command the resources to battle the irreligious trends building in American society during the last decades of the twentieth century. Nor were they prepared to pass on to the younger generation a synthesis of old and new Catholicisms, old and new Americas, that they themselves had not yet achieved.

---

[10] See, for example, Mary Perkins Ryan, *Are Parochial Schools the Answer? Catholic Education in the Light of the Council* (New York: Holt, Rinehart and Winston, 1964) 13; John E. Corrigan, "Catechetics for Christian Living," *Worship* 39 (May 1965).

Instead the social thinning of American Catholicism—the virtual collapse of the old associational networks fostered by the immigrant neighborhoods, devotional societies, ubiquitous parochial schools, and family religious practices—was accompanied by a theological and institutional decentering of the faith. Symptomatic of the fragmentation that followed was an ideological struggle that came to resemble a Catholic version of America's "culture wars." The assortment of professional interpreters and expositors of the faith—the religious, the lay and clerical theologians, the public intellectuals of the Church, the catechists and directors of religious education—split into "liberal" and "conservative" camps, with reforming movements of spirituality and activism such as Call to Action, Womanchurch, and Pax Christi positioned on the left, and Cursillo, Catholics United for the Faith, and Opus Dei, among others, occupying the right half of the ideological map.

The disputes about the legacy of Vatican II that have colored the life of the Church are mostly the concern of preconciliar Catholics and their boomer children. That these disputants and disputes seem increasingly irrelevant to the coming generation seems not to lessen their capacity to absorb the time and energies of Catholic publishers, educators, diocesan administrators, pastors, and parishioners.

Not all points along the spectrum are equally represented—or equally vocal—in most postethnic parishes, colleges, and other Catholic organizations. Ultraconservative or traditionalist Catholics, who deem the pastoral application of Vatican II a disaster, like to cite authoritative (usually papal) teaching against their insufficiently vigilant coreligionists. But most have abandoned their parishes and migrated to an "orthodox" parish, chapel, college, or seminary after their response to Sheilaism—the restoration of the Tridentine Mass, preconciliar devotional practices, and traditional theology—failed to appeal to more than a small minority of American Catholics.

Those who usually call themselves conservatives, by contrast, tend to work within the parish, where some function as self-appointed guardians of orthodoxy. Others join or support organizations such as the Catholic Campaign for America, or the Catholic League for Civil and Religious Rights, where they contest anti-Catholic and irreligious forces in mainstream society. Conservative activists acknowledge the decline of support for traditional religion in the larger culture, but they believe that Catholics, if not entirely impervious, should rise above the situation and provide leadership toward the moral regeneration of the Church and nation. They feel a profound sense of regret, shading into outrage, over certain postconciliar developments, including the rise in moral relativism and fundamental theological illiteracy on the part of significant segments of the laity; the blurring of the distinctive features of religious identity, making it difficult to distinguish Catholics from mainline Protestants in mutually useful ways; the flight from ordained and religious life; and the weakening of the status and authority of the institutional Church.

Those who call themselves "progressives" or "liberals" expend their energies on preserving and extending the reforms of Vatican II. Some pastoral leaders and parishioners in this camp worry that the hierarchy, with notable exceptions, has been insufficiently attentive to the pressing task of empowering lay leadership. The bishops, they charge, have been slow to provide adequate financial and moral support to laity seeking advanced degrees or other training in ministry. Progressives themselves tend to support or staff advocacy groups pursuing internal Church reform, such as Call to Action, Women's Ordination Conference, and organizations dedicated to promoting the rights of homosexuals, retired priests, and other aggrieved minorities within the Church. They seek to move the Church toward positions consistent with the spirit of the Council as articulated by feminist, liberationist, and ecumenical theologians in recent decades.

Progressive Catholics are also defined by a commitment to raising parishioners' awareness of Catholic social teaching and increasing their sensitivity to the concrete demands of justice. Activism on behalf of the poor and the dispossessed is their forte. Some join or support lobbying and policy organizations such as Network and Pax Christi; many commit themselves to advocacy in pursuit of the elimination of racism, human rights violations around the world, and other forms of social discrimination.[11]

While the articulation of "liberal" and "conservative" perspectives may have been a necessary and even healthy means of coming to terms with the most important ecumenical council

[11] On the Catholic culture wars, see the essays in *Being Right: Conservative Catholics in America*, ed. Mary Jo Weaver and R. Scott Appleby (Bloomington, Ind.: Indiana University Press, 1995), and *What's Left: Liberal Catholics in America*, ed. Mary Jo Weaver and R. Scott Appleby (Bloomington, Ind.: Indiana University Press, 1999).

in four hundred years, the consequent internal disputes distracted some of the Church's best minds, thereby weakening its public presence at a time when American society needed strong and unified religious and moral leadership. No simple cause-effect relationship explains these simultaneous developments: the advent of a post-Christian America cannot be blamed on the intramural squabbling that preoccupied Catholics and other Christians; nor, on the other hand, can the turmoil of the American 1960s, the disillusionment of the 1970s, and the hedonism of the 1980s be held entirely accountable for the dissension and divisions in the American Church.

Future historians will address the question of cause and effect. For our purposes it is the results of the simultaneous revolutions in Church and society that matter. In this regard, the besetting preoccupation of American Catholics as the new century dawns will not be the clash of postconciliar visions of authority, lay involvement, or women's rights in the Church. Rather, the Church will be engaged by a far more profound and disturbing crisis of belief and meaning. In light of the extent and depth of this crisis, the attention given to "Catholic culture wars" will come to be seen as an unaffordable luxury.

Beyond the Culture Wars, a Crisis of Meaning

By way of summary, let us consider the world that the upcoming generation of Catholics is poised to inherit. For theists—believers—living at the end of the twentieth century, the secularization process has reached an alarming stage. The operative agnosticism of the majority of professional, corporate, artistic, and intellectual elites in the United States has decisively penetrated the mainstream media as well as political, educational, and cultural institutions. It has shaped popular sensibilities to such a degree that American culture, while not systematically or comprehensively hostile to religious faith, nevertheless undermines its plausibility structures, erodes it ethical foundations, and debases its public manifestations.

Contemporary popular American culture, driven by the secular media and Madison Avenue, trivializes religion, commodifies the spiritual, confuses accidents for substance, absorbs and flattens potentially subversive ideologies, promotes a consumerist approach to traditions of wisdom, glamorizes artifice, scorns self-denial, creates need and exploits desire, celebrates superficiality, and courts violence. Otherwise, it poses no serious threat to Christian faith.

This familiar litany of cultural complaints notwithstanding, I perceive no conspiracy against religion by secular humanists or anyone else. Rather, among too many Catholics there exists a widespread attitude of indifference, whether inspired by assumptions about the irrelevance of the Church or, among younger Catholics, by disillusionment with its unfulfilled promises. Outrage at hypocrisy on the part of Christianity's supposed practitioners, surveys indicate, also has a powerful, alienating effect.[12]

One result of the social thinning of American Catholicism has been a lowering of the religious literacy of younger Catholics. Hastened ironically by the extended period of experimentation in religious education, the dumbing down of Catholic Americans qua Catholics left the generation born after the Council—people who are now in their teens, twenties, and thirties—groping for a way to integrate a Catholic sensibility into their lives. That sensibility now must be achieved, in other words; it can no longer be taken for granted.

Religious educator Tom Beaudoin describes the anxieties of his generation of Catholics, who constitute slightly more than one-fifth of Generation X, the eighty million Americans born between 1962 and 1982:

> While we are a multicultural generation, racism still infects our relationships. While we are a generation that has been generally open to the equality of women, sexism still works subtly even among our most intimate friends. While we are more progressive than any previous American generation in accepting various sexual orientations, the roots of homophobia still run deep, and run religious. We inherit homelessness, illiteracy, spousal abuse, drug abuse, and a hypersexual culture from our parents.[13]

America's thirteenth generation, the most diverse yet, is approximately 70 percent white, 13 percent African American, 12 percent Hispanic, 4 percent Asian, and 1 percent Native Ameri-

---

[12] The former attitude, implying Christianity's irrelevance, is succinctly expressed in a recent article in the *New York Times* which includes "eternal life" among the ideas that have outlived their usefulness. Janny Scott, "Lofty Ideas that May be Losing Altitude," *New York Times* 1 November 1997, A–19.

[13] Tom Beaudoin, *Virtual Faith: The Irreverent Spiritual Quest of Generation X Catholics* (San Francisco: Jossey-Bass, 1998).

can or other ethnicity (young Catholics are somewhat more Hispanic American and less African American than their generational cohort).[14] The majority hails from a middle-class background and is the most educated in American history, but it came of age in a time when real wages were declining, despite the fact that Americans worked an average of one month more per year than they did in the 1960s. Nearly one in three college graduates of the 1990s took a job that did not require a college degree—up from one in ten in the 1960s. In 1993 AIDS was the top killer of young adults in sixty-four cities and five states. On *every day* of that year 25 percent of all African American men in their twenties were either in prison, on probation, or on parole; there were more than 2,500 divorces or separations; ninety children were taken from their parents' custody and committed to foster homes; 13 Americans age 15 to 24 committed suicide and another 16 were murdered; 3,610 teenagers were assaulted, 6,530 were robbed, and 80 were raped; 500 adolescents began using illegal drugs and 1,000 took up drinking alcohol; 1,000 unwed teenage girls became mothers and 2,200 kids dropped out of school. While young Catholics accounted for a relatively small fraction of these statistics, they were nonetheless shaped by the urban and suburban environments that produced them.[15]

In this milieu a crisis of religious meaning binds GenXers together. In surveys conducted from 1990 to 1992, statistician George Barna found that, while 53 percent of GenXers defined themselves as "religious," 70 percent said that "absolute truth does not exist." Young Catholics are less cynical, writes Beaudoin, but many join their generational cohort in feeling alienated from their parents' world of affluence and "modernity." They evince far less trust in reason and "progress," and are skeptical of grand narratives that attempt to enfold within one philosophical vision or worldview the diversity, competitiveness and acquisitiveness, chaos and violence, of the world they know.[16]

---

[14] Geoffrey T. Holtz, *Welcome to the Jungle: The Why Behind Generation X* (New York: St. Martin's Griffin, 1995) 191, 271. The figures are for those born between 1965 and 1974.

[15] Rob Nelson and Jon Cowan, *Revolution X: A Survival Guide for Our Generation* (New York: Penguin Press, 1994) 209–221, passim.

[16] George Barna, *Baby Busters: The Disillusioned Generation* (Chicago: Northfield, 1994) 69; Beaudoin, *Virtual Faith,* 24.

More so than for their parents or grandparents, young Catholics' religious sensibilities have been affected by morally unsettling trends in the secular mainstream culture. Their generation is coming to maturity, Beaudoin explains, in a media-driven and cyberspace culture that trades in images, symbols, and simulations. Radicalizing an insight inherited from their boomer parents, many young people suspect that the constructed self is the only self. Almost half of the GenXers, Barna found, "believe that the values and lifestyles shown in movies, television programs, and music videos are an accurate, representative depiction of the way Americans live and think these days."[17]

The GenXers tend to ask not, "What can I do for my Church and my faith?" or, "What can it do for me?" but, "Is there any discernible purpose to this existence, to the madcap rush for material riches and 'success'?" Whereas preconciliar Catholics and their boomer offspring shared, beneath their surface animosities and contrasting pieties, a simple trust in the holiness and permanence of the Church (despite its manifest temporal flaws), the generation coming to maturity today has not internalized this assumption. From her perspective as a self-described GenX Catholic, a lawyer in her thirties comments:

> Catholics formed prior to and even during the Council seem to take for granted that the Church has always been, is now, and forever shall be a historical force, a relevant institution in American society, and of course much more—the means of their salvation in Christ. Catholics of my parents' and grandparents' generations feel this to the tips of their fingers and toes; it's bred in their bones; they exude Catholicism and speak unselfconsciously from its depths. There is such a taken-for-grantedness about it all that is so foreign to me and my peers. *My* generation is not asking, What should we do about the role of women in the Church? What about the creeping infallibility of the papacy? They are asking: Is Richard Rorty right?[18]

They are asking, that is, whether we must abandon the notion of an objectively ordered universe and all claims to knowledge that appeal to the authority of universal and abiding principles. In staking out his position within the company of thinkers known as antifoundationalists, Rorty, an influential philosopher at the

---

[17] Ibid., 71.

[18] M. Kathleen Caveny, interview with the author. Caveny is a professor of law and medical ethics at the University of Notre Dame.

University of Virginia, argues that metaphysics has finally run its course. Modern science, he concludes, has undermined the Cartesian claim that we find an ineluctable truth and basis for certainty of knowledge by turning inward and examining the process of thought itself. Accordingly, moral "truth" remains merely subjective; neither religion nor morality has the authority to impose limits on the possible results of empirical inquiry. Philosophy is, for Rorty, continuous and coterminous with science. Thus the philosopher must abandon belief in "the mind" as an independent and transcendent reality, just as he must abandon "knowledge" as something about which one ought to have a "theory" and that has "foundations."

According to this way of thinking the quest for certitude and common first principles is quixotic. It, too, must be abandoned in favor of an open-ended dialogue in which hermeneutics (theories of interpretation) are not a method for uncovering "the Truth," but rather a style of philosophy that enables an ongoing exchange of views about what is meaningful in individual lives, in disciplines and cultures. Rorty has described such a dialogue as a "way of coping" with the realization that we no longer sit atop a pyramid of knowledge built on rock-solid epistemic foundations but instead are marooned on a raft tossed about by the churning waters of history, context, and contingency, our goal being to keep the fragile life preserver intact, presumably by constantly chattering about it.[19]

Rorty himself is a liberal whose affirmation of humanity prevents him from sliding off the raft into the abyss of nihilism. Imagine, however, a generation naïve yet cynical inheriting a world, the ground in Being and transcendent meaning of which is denied by its most influential interpreters. Imagine, also, the havoc antifoundationalism visits on the Catholic orientation to reality by denying any transcendental standpoint from which one can judge human belief and behavior. Such skepticism undermines the plausibility of belief in the existence of an Objective Moral Order—a phrase by which the Catholic bishops have indicated that the Church's moral teaching is rooted not in historically contingent philosophizing but in the very fabric of

[19] John E. Thiel, *Nonfoundationalism* (Minneapolis: Fortress Press, 1994) 24–35; Richard Rorty, *Objectivity, Relativism, and Truth: Philosophical Papers*, vol. 1 (Cambridge, U.K.: Cambridge University Press, 1991).

being. Yet for Rorty and the company of modern thinkers influenced by antifoundationalism, the "Objective Moral Order" and other metaphysical assertions have no place in public discourse because they cannot be demonstrated empirically. Such notions, Rorty has written, are "a religious conversation stopper."[20]

How, then, is the Church to respond to an end-of-century nihilism that finds voice not only in public philosophers' esoteric debates but in the lyrics of the popular rock bands, in the current cinema, in the cynicism of our political discourse, and in our own unexamined personal attitudes? In this milieu, is it really surprising to observe younger Catholics raising to the level of operating principles the suspicion of authority and tradition entertained by their skeptical and metaphysically challenged but still believing boomer parents?

For Catholics born in the 1980s and 1990s, writes DePaul University's Robert Ludwig, "The television in particular and the datasphere in general have become surrogate *ministers* for millions of impressionable kids raised without systematic religious instruction or with negative modeling about the value of a life of faith."[21] For these young Catholics a postmodern simulacrum of piety, which I have elsewhere termed "Virtual Catholicism," threatens to displace the institutional Church and its rich treasure-trove of moral wisdom and spiritual discipline. This is religiosity marketed through popular songs, television and movies, breezy bestsellers, and the worldwide web. At its most spiritually deadening, Virtual Catholicism offers its practitioners a pose rather than a plunge into mystery, a passing encounter with the hard-won truths of the faith, and a brushing up against the symbols and stories of the tradition as these are selectively recycled through MTV, cyberspace, and popular art. While a superficial approach to the gospel is nothing new—"Catholicism Lite," as every pastor knows, is one of our most abiding traditions—Virtual Catholicism is more formidable a rival to mature faith because it has arisen as an intentional response to the experience of dislocation and drift. Resembling a high-tech, cyberspace version of what Chicago's Joseph Cardinal Bernardin

---

[20] Richard Rorty, "Religion as a Conversation Stopper," *Common Knowledge* 3/1 (Spring 1994) 1–6.

[21] Robert Ludwig, *Reconstructing Catholicism for a New Generation* (New York: Crossroad, 1995).

memorably criticized as "supermarket Catholicism," it is a dis-
embodied, disembedded form of religion that has arisen in response to the historical fragmentation, scattering, and ideological
hardening (into camps of "left" and "right") of the Church's actual formative communities.

As an intentionally superficial phenomenon, Virtual Catholicism has no strategy for drawing young Catholics into a more
authentic encounter with the depths of Christian faith. Rather
it coexists with other, more powerful formative agents in the
culture, some of which are reconcilable with Christianity, others resolutely hostile. Yet young Catholics want to be drawn in.
Data from the National Opinion Research Center at the University of Chicago suggest, for example, that the members of Generation X are no less religious than their boomer parents; in
fact, they have slightly more confidence in organized religion,
are more likely to attend church and, it may be expected as they
grow older, to participate in the parish. Ludwig's experiences as
a campus minister confirm these data. Younger Catholics' fas-
cination with media and cyberspace, he explains, reflects a concern with *presence*—how people are to be present to one another,
how the sacred is present within the profane, how community
is present to the individual. He argues that young Catholics are
not abandoning their faith but taking it into their own hands by
accessing the use of religious signs and symbols within their
popular culture. Their lack of familiarity with the actual doctrinal content of the tradition means that they can take the
process only so far, however; the music videos and cyberspace
discussions draw almost exclusively on popular religious imagery that demands no esoteric theological knowledge—for example, Adam and Eve, Handel's *Messiah,* the Holy Family—and
has been dissociated from its context within the Christian symbol system.

The challenge for priests and ministers of the gospel in the
current era, then, is to recontextualize Christian images, symbols, and doctrines for believers of all ages, thereby (re) initiating them into a coherent and profound worldview and set of
practices that serve authentic human flourishing. Pastoral and
intellectual leaders of tomorrow's Church must speak to the
metaphysical doubts and superficial samplings of boomer and
buster Catholics alike. They must be sophisticated evangelists
to a *Catholic* diaspora. This is not a call to abandon the fight for
justice in the Church and in the world, but it is to remind
priests and ministers in training that a new set of fundamental

educational and pastoral challenges awaits them. Although people want to belong, they are shy of making commitments that would distract them from other pursuits that they mistakenly believe are more life-enriching. In our time it is not spirituality that is in danger but religiosity—the spiritual life lived in communion and community with others. The Catholic life imposes certain obligations on the individual: to observe binding norms, practice shared disciplines of prayer and self-sacrifice in service to others, and meet the bracing demands of moral transformation. Such challenges, the preparation for which has perpetually defined the task of religious education and spiritual formation, must be approached in startling new ways by assimilated white middle-class Catholics.

The Assimilating Catholics

On this point, at least, much the same could be said of the Hispanic minority, which is projected to grow toward majority status in the next century, and of Asian and African-American Catholics, whose attitudes and sensibilities have been shaped not only by the dominant white American culture but by their own distinctive ethnocultural traditions, some of which remain strongly influential. These various groups are assimilated at different levels to the overarching American culture; in that respect, their pastoral needs differ somewhat from those of postethnic Catholics, who had blended decisively into the mainstream by the 1960s. The rise of theologies of inculturation coincided with heightened political self-awareness on the part of American minorities and their growing sophistication in articulating and advancing their claims to political—and pastoral—attention. During the decades following Vatican II, each of these religious subcultures sought to strike the proper balance between developing its own distinctive theologies and fostering distinctive Mexican-American, Korean-American, Filipino-American, and other such communities, on the one hand, and seeking greater fellowship and unity with segments of the broader Church, on the other. Pastoral and intellectual leaders of the Hispanic communities, for example, have been engaged in developing theologies that both reflect and bridge the differences between the various Latino cultures.[22]

[22] See, for example, Orlando Espín, *The Faith of the People: Theological Reflections on Popular Catholicism* (Maryknoll, N.Y.: Orbis Books, 1997).

While the requirements of inculturation remain strong in these precincts of the United States Church, Hispanic, Asian, and African-Americans have the same basic pastoral needs—for catechesis, religious education, moral formation, sacramental presence, and so on—as do postethnic white Americans. Nor is the crisis of meaning restricted to any one group. The homogenizing effect of the media and the marketplace is far-reaching, penetrating Hispanic and Asian enclaves in large urban centers such as Chicago, Los Angeles, and New York. How can Hispanic and Asian Catholic subcultures resist the secularizing forces of the dominant culture in the United States? How will these subcultures become integrated more fully into one religious body in the years ahead? As a multicultural, multiethnic community seeking to fend off the spiritual side effects of living alongside a "culture of disbelief," the American Catholic Church must locate and solidify the "common ground" underlying Hispanic, Asian, African, and European theologies, religious experiences, liturgical forms, and ideologies. Priests and ministers must be visible signs of unity, reaching out to incorporate a variety of Catholic styles and sensibilities.

And While You're At It

Lest the picture painted here become unjustifiably bleak, it is important to acknowledge that the discourse of decline is an incomplete and therefore unsatisfying description of the American Church in the postconciliar era (just as a discourse of disbelief tells only part of the story of contemporary America). Indeed, future historians might judge the turn of the twentieth century to be the passage to a renewed United States Catholicism. The extraordinary accomplishments of the postconciliar American Church give rise to such expectations. These accomplishments include the consolidation of a century of institutional growth that has seen the Church become the nation's largest non-public provider of education and health care; the gains made in ecumenical relations and, more profoundly, the vastly improved attitudes toward "non-Catholics"; the development of a broad range of dynamic lay ministries at the parish level; and the articulation of a clearly defined set of principles by which Americans might pursue "the common good," at the center of which is a consistent ethic of life. American Catholics are better educated than at any time in the past, and at the dawn of the twenty-first century there are more laypeople studying for advanced degrees in theology and ministry than ever before in the history of Roman Catholicism.[23]

The Church remains remarkably active in service to its members and to Americans beyond its faith community. Perusing the index of *Origins,* the weekly publication of representative documents and speeches compiled by the Catholic News Service, one is overwhelmed by the initiatives taken at the national, diocesan, and parish levels in 1994–1995. Perusing only letters *A* through *C,* one notes the impressive range of Catholic service to Church and society: providing alternatives to abortion; staffing adoption agencies; conducting adult education courses; addressing the pastoral needs of African-American Catholics; funding programs to prevent alcohol abuse; implementing a new policy on altar servers and guidelines for the anointing of the sick; lobbying for arms control; eliminating asbestos in public housing; supporting the activities of the Association of Catholic Colleges and Universities (227 strong); challenging atheism in American society; establishing base communities (a.k.a. small faith communities); bringing aid to war victims in Bosnia; conducting Catholic research in bioethics; publicizing the *Catechism of the Catholic Church;* battling child abuse; strengthening the relationship between Church and labor unions; deepening the structures and expressions of collegiality in the local and diocesan church.

These items merely suggest the direction of Catholic energies in the 1990s. They do not include, for example, Catholic Charities' extensive network of 1,400 charitable agencies serving 18,000,000 people; the Catholic Health Association's 600 hospitals and 300 long-term care facilities serving 20,000,000 people; or the Campaign for Human Development's efforts to organize and empower the poor, with 200 local antipoverty groups working to improve policies, practices, and laws affecting low-income individuals.

This chronicle of Catholic engagement tells only part of the story, however, masking concerns about the gradual depletion of the resources and personnel needed to maintain these programs and their Catholic identity. The shortage of priests and women religious, the graying of the leadership of Catholic agencies and institutions, and the apathy of sizable sectors of the laity are among the obstacles on the road ahead.

---

[23] Bernard J. Lee, *The Future Church of 140 B.C.E.: A Hidden Revolution* (New York: Crossroad, 1995) 9–10.

Only a small percentage of the Catholic population actually participates in or contributes to the range of services and pastoral initiatives celebrated in the *Origins* catalog of activities.[24] By other markers as well, increasing numbers of lay Catholics seem detached from the central beliefs, religious practices, and everyday ministries of their Church. Less than one-third of the United States Catholic population regularly attended weekly Mass during the nineties. A 1993 Gallup poll found that, of those who did, only 30 percent believed that they were actually receiving the body and blood of Christ in the Eucharist; and only 21 percent under age fifty so believed. Meanwhile one-fourth of Catholics affirmed that Christ becomes present in the bread and wine only if the recipient believes this to be so. One need not be a stickler for orthodoxy to be alarmed by such attitudes toward the doctrine of the real presence of Christ in the Eucharist—the central affirmation of the worshiping Catholic community. To describe the situation as a catechetical crisis seems warranted.[25]

The enormous untapped financial, personal, and intellectual resources of the laity prompts soul-searching. Is the poor record of resource mobilization attributable to a lack of generosity on the part of most baptized Catholics? Given the prodigious record of lay support for Catholic schools and hospitals, this seems a

---

[24] Catholic giving reached a new low in the 1990s. In 1995, as in every other year for more than a decade, giving as a percentage of income to all mainline churches, Protestant as well as Catholic, declined. Yet Catholics fared much worse than all of the Protestant congregations studied, including those supporting private schools. A 1992 study by Joseph Harris of 330,000 Catholic households from 280 Catholic parishes, for example, found that, whereas the average family income was $41,000.00, the average annual contribution to the parish—not including school tuition—was $276.51, less than one percent of total income. Furthermore, "the sense of personal ownership of the charities of the church has declined," reports Mary J. Oates in her study *The Catholic Philanthropic Tradition in America* (Indianapolis, Ind.: Indiana University Press, 1995) 26: "A paradox faces Catholic philanthropy. By adopting secular standards in organization and fundraising, and by relying heavily on extra-ecclesial funding, [the Church] has vastly expanded its capacity to assist the poor and to offer high-quality services. Yet in critical ways these strategies compete with primary religious values."

[25] R. Scott Appleby, "Crunch Time for American Catholicism," *Christian Century* 113 (3 April 1996) 370–76.

difficult case to make. Do pastoral leaders possess the self-confidence necessary to welcome a diversity of gifts from the laity—including vigorous leadership at the parish and diocesan levels? Some commentators have suggested that lay Catholics, especially the significant portion with advanced degrees, want the Church to become more open to lay participation in decision making.[26] Others complain that some pastors' attitudes or personal styles lend credibility to charges of an inherent sexism in the Church. Is preaching inspired, liturgy welcoming, spiritual guidance available? Among the newer immigrant groups, are pastoral leaders sufficiently attentive to linguistic and other ethnic particularities in worship and education?

A snapshot of the American Church on the eve of the new millennium offers a mixed picture. On the one hand, the broad range of pastoral ministries and social action programs involve informed, dedicated, and faithful Catholics from almost every corner of society. The Catholic culture wars notwithstanding, Catholic institutions follow a clearly defined set of principles by which to pursue the common good. Since the Council the American bishops have produced a striking series of pastoral letters, acclaimed not only by Catholic intellectuals working in universities and the media, but also by influential segments of the non-Catholic elite in the United States. In its pastoral life, moreover, the United States Church embodies compassion, sustains a gentle sense of irony, and presents a remarkable witness to the possibilities of holiness in everyday life. Priests, sisters, and lay ministers serving the parishes continue to baptize, confirm, educate, and be educated by a bewildering variety of American Catholics drawn from dozens of racial and ethnic backgrounds. Most remarkable, perhaps, they balance loyalty to a universal Church and its pontiff, who is not ministering daily to the North American cultural environment, with the demands of a lay population often unrealistic in its expectations of the clergy or merely indifferent, distracted by a culture of self-absorption.

On the other hand, one finds a thin layer of dedicated but aging professionals at the pinnacle of the Catholic organizational pyramid—priests overworked to the point of exhaustion and thus an increasingly unstable base of operations. The Church is rela-

---

[26] See the various perspectives included in *A Democratic Catholic Church: The Reconstruction of Roman Catholicism*, ed. Eugene C. Bianchi and Rosemary Radford Ruether (New York: Crossroad, 1992).

tively ineffective in mobilizing resources not only politically and socially but also pastorally and ecclesially. If the challenges to belief and meaning posed by American society are to be met, Catholic leaders must develop new strategies for capturing the religious imagination of the faithful and enlisting them in the Church's work.

The local church remains the great strength of American Catholicism. Most parishes have a non ideological core of gifted and dedicated pastoral and lay leaders who staff an array of programs and activities that appeal to the various generational and cultural sensibilities sketched above. Despite splintering of some Catholics into entrenched ideological camps of "left" and "right," most conservatives and progressives coexist rather peaceably within a broad "middle" encompassing the vast majority of active parishioners. Through their scriptural, sacramental, educational, and pastoral offerings, the most successful parishes sustain a coherent religious culture—a "world" whose imagery and symbols bespeak a real (not merely superficial or simulated) presence of the sacred.

Thus United States Catholics have come full circle. Like their coreligionists of the early American republic, today's Catholics live in a society that puts their Christian faith to the test on a daily basis; yet they continue to build and sustain vital communities of shared faith and common purpose. They do so increasingly in the absence of the tight ethnoreligious enclaves and material interdependence that characterized the immigrant Church. At its best the contemporary parish provides the space for reordering priorities, recommitting oneself to the service of others, reintegrating partial truths within a comprehensive system of belief and moral purpose, and rejecting the moral vacuities of American consumerism, racism, and classism.

If the Church is to flourish in the twenty-first century, a new generation of priests and lay ministers must emerge to renew the foundations of Catholic belief and practice. Their work will be fundamental in that they can no longer take for granted a measure of religious literacy among those Catholics who do not participate in formative Catholic institutions, the parish foremost among them. Depending on one's attitude toward hard work against daunting odds, serving the people of God as a priest or lay minister in such times will be either an exhilarating opportunity or an excruciatingly difficult calling. Recent history suggests that it will yield a full measure of both experiences.

B. Reaping Harvests, Sowing Seeds: Vatican Influences and National Developments in United States Seminaries from the Mid-Nineteen Eighties to the Present

Rev. James Walsh

Just as effective priestly ministry has changed and evolved in response to a changing and increasingly complex world over the past thirty years, so too has the art and practice of priestly formation. It is not surprising that the *Program of Priestly Formation (PPF)*, the normative set of guidelines for seminaries approved by the United States Bishops' Conference and the Holy See in 1971, was revised in 1976, 1981, and 1993.

Vatican II's decree on the training of priests, *Optatam totius* (On the Training of Priests), called on each national conference of bishops to develop its own program based on *Ratio fundamentalis institutionis sacerdotalis*, the set of guidelines for priestly formation promulgated by the Vatican Congregation on Education in 1970, and to review and revise that program on a regular basis. The United States Bishops' Conference has charged its own Bishops' Committee on Priestly Formation with the task of reviewing the program periodically and bringing recommendations for revision to the total body of United States bishops for approval. That process has taken place on a regular basis since 1971.

The *PPF* is normative for seminaries in the United States. It is also a living document. As seminary faculties and administrations implement the revised guidelines and emphases of each new edition, new insights, needs, directions, and areas for additional development come to light. That development is further influenced by insights and directives from the Holy See as well as by the experience of seminary personnel engaged in the actual ministry of priestly formation.

In the mid-1980s the seminaries in the United States, as well as in other countries, were in the midst of the Vatican Visitation of seminaries. Rectors and bishops also gathered to discuss some significant concerns about priestly formation. Studies of seminarians and seminaries were conducted. In 1990, the International Synod of Bishops on "The Formation of Priests in the Circumstances of Today" took place in Rome. Pope John Paul II issued his landmark exhortation *Pastores dabo vobis (PDV)* in 1992. These events influenced the development of the fourth edition of the *PPF* (1993) and seminary life as we observe it today.

A brief survey of these Vatican influences and seminary developments across the country, and the consequent changes in the fourth edition of the *PPF* will provide a context for looking at the changes that have occurred in United States seminaries since the mid-1980s.

The Vatican Visitation

On June 21, 1981, Pope John Paul II mandated an apostolic visitation of all United States seminaries. William Cardinal Baum, former archbishop of Washington and recently appointed prefect of the Vatican Congregation for Catholic Education, supervised the project from the Vatican. Within the United States this ambitious undertaking was coordinated by Bishop John Marshall of Burlington, Vermont.

These visits were to be an opportunity for seminaries to do some intensive self-assessment and to be evaluated by a team of bishops and seminary personnel selected by Bishop Marshall from within the United States. The norms for the evaluation were given in the 1981 edition of the *PPF*. Bishop Marshall sent specific instructions to the chairs of the teams based on his reading of the preliminary documentation sent from each seminary. The visitation process included a preliminary seminary self-study; a four-and-a-half-day visit by the evaluation team during which faculty, students, alumni, and board members were interviewed, and seminary life and worship observed; a preliminary set of commendations and recommendations reported orally by the visiting team to the bishop and seminary administration on the last day of the visit; a written report from the visiting team to Cardinal Baum sent on to the bishop or superior responsible for the seminary; and finally a letter from Cardinal Baum to the bishop or superior concerning the report.

Upon completion of the visits to the freestanding seminaries in 1986, Cardinal Baum sent a letter to the bishops of the United States reflecting on the visits. While commending the majority of seminaries for "serving the Church well" and describing them as "characterized by good leadership on the part of their rectors,"[27] he also voiced some concerns.

---

[27] The text of Cardinal Baum's letter to the United States bishops, "The State of U.S. Free-Standing Seminaries," *Origins* 16 (October 15, 1986) 315.

Cardinal Baum's most serious counsel was that a clearer concept of ordained priesthood be developed.[28] Closely connected with this emphasis on priestly identity was his recommendation that seminaries promote the specialized nature of priestly formation. Related to priestly identity, too, was his concern about the growth of programs other than priestly formation within seminaries. Thus he cautioned seminaries against forming all ministers together, that is, mixing clerical and lay students. For he noted that "in some seminaries [this] has led to a fragmentation of the enterprise, confusion about priesthood, and a lowering of theological standards."[29] He added that the very identity of a seminary is strengthened by a significant number of priests on the seminary faculty.

In the area of intellectual formation, Cardinal Baum stated that there were some instances of dissent from the magisterium in the teaching of moral theology. Yet he observed that confusion about the magisterium is a more common phenomenon than dissent.[30] He also suggested that rectors were being stretched too thin when asked to be fund-raisers, recruiters, and public relations officers in addition to their primary role as internal leaders of their seminaries.[31]

In 1990 at the conclusion of the visits to the religious-order seminaries, Cardinal Baum issued a joint letter with Jerome Cardinal Hamer of the Congregation for Institutes of Consecrated Life and Societies of Apostolic Life. That letter reiterated the main themes from the letter regarding freestanding seminaries but also called for clear lines of authority between bishops of the diocese, superiors, presidents, and boards at both union and collaborative theologates.

Assemblies of Rectors and Ordinaries, 1983 and 1986

While the seminary visits were taking place, rectors, bishops, and provincials of men's religious orders were meeting to discuss some aspects of priestly formation that all felt needed attention. The first Assembly of Rectors and Ordinaries met at Mundelein, Illinois, in 1983, and the second at Seton Hall University, New Jersey, in 1986. Those assemblies provided occa-

---

[28] Ibid.
[29] Ibid.
[30] Ibid., 322.
[31] Ibid., 317.

sions for Church leaders in the United States to review and discuss issues pertaining to seminary formation.

One of the issues discussed at the 1983 assembly was the multicultural Church and its implications for priestly formation. Two major questions were asked about this multicultural reality:

- What adaptations should be made in the priestly formation program to serve multicultural seminarians?
- How does the seminary prepare all seminarians to serve in a multicultural Church?

In the discussions it became clear that there was a need for better data on seminarians and seminaries. As a result, over the past ten years the Lilly Endowment Inc. has funded a number of significant studies by the National Conference of Catholic Bishops (NCCB) and the Seminary Department of the National Catholic Educational Association (NCEA) as well as the first comprehensive study of seminaries by Sr. Katarina Schuth.[32]

The first Assembly of Rectors and Ordinaries also considered the screening and selection of candidates, and what seminaries and vocation directors could do to enhance the quality of the seminary population. They recognized the need to identify those applicants with serious psychological problems in order to keep them out of the seminary. There was even some talk of regional screening centers. Today the screening and selection of candidates continues to be done at the local level by the bishop, the

---

[32] Katarina Schuth, *Reason for the Hope: The Futures of Roman Catholic Theologates* (Wilmington: Michael Glazier, Inc., 1989).

Raymond Potvin, *Seminarians of the Eighties: A National Survey* (National Catholic Educational Association, Seminary Department, 1985 [funded by the Lilly Endowment Inc.]).

Eugene Hemrick and Dean Hoge, *Seminary Life and Visions of the Priesthood: A National Survey of Seminarians* (National Catholic Educational Association, Seminary Department, 1987).

Eugene Hemrick and Robert Wister, *Readiness for Theological Studies: A Study of Faculty Perceptions on the Readiness of Seminarians* (National Catholic Educational Association, Seminary Department, 1993 [funded by the Lilly Endowment Inc.]).

Eugene Hemrick and James Walsh, *Seminarians in the Nineties: A National Study of Seminarians in Theology*, 1993 (National Catholic Educational Association, Seminary Department [funded by the Lilly Endowment Inc.]).

vocation director, and the seminary, with help from national resources and publications.[33]

The 1983 assembly called for the development of an effective and collaborative process conducted by the diocese and the seminary for the continuing education and formation of priests after ordination. Rectors and bishops realized that a seminary program could only accomplish so much within the normal time frame of seminary formation. Everything a priest should know and every pastoral skill required for a lifetime of ministry could not be squeezed into a four- to six-year seminary program.

The most sensitive issue discussed was the tension caused by the conflicting ecclesiologies or understandings of the Church and its mission found among faculty, bishops sending candidates to seminary, vocation directors, and the seminarians themselves. Closely related to this issue were those of priestly identity, the theology of Holy Orders, and the relationship between priestly formation and lay ministry formation programs.

The 1986 assembly at Seton Hall University once again discussed the theology of priesthood along with three other matters: the place of academic freedom in the seminary, the differences between religious and diocesan formation, and the necessarily collaborative nature of priestly ministry now together with its implications for priestly formation. The Lilly Endowment Inc. funded study groups sponsored by the NCEA Seminary Department, which focused the 1989 NCEA Convention around these issues.

Priestly identity and the theology of Holy Orders was the main theme at the convention. Who is the priest in the midst of the baptized, and what is his special ministry in the midst of a ministering community? This was the central question addressed in Cardinal Baum's letter following the seminary visits. It is significant that the same question was also a major concern of those charged with the ministry of formation at the local level, that is, ordinaries and rectors/presidents.

The Bishops' Committee on Priestly Formation decided to initiate a dialogue with scholars on this theme, and later issued a paper entitled "The Doctrinal Understanding of the Ministerial Priesthood." This document served as the basic position paper

---

[33] Melvin Blanchette, S.S., "On Screening Seminarians through Behavioral Assessment and Psychological Testing," *Seminary Journal* 3 (Spring 1997).

for chapter 1 of the 1993 *PPF*. The papers resulting from the dialogue were published in *Priests: Identity and Ministry*, edited by Robert Wister.[34]

International Synod of Bishops, 1990

In 1990 an assembly of representative bishops met in Rome for an international synod on "The Formation of Priests in the Circumstances of Today." Preparation for the synod involved consultation and conversation among bishops and rectors from around the world concerning the question, What is the identity and mission of the ordained priesthood, and what are the implications for priestly formation? The purpose of the synod was to "summarize the nature and mission of the ministerial priesthood as the church's faith has acknowledged them down the centuries of its history and as the Second Vatican Council has presented them anew to the people of our day."[35]

Pastores dabo vobis, *1992*

As a follow-up to that synod, Pope John Paul II issued the apostolic exhortation *Pastores dabo vobis*. Devoting the second chapter of the exhortation to the nature and mission of the ministerial priesthood, he pointed out that it is within the Church's mystery, as a mystery of trinitarian communion, that the specific identity of the priest and his ministry is revealed.[36] Thus he stated, "Indeed, the priest, by virtue of the consecration which he receives in the sacrament of orders, is sent forth by the Father through the mediatorship of Jesus Christ, to whom he is configured in a special way as head and shepherd of his people, in order to live and work by the power of the Holy Spirit in service of the Church and for the salvation of the world."[37] The priest's fundamental and primary relationship is to Jesus Christ, but intimately linked to this relationship is the priest's relationship with the Church.[38]

This exhortation affirms that the mission of the seminary embraces four dimensions of formation: human, intellectual,

---

[34] Robert Wister, ed., *Priests: Identity and Ministry* (Wilmington: Michael Glazier, Inc., 1990).

[35] *PDV*, #11.

[36] Ibid., #12.

[37] Ibid.

[38] Ibid., #16.

spiritual, and pastoral. These dimensions of formation are all directed toward the priest's assuming, by means of sacramental ordination, the representative, leadership role in the Church by which he acts *in persona Christi capitis,* in the person of Christ the head of the Church.[39] As the footnotes to the 1993 *PPF* show, *PDV* had a major impact on the fourth edition. It continues to guide and inspire the work of priestly formation.

In *PDV,* Pope John Paul II notes that a suitable human formation is the necessary foundation for the whole work of priestly formation.[40] His highlighting of human formation in the exhortation has inspired seminary administrations and faculties to engage seriously the implications for priestly formation. The Pope's image of the priest's human personality as a bridge rather than an obstacle for others in their meeting with Jesus Christ has had a stimulating effect. Indeed that image has served as the theme for a NCEA Seminary Department convention and an annual meeting of the National Association of College Seminaries.

The development of guidelines for human formation is not part of the fourth edition of the *PPF.* However, the Bishops' Committee on Priestly Formation has already determined that a section on human formation should be added to the next revision of the *PPF.* Thus a seed for the fifth edition has already been sown by Pope John Paul II, and is bearing fruit in the minds and hearts of seminary staffs as they reflect on its implications for seminary life.

Fourth Edition of the Program of Priestly Formation, *1993*

In 1988 the Bishops' Committee on Priestly Formation decided to undertake the revision of the third edition of the *PPF.* The formal process began with a lengthy period of consultation with bishops, superiors, rectors, and other seminary administrators. The National Conference of Catholic Bishops approved the fourth edition of the *PPF* in November 1992, the Congregation for Catholic Education ratified it in December 1992, and it was published in early 1993.

In the fourth edition the bishops affirmed the current direction of seminary programs as per the third edition, but the document was rearranged and some new sections and guidelines

---

[39] Ibid., #43–62.
[40] Ibid., #43.

added. The changes were illustrative of what was already starting to occur in seminaries or, at least, to be discussed among
seminary administrators. Moreover, because of the normative
character of the *PPF,* the recommended changes in the fourth
edition will explain many of the actual changes in the individual seminaries since its publication.

The most significant change was a new emphasis on priestly
identity and the theology of Holy Orders. Responding to the need
for a clearer theology of the priesthood, the bishops set forth a
doctrinal understanding of priesthood in chapter 1, and called
for each seminary to include in its mission statement a "brief
summary of the Church's doctrinal understanding of the ministerial priesthood."[41] Related to this emphasis on priestly identity was the insistence that the priesthood is unique in the
Church and therefore ought to have its own specialized programs
of learning and formation.[42] In implementing this directive, seminary administrators have been trying to balance it creatively with
the imperative to form priests who are able to work collaboratively with the laity.

Another new emphasis was on formation for celibacy and
permanent commitment. Because "the social climate in the U.S.
. . . creates an atmosphere that renders celibate commitment
less intelligible and its practice more difficult, . . ."[43] extensive
attention is given in this edition to the preparation of seminarians for celibate living."[44] Actually this extensive attention was
already being invested at many seminaries through workshops,
planned formation sessions, group discussions, rectors' conferences, and so on.

The fourth edition also recognized four themes, or topics, of
significance to the life of the Church in the United States and
the future ministry of priests. In earlier editions these themes
had been presented as new emphases and considered separately.
In the fourth edition they were integrated throughout the text.
The themes thus treated are

- the changing ethnic and racial fabric of the Church in the
  United States;
- peace, justice, and respect for life;

---

[41] *PPF,* #250.
[42] Ibid., #12.
[43] Ibid., #16.
[44] Ibid., #17.

- ecumenism and interfaith relations; and
- collaboration.

Spiritual formation was placed first in the fourth edition to underscore its primary importance. The importance of professional training for spiritual directors was a new emphasis, and the requirement that seminarians have a priest as a spiritual director was a new norm. Some rectors had difficulty with the short-term implementation of this directive because they had to replace nonordained spiritual directors, who were professionally trained, with ordained spiritual directors, who often were not.

"The conversion of mind and heart"[45] remained the goal of intellectual formation. While omitting the model curricula included in past editions, the 1993 *PPF* did name specific required areas of study such as the theology of the priesthood. In the faculty section, there was a newly expressed hope that "priest faculty members should teach significant portions of the course of studies in the major theological disciplines."[46]

Regarding pastoral formation, the specifically priestly dimensions of pastoral work, that is, the sacramental and spiritual,[47] were newly emphasized.

The bishops' emphasis on a strong priestly identity can be found in each of these sections on spiritual, intellectual, and pastoral formation specifically in the new requirements that seminarians have a priest as a spiritual director, that priest faculty members teach a major portion of the theological curriculum, and that pastoral formation highlight the specifically priestly dimensions of ministry.

Rectors/presidents were exhorted to maintain close contact with the bishops and religious ordinaries of the dioceses and religious institutes served by their seminaries. The fourth edition also cautioned that the rector should not have additional outside obligations detracting from his primary role as leader of the internal life of the seminary, pastor, and priestly model.[48]

The 1993 edition of the *PPF* contained a new article on priesthood in the context of religious life, in which it was said that "formation for religious life must always take into account the

---

[45] Ibid., #333.
[46] Ibid., #487.
[47] Ibid., #398.
[48] Ibid., #462.

charism, history, and mission of the particular institute, while recognizing the academic and pastoral requirements incumbent upon all who are called to ministerial priesthood."[49] The *PPF* also stated that religious who are called to priesthood exercise that ministry as an expression of their religious charism. It acknowledged their different processes of spiritual formation.

Addressing the continuing education issue raised at the 1983 Assembly of Ordinaries and Rectors, the fourth edition of the *PPF* added a new section entitled "The Continuing Formation of Priests," which presented growth and development as lifelong processes. It urged dioceses and orders to establish continuing education programs for priests.[50]

The most important programmatic change in the fourth edition was the insertion of a whole new section on Pre-Theology Programs.[51] The bishops required the seminaries to establish two-year programs for those candidates with no previous college seminary background. Over the years seminaries had been responding to the needs of men applying for admission to the seminary at the theologate level. Many did not have the necessary philosophical, theological, or spiritual background. Many had little experience or knowledge of Catholic culture and tradition. Seminaries gradually introduced programs to prepare admitted candidates for theological studies.

In the interest of building an adequate philosophical foundation for the study of theology, the fourth edition of the *PPF* raised the entrance requirements from 18 to 24 semester credits in philosophy and specified the areas to be covered. To ensure a basic knowledge of the Catholic faith and tradition, the requirement of 12 credits in "religious studies" was replaced with 12 credits in specified areas of "undergraduate theology."

In the same section on pre-theology, the *PPF* also encouraged seminaries to institute intensified periods of introductory spiritual formation, without specifying or mandating. In fact seminaries employ different approaches to introductory spiritual formation during pre-theology, as this study will show. The whole pre-theology program is undergoing development and evaluation as seminaries gain more experience to learn which strategies and programs are most effective.

[49] Ibid., #87.
[50] Ibid., #549–572.
[51] Ibid., #209–248.

Developments since Publication of the Fourth Edition, 1993–1998

The *Catechism of the Catholic Church* was published in 1994. Cardinal Baum in his 1986 letter to the United States bishops had noted that at times there seemed to be confusion in some seminaries about what the Church teaches. Like previous editions, the fourth edition of the *PPF* continued to stress that "sound theological training teaches seminarians to value the special role of the Magisterium in Catholic theology as the authoritative teacher."[52] The *Catechism* now serves as a point of reference for those engaged in seminary education, according to Cardinal Pio Laghi, prefect of the Vatican Congregation for Catholic Education, who made the point in an address given at the University of Toronto in April 1997. While judging the document's level of discourse to be below that pertaining to theological study in a seminary, he nevertheless declared it a sure and concise statement of the Church's teaching.[53]

Screening and testing of candidates for the priesthood continues to be a major concern. A related issue for Cardinal Laghi and many rectors is the application for admission to one seminary by candidates who have been dismissed from another. At the request of Cardinal Laghi, the Bishops' Committee on Priestly Formation is currently working on procedural norms for handling such cases.

The continuing education of priests after ordination, and the transition of the newly ordained from seminary to priestly ministry, are becoming critical issues with seminary programs being pressured to fit more and more academic, pastoral, and spiritual formation into five or six years. Both matters have been discussed at two recent national meetings of rectors. They are also the subject of conversations between the Seminary Department of the National Catholic Educational Association and the National Organization for the Continuing Education of Roman Catholic Clergy, as well as within the Bishops' Committees on Priestly Life and Ministry and Priestly Formation.

Priestly identity and the theology of orders continue to be topics of discussion and reflection among seminary staffs, as evidenced by the theme of the 1997 Midwest Association of Theo-

[52] Ibid., #359.
[53] Pio Cardinal Laghi, "Horizons and Limitations of the Catechism in Education," *Origins* 26 (April 24, 1997).

logical Schools' annual meeting of rectors, deans, and faculty from the Catholic theologates in the Midwest and West: "Digging Deeper: Toward a Fuller Theology of Orders."

Finally, the issue of human formation raised by Pope John Paul II, with its implications for seminary life, remains a focus of attention for the Bishops' Committee on Priestly Formation and within United States seminaries. It will also be featured in the next edition of the *PPF*.

Conclusion

Incorporating the teaching of Pope John Paul II on ordained priesthood, the fourth edition of the *PPF* is the normative guide in the United States to priestly formation. It addresses the concerns raised by Cardinal Baum following the Vatican visitations, in addition to those of bishops and seminary personnel that have surfaced during the actual ministry of seminary formation over the past ten to fifteen years. As seminary staffs have implemented and incorporated the recommended changes, they have acquired new insights that inform their ongoing discussions with one another and with the bishops. From those discussions new recommendations for effective priestly formation are emerging.

The wisdom of the past and present is being harvested at the same time that seeds of future developments are germinating and beginning to bud. Implementation and revision of the present *PPF* are in constant process as the portion of the Church charged with the responsibility for priestly formation continues to pursue the best means of accomplishing it.

C. The Priest as Parish Leader: A Contextual Analysis

Dr. Victor Klimoski, The Saint Paul Seminary School of Divinity, University of St. Thomas

For seventeen years I have participated in interviews of prospective seminarians by which, among other things, we attempt to discover the applicant's motivation. Interviews often begin with the simple question of why the applicant wants to be a priest. Listening carefully to the replies to that question, I have noted that the majority of responses fall into the personal helping category: "I want to help people find God," "I want to help people know Jesus," "I want to help people in times of need," or "I want to help people by providing the sacraments." Rarely have applicant responses mentioned parish leadership, formation of community, calling people prophetically to live just lives, evangelization of the wider society, or enabling the ministries of the laity.

There is nothing wrong with the desire to be personally helpful, nor is it necessarily reasonable to expect that applicants fully appreciate the public demands on ordained leadership. After all, it is the task of seminary formation to expand the student's horizons and to help him embrace an understanding of priesthood that moves back and forth between one-to-one helping and the expectations of leadership in a public forum. While one might argue that it is the very personal character of ministry that draws many to priesthood, an essential part of the formation task is to establish that such personalism never substitutes for the requirement that pastors provide decisive, informed public leadership. Personal and public understandings of ministerial leadership are not opposed to each other, but they do exist in tension. This essay attempts to identify that tension by reflecting on the expectations that parishioners tend to have of their parishes and "their priests."

The sense of proprietary ownership of the priest is not just a colloquial expression. Parishioners generally believe that priests are ordained to be among them in service. They rely on their priests for spiritual leadership; for linking faith and life; for centering the parish community; and for recognizing the challenges they face in raising families, cultivating a marriage or other relationships, earning a living, staying true to their values, growing old, and dealing with their fears. They want *their priests* to be wise enough to envision a faithful response to the gospel and compassionate enough to realize what that entails.

The expectations of parishioners derive from memory and culture. It is the memory of the faith community that generates images of the priest. Some images are based on theological definitions, but most are the products of legend passed down from generation to generation. "That one was a fine priest," grandmother might say over a Sunday meal as she relates stories about priests who carried out their ministries in ways that set them apart from the ordinary. My own parents hosted every priest who ever served our small rural parish during my childhood and youth. Those relationships as interpreted by my parents gave me clear criteria for determining whether the current pastor was good or unacceptable. A result of communal memory, such standards are notably unobjective; yet their influence is significant.

The expectations that are shaped by culture have a similar impact, though they are far more subtle at least in the initial analysis. We would like to believe that religion and its practices stand aloof from the formative pressures of the larger society in which we live. Our views of the Church, of parish life, of priests, and of lay ministers come to us, so we may think, from a theological core of ideas carefully cultivated and systematically indoctrinated into the Catholic imagination. We are Americans, however, living in a complex, urbanized society where information rules the public square, and where tastes, points of view, and definitions of the good, the true, and the beautiful can be transformed within twenty-four hours. A colleague who works closely on issues of media and culture, for example, asserted that in the space of less than a day, Diana Spencer changed status from elite, self-absorbed socialite fallen from the House of Windsor to princess of the worldwide proletariat.

It should not surprise anyone, then, that our views of religion and its official representatives are winnowed to a significant degree by the winds of modern culture. How people belong to a Catholic parish and expectations that membership generates are profoundly influenced by the attitudes, values, and dispositions we carry as late-twentieth-century Americans. We are accustomed to examining and judging the behavior of our public leaders. We have been conditioned to deal with issues on the basis of brief sound bites and high visual impact in the conviction that opinions are relatively neutral. As a result, our criteria for what makes a good pastor or good parish bear the marks of how we assess almost every other aspect of modern life.

1. What Does a Parish Look for in Its Priests?

It would be presumptuous to make sweeping generalizations about what a parish wants in a priest. Expectations vary for a host of reasons. A parish, for instance, that has long resisted change and prides itself on adherence to older modes of worship and Catholic observance will look for clergy who hold compatible views. Another parish ten miles away, based on the ideal of a fully empowered laity, will prefer clergy who can cultivate a broad array of ministries. Expectations of priests vary as well within parishes. Older parishioners, for example, are often able to tolerate behaviors in their pastors that can quickly become an obstacle to the cooperation and participation of younger members. These intraparish variations emerge as well according to the level of involvement and length of association one has with the parish. Those who are deeply involved in parish life, or have a long association with a parish, tend to balance their expectations of a pastor with their more fundamental commitment to the parish community. As a result, they may be more tolerant of variations in pastoral leadership styles than those less committed to the parish or those more recently arrived who have only occasional contact with the pastor either in a liturgical setting or in sporadic personal encounters.

Finally, expectations of priests will often vary according to one's life circumstances. In the course of my parish research, I have noticed that people's participation in a parish seems to follow a cycle marked by levels of activity based on needs, limitations of time and energy, the state of one's spiritual development, attitudes toward particular church issues, and other factors that draw one into parish life or prompt one to stay on the periphery. When people have distanced themselves from parish involvement, having someone say Mass unobtrusively and preach sensibly may embrace the fullness of their expectations. When for a variety of reasons that distanced relationship shifts to one more invested in parish life, expectations of pastoral behaviors can refocus on issues of leadership, engagement with the community and its larger society, or insights into cultivating spiritual growth amidst the clamor of modern culture.

2. A Model for Interpreting Parishioner Membership and Resulting Expectations of Priests

This range of variables influencing parishioner expectations of priests has generated a model that might be helpful for analyzing those expectations in light of different categories of parish membership (figure 1). The model has developed as a result of reflection on my recent research in two parishes, my observations drawn from broad research on Catholic life in the United States, and my impressions from working with students who are also professional lay ministers. The model describes the ways in which people relate to an "average parish" as members. "Average" here allows for the fact that the model does not describe every parish but offers a heuristic structure as the context from which parishioner expectations of priests emerge.

At the center of this model are *insiders*, that group of parishioners who are deeply involved in parish life, who would define the parish as one of their primary areas for social life and commitment, and have personal access to the pastor and members of his staff. They often comprise the people who occupy positions of leadership or have been removed from leadership by another group of insiders. They may be liberal or conservative in their outlook, may have active or dormant influence in parish decision-making, tend to be very aware of the internal workings of the parish, and have strong opinions about parish practices and policies. *Insiders* will usually also be aware of larger church issues, especially those affecting polity and shaping attitudes. *Insiders* tend to be older, long-term members of a parish with an extensive record of contributed service. However, an *insider* might also be a relative newcomer to the parish who makes getting involved in the parish a priority, and gaining access to influence a part of his or her personal agenda. *Insiders* are a primary source of feedback for pastors and staff members. As a result, they tend to be thought of as representing "parish opinion" on important matters.

Figure 1
A Model of Parishioner Membership

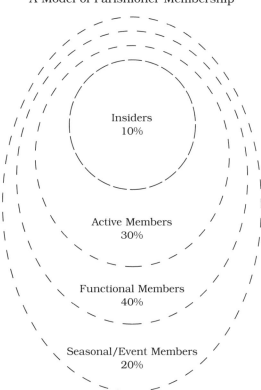

Insiders
10%

Active Members
30%

Functional Members
40%

Seasonal/Event Members
20%

Active members are those people who regularly attend Sunday Mass and can be counted on to volunteer for parish-sponsored activities or events. They tend to be steady in their connection to the parish without much interest in getting enmeshed in its internal workings or politics. Because of their loyalty and commitment, *active members* may become *insiders* but do not do so necessarily. Often content with the extent of their participation, they look to the parish both for family spiritual resources and for the opportunity to make social connections with others who share their values and their desire for some type of community.

Functional members include a wide variety of people. Membership is functional in the organizational sense of the term coined by early twentieth-century social theorist Ferdinand Tonnies. He identified two essential forms of social arrangements: those based on a familial model according to which the quality and depth of relationship takes precedence in determining group interaction, and those based on an organizational model according to which specific contractual-like outcomes define the relationship one has with the group. *Functional members* may be individuals who belong to the parish primarily to have a place to go on weekends for Mass or to receive the sacraments. They may or may not participate in programs or social events of the parish. If they do, it is to answer a specific need: The children need religious instruction, they are going to get married, they have experienced a death, or they like to sing and enjoy the current choir director. Some *functional members* may become *active members* especially if, as mentioned above, they are among those who have previously cycled out of active involvement for some reason. The functional purpose that brought these people to the parish may be an occasion for them to reestablish themselves as *active members*.

Finally there are *seasonal/event members*. Interestingly these individuals will likely identify with a particular parish and may even contribute financially from time to time, but their participation is limited to traditional Christmas and Easter liturgies or to events involving family, friends, and neighbors. They seldom, if ever, have direct contact with the pastor or with members of the pastoral staff, and tend to express skepticism about the value of organized religion, even if married to a spouse who is at another level of membership. Individuals who have been burned by their experience at some other level of membership may retreat to *seasonal/event membership* in an attempt to regroup and reconsider how they will relate to the parish (or a parish) in the future.

The dotted lines in the model (figure 1) represent the permeability of membership categories. People seem to move in and out of categories as their lives change, as pastoral leadership changes, or as they experience the need (or lack of need) for the parish in their own spiritual and human development. The denser line around *insiders* suggests that it is less susceptible to penetration than other categories are. *Insiders* are tempted to be exclusive. They enjoy being at the hub and exercising influence on pastoral decisions. Access to the circle of insiders is guarded carefully by them. "We are just looking out for the good of the whole parish," an *insider* might say while promoting his or her own agenda with fierce determination.

3. Significance of the Model for Contextual Analysis of Pastoral Leadership

While one may take issue with aspects of this model, including the definition of categories and the distribution percentages in an "average parish," it seems evident that a larger percentage of parishioners relate to the parish from a distance than from close involvement. Given this assessment, priests who view parishes primarily as congregations of *insiders* and *active members* may be surprised at the lack of response to their initiatives. Moreover if the leadership style of the parish pastor is premised on having a congregation made up of *insiders* and *active members*, the priest's leadership may fail to motivate a majority who consider the parish theirs but in ways quite distinct from those more intimately involved with parish life.

The model suggests that the "personal helpfulness" approach to ministry can distract the priest from considering how he as leader will span the categories of membership and draw people into a meaningful, sustained relationship with the parish as a center of faith and fellowship. The model is a reminder that the ideal parish may well exist in one's mind only, or in a remembered past that does not correspond to the reality of the modern "average parish." The "average parish" calls for skills to assess, analyze, and strategize in contexts made complex by the types of relationships that define them. It would be tempting to surround oneself as a pastor with nothing but *insiders* and *active members*, despite the tensions that can exist with those groups. An experienced pastor reviewing this article suggested that, while focusing exclusively on *insiders* and *active members* may be shortsighted, it is often from those groups alone that the pastor receives affirmation and feedback. Their commitment will obviously remain an important force in setting the agenda for pastoral leadership. But if the modern parish is to be successful in its efforts to offer an alternative mode of social life and affiliation, and serious about evangelization, then its leadership needs to attend carefully to the other voices that comprise parish membership.

4. Factors Shaping Contemporary Catholic Parish Life

Apart from the impact of different levels of parish membership, what other factors influence expectations of a priest's pastoral leadership? From my research and reflection, five such factors seem to stand out.

The first factor has to do with the very *meaning of parish membership*. The minimal criteria entail signing up, receiving and using contribution envelopes, and attending Mass. If one asks Catholics why they belong, their answers are often intuitive and idiosyncratic. Many would connect membership with their responsibilities as baptized Catholics. Beyond that there is no broad consensus on how membership connects one to a community of believers, or images the larger Church, or is the environment in which one encounters the Lord. Catholics are as likely as other Christian believers to assert that, while membership may be important, their spiritual lives do not depend on it.

This assertion reflects shifts in religious attitudes within American society directly related to notions of individual freedom that have flourished during the past thirty years. Wade Clark Roof's research on the baby boomers provides persuasive evidence that the freedom to make up one's own mind on virtually every issue is now taken for granted no matter where one falls along the liberal-conservative continuum. Thus membership in a parish is no longer assumed to be the principal means of gaining access to a spiritual relationship with God. Moreover what I as an individual determine is sufficient for parish membership takes precedence over external criteria imposed by an institutional authority (see factor 4 discussed below).

The uncertainty over the meaning of parish membership also reflects the fact that membership in a particular parish is no longer passed down as part of a family legacy. Where one was baptized, catechized, confirmed, and married will likely not be the same place where one goes to church. As parish memberships change with each change of household location or as a result of revising one's preferences regarding liturgy, programs, or leadership, membership becomes a matter of personal choice rather than communal obligation, even though one of the reasons for membership is to find community.

For many people today the desire for community is more theoretical than real. Few will have grown up, as I did, in a small town where the parish was a critical social center. Those who belonged to my parish knew that their grandparents had built the parish from the ground up. Parishioners knew each other, knew each other's business, participated in raising each other's children, and shared a common history. When I think of parish as community, my attitudes are therefore strongly influenced by this profound experience of community. The language of community that so characterizes our current descriptions of parish life, however, has less of a personal reference point for people. Drives toward independence and anonymity contribute to a bittersweet tension between wanting to draw close to a group of people with the purpose of forming affiliative relationships, and resisting the intrusions that can occur when such relationships exist. While there are cognitive aspects to the notion of community, it is ultimately an affective phenomenon. Therefore the finely crafted parish mission statement affirming the parish as a place of hospitality must be matched by consistent actions that create a feeling of being welcomed and of belonging to the group.

A second factor in contemporary Catholic life is *the general absence of a systematic understanding of Roman Catholicism.* This absence reflects both the movement away from catechism-based instruction of the young that emerged in the 1970s without an adequate substitute, and the relative absence of a sustained commitment to adult formation in Roman Catholicism. Consequently people's formal belief systems tend to be more thematic than systematic, to be directed by ideological preference, to be often predominantly subjective, and to find their reference point in personal history and experience. This does not mean that Catholics are religiously illiterate; they simply are no longer trained "by the book." Their religious conclusions reflect a distillation of what they have received from the Church in terms of formal religious instruction (which typically ends in high school) and evangelical exhortation interacting with their own analyses of personal and societal experiences. Laity have formed opinions on a wide range of issues and will not be persuaded to abandon their conclusions unless the contrary evidence is compelling and persuasive. Even the most conservative Catholic is far less docile than his or her predecessors in faith of two generations ago.

This independence of mind is in part the consequence of a well-educated citizenry. Priests no longer preach to peasant audiences made up of those whose only source of authoritative data stands in the pulpit. Rather, congregations are populated by large numbers of college-educated and professionally trained men and women who have access to news and information on a twenty-four-hour basis. Although these people may not have had a formal course of study in theology, there is an avid readership among the laity for religious books and articles, especially in the area of spirituality. Despite our inattention as a Church to the lifelong education of adults in the faith, Catholics are thinking critically about nearly every issue important to a theological view of reality. In addition, as Americans we are overwhelmed with information. We might argue about the quality of its sources or the discipline to deal with it critically; nonetheless we know more and are exposed to more more quickly, and from more sources, than our predecessors of even two generations ago. The impact this has had and continues to have on an intellectual sense of what it means to be Catholic has yet to be imagined or addressed sufficiently.

The third factor to be noted about contemporary Catholic life is *a decline in tolerance and acceptance of difference.* Although the acceptance of differences of opinion within Catholicism has had an uneven history, there was a consensus once that, however we might approach this or that question of faith and practice, we were bound together somehow by our common Catholic identity. Increasingly that is not the case. Someone recently reported the existence of a website dedicated to ferreting out those who are perceived to lack the full measure of orthodoxy. A series of questions is offered as well as a full menu detailing how to report up the chain of command those who fail to meet the test. The Mother Angelica phenomenon offers another example of mistrust and distrust of other Catholics being acted out in the name of loyalty to Rome. On the Left one finds journals and periodicals in which any conservative position is skewered as reactionary and recidivist. Until a few years ago I believed that such acrimony would fall away before the Eucharist and that people divided by their points of view would find a common home in sacramental celebration. Yet just the opposite appears to be true.

The Eucharist has become the premier battleground for allegiance to this or that position. One selects with care where and with whom one celebrates the Eucharist.

This gloomy perspective on our ability to think beyond differences must be read in light of a sign that is far more hopeful. The Catholic Common Ground Initiative launched by the late Cardinal Bernardin touched a live nerve among many Catholics. The motives behind this effort to bridge hostility among Catholics strike some as not only the search for common ground but also the attempt to reclaim what was once Catholic common sense. Civility in argument, efforts to listen authentically, the assumption of good will, and an adherence to core values drawing on our deepest religious beliefs are hardly revolutionary incitements by the late cardinal and the colleagues he invited to help launch Common Ground. They are the soul of Roman Catholicism at its best.

A fourth factor that exerts a significant influence on contemporary Catholics is their *attitude toward authority*. The cultural shift that occurred in Western society over the past thirty years has engendered a nearly reflexive antiauthoritarian disposition. If not antiauthoritarian, it is minimally very selective when deciding whose word counts on any matter. This frame of mind spans the ideological continuum, with conservatives and progressives alike exercising varying degrees of selectivity as to what they will or will not accept from someone in authority. In one parish that prides itself on lay leadership, any exercise of leadership from the pastor is denounced as a retreat to pre-Vatican II thinking. There are priests, many newly ordained, who vow that they will "simply lay down the law" and thus regain control over an unruly laity. Some laity welcome that sort of pastor rule; most perceive it as odd and then respond either by ignoring it, going dormant, moving to another parish, or even looking into another denomination. There is little to suggest that this attitude toward authority will be reversed culturally any time soon.

Such varied attitudes toward authority should not evoke acquiescence, a communal throwing up of our hands and hoping for the best. Instead we need to struggle with the meaning of authority and the ways in which authority functions. The era of "because Father says" is dead, though remnants can be found in most dioceses, and informal reports from seminaries suggest that a number of candidates are ready to be its advocates. These data do not validate a movement to reclaim a relegated style of parishioner management. Yet they may delay a serious attempt to reengage Catholics around the thoughtful consideration of the many forms of authority and the role of authority in serving unity and fellowship for the sake of the Gospel.

Finally, a discussion of key factors shaping contemporary Catholic life would be incomplete without addressing the issue of *cultural diversity*, which plays out on at least two critical levels. The first level involves the profound impact of ethnicity and gender on our experience as Americans living at the end of the twentieth century. Those of us who grew up on the rhetoric of the American melting pot have lived to see that that notion was shortsighted at best, malicious at worst. This essay has been written from my own experience, which is basically that of the majority group. My worldview has been little influenced by the experience of ethnic groups who are not white in color or European in heritage. My father was an immigrant from Lithuania who refused to speak about the Old Country and its ways because we were destined to forget all that in order to become Americans. The new immigrants—and those ethnic groups who predated the surge of migration in the last two centuries—are not as docile. They embrace their Americanism without repudiating their pasts. The images, the myths, and the ways of understanding human history are no longer controlled by the majority group. Even in the Midwest, where we sometimes act as though the tides of ethnic change will never touch our shores, we are awakening to the challenges of being receptive to the new immigrants and to ethnically diverse peoples in a spirit not merely of toleration but of openness to new insights into what it means to believe in and live out of the Gospel. We have yet to be fully tested or to understand fully the impact of this shift in cultural assumptions.

Regarding gender, we continue to struggle with how to think about gender differences and perspectives in other than an accommodationist fashion. That is, we have yet to become theologically aware of how mutuality between women and men informs who we are and nurtures our potential as human beings in our quest to realize the Gospel and its imperatives. We are eager for "peace" on this issue without, it seems, grappling with the fact that it is women who are most active in the Church in terms of participation, volunteering, and lifetime careers of service. The attempts to equate feminism solely with the most radical political agenda fail to consider how women's ways of knowing and being enable all of us to delve deeper into the mystery of God and the message of the Gospel.

The second level of cultural diversity has to do with ways of learning. Many of us assume that the main conduit for learning is the written text. We cherish books and the written word as the preeminent way in which ideas are shared and contribute to our progress. The text represents discipline and a careful analysis of ideas based on a culling of information and argument. There are those who point out, however, that text is only one way of learning. For many people—including those raised in cultural settings other than white and Western—learning is largely oral-based. It rests on the communication of traditions passed from generation to generation through stories that embody key values, ideals, and convictions. Even within the majority culture of the United States, the power of the written text competes with and is often overshadowed by the visual media. It is unproductive to skewer television—the primary agent of visualization—which is simply a permanent fact of contemporary life. People have become accustomed to receiving critical information visually, and using that information as an important source in reaching conclusions about a host of social issues. We can lament that people do not read more; the fact is they do not. Lament is a feeble response when hard thinking about strategies for learning is what is called for. We may deplore her results, but Mother Angelica fully understands that the medium is often the message.

5. What Do People Expect from Parish Membership?

While these five factors shaping contemporary Catholic life pose major challenges to new generations of clergy, they do not exhaust the subject of what Catholics expect from their priests. On the contrary, they are best read as a backdrop against which to understand expectations of priests that seem fairly common in parish communities. This has certainly been the import of my own research in two urban parishes. Generalizing from that limited formal study of parishes as well as from other research on Catholics, I would identify a relatively short list of expectations Catholics have of "their priests." These expectations are often channeled through their expectations of the parish. Although the priest is not the parish, it is clear that as public leader he influences the ethos of the parish significantly. He should not be expected to bear full responsibility for creating a vibrant parish; that would be theologically and pastorally shortsighted. In fact a pastor recently told me that his success will be measured by the extent to which efforts developed during his tenure continue after he is reassigned. Yet the priest cannot minimize his responsibility for holding up a "vision" before the parish and for eliciting or mentoring the talent to make the vision real.

People expect a *consistent, tangible sense of welcome and hospitality* from the parish, even if they are only functional members. This involves being recognized, valued, and made to feel at home. People are keenly aware of situations in which they are shunted aside or merely tolerated. They may anticipate such treatment in other settings but take great offense when it occurs in the local parish. This expectation expresses people's search for community—their wish to relate to others with whom they share certain values and convictions, and to belong to a group where their presence or absence matters. This expectation escalates the importance of the priest's leadership role in forming community. He cannot assume that hospitality just happens or that it automatically arises from a schedule of liturgies, a roster of programs, a physical gathering place, and well-advertised opportunities to become involved. Forming community requires deliberate, purposeful action toward building and cultivating relationships in an environment in which diversity, not commonality, is the rule. The task is not the pastor's alone, but he sets the tone and demonstrates how a particular assembly of people, or collection of strangers, becomes a community of friends.

Parishioners expect a *meaningful liturgical experience.* This is a prickly expectation because it elicits equally passionate responses from those who prefer a quiet, traditional liturgy on the one hand, and from those who prefer stimulating, energizing, and lively services on the other. Most want something that will touch their hearts and move their souls. The debate seems endless over whether to follow the established forms, revert to older forms, or adapt forms to particular needs and settings. While that debate continues, parishioners are frustrated if what happens in the church sanctuary depends entirely on the tastes of the pastor or liturgist rather than on whether the liturgy helps evoke a feeling of God's presence as people gather to worship or equips them to live their lives in faithfulness.

Similarly parishioners expect *homilies that relate to their lives and experience.* More precisely they are looking for some direction in life, for spiritual insight, and for interpretation of what is happening around them. They expect the homily to speak to the issues of the day, illuminating the ordinary and extraordinary events that comprise our collective life with the in-spired language of the Gospel. Priests who shortchange their preparation of homilies, fail to continue their studies, or rely on a cute story to replace substance unhinge even the best litur-gies. A poorly preached homily is best left unsaid.

Parishioners expect the parish to be *active in responding to the formation needs of children, youth, and young adults.* I have not found that parents are asking the parish to replace their own efforts to form their children. There is, however, a perva-sive sense that this task exceeds the skills of any family alone. Like so many other aspects of our life, religious formation com-petes in a tough environment for time and attention. Parents feel the challenge of doing the job right, and expect the parish to be innovative and aggressive with programming that sup-ports, builds on, and extends their own efforts. In research focus groups of parishioners, I have listened to the poignancy with which many describe their desire to pass on their legacy of faith and their apprehension that the gift may be lost.

Parishioners expect the parish to be *active in reaching out to those in need.* The Church's convictions about justice and char-ity continue to motivate Catholics to demand of themselves and of their parishes some kind of action on behalf of the poor and marginalized. Sometimes the action is superficial and conscience-easing; sometimes it focuses on good deeds while ignoring bad systems. Nonetheless, even among those opposed to activist re-sponses to poverty and related social-justice issues, there is an expectation that the parish should enact compassion toward the poor.

Parishioners expect a *leadership style that strikes a balance between antiquated authoritarianism and modern laissez-faire egalitarianism.* Authoritarianism is antique because it assumes that people need to be controlled and are unable or illequipped to think through issues, much less contribute to a solution. Some-one recently recounted his experience on his parish council, whose members were highly trained, accomplished leaders in their own professions. The pastor consistently treated them like school children, insisting on his prerogative of making the final decision before the outlines of an issue were identified and care-fully discussed. Even when the discussion would have benefited from the expertise of council members, the pastor imposed his authority without taking counsel and sometimes despite the best advice offered. Within six months the council ceased to meet.

Equally annoying to many parishioners is the pastor who, in eschewing authoritarian tendencies, withdraws from playing a leadership role in the parish. He defers to others when making decisions, refuses to intervene in controversies demanding negotiation, and insists that his role is primarily sacramental rather than governmental. In the name of empowering the laity, the laissez-faire leader creates a centerless organization. The most vocal, most dominant members of the parish exercise undue influence in parish life and often actually discourage full, broad participation by parishioners. In some instances when the laissez-faire pastor is forced to act, he too often does so out of the only model he remembers: authoritarianism.

The middle ground lies in understanding the authority that comes with one's role as leader and using it wisely as a formative force in parish life by remaining clear about how decisions are made. Parishioners expect to be consulted on major issues and to be informed on all other issues that affect parish life, programs, and policies. They expect to understand a decision that chooses one option and rejects another apparently preferable one. Few are the parishioners who believe that "Father knows best about everything." The coercive use of authority or a seeming abandonment of any use of authority does not help people gain an insightful appreciation of the role authority plays in healthy community life.

These observations about authority would be incomplete without acknowledging the bind in which priests find themselves at times when they exercise *theological* authority in the decision-making process. While Father does not know everything, he has been trained to be well-grounded in theology and church teaching. He is expected to ensure that decisions about parish life and practice give serious consideration to the theological implications implicit in options that may be available. Priests who in doing this call into question, or need to oppose, what an individual or group of parishioners wants can too readily be dubbed "authoritarian" because the result runs counter to their preferences.

Parishioners expect their pastors to have a *broad empathic understanding of their lives.* Thus they want pastors who are approachable, able to listen without prematurely taking sides, and tolerant of people's willingness to live with ambiguity even as they search for clarity. Priests who are patently ideological immediately distance themselves from those in the parish who do not share their ideological persuasion. People quickly learn that he belongs to "them," and indeed the ideological pastor will find comfort and safety among those who share his view of the world. Unfortunately that same pastor undercuts his ability to minister to the entire parish, to serve as mediator for the sake of the truth, and to call all people to a common adherence to gospel values.

Along these same lines, people expect their priests to be healthy, whole, and well-integrated. These qualities undergird approachability. Someone who is working out his life adjustments by way of the congregation often ends up being a divisive force. Unresolved issues come out sideways, often expressed in intemperate anger or the formation of relationships that isolate the pastor from other than select groups. Even if people do not want their priest as a buddy, they do want him to have the qualities of character that they would find in a trusted friend.

6. Implications for Seminary Education

The present context for parish leadership is both challenging and exciting. Although it often differs radically from anything that anyone of my parents' generation remembers, it remains a place where good-hearted people gather to worship God, deepen their faith, find community, and live out their highest ideals. Although they are good-hearted, modern parishioners are not docile. They are products of their culture who more than ever before understand at least intuitively the voluntary character of church membership. They are clearer about their spiritual needs, and act to meet those needs whether or not they are affiliated with a parish. They are generous in their affection for the parish and its leadership but equally open in their judgments of parish and leadership performance. What might all this suggest for seminary formation? Let me offer three brief recommendations.

First, raise standards for admission and increase formation expectations. For a priest to exercise parochial leadership is an exacting task. The pastorate is not for amateurs or for those who see priesthood as embodying their privatized notions of ordination. The temptation is strong to compromise standards and lower the expectations for significant formational development when the pool of candidates is small. We must do neither. Both at the admissions stage and throughout formation, students need to be challenged beyond private, ideological, or vague notions of the public role the parish priest plays in carrying forward the mission of the Church. Students in formation must be required to demonstrate the maturity and conviction needed to move into their leadership roles. Being satisfied with minimal development or rationalizing that students' good intent compensates for leadership deficiencies is in the end a disservice to the student and the Church.

Second, intensify the relationship between seminaries and parishes. If the environment for parochial leadership is as demanding as I have indicated, the seminary needs to remain closely associated with parish life. Pastors, staff, and parishioners should become vital participants in the formation process, not simply during internship assignments but throughout a student's seminary years. Association with parishes reminds students of the real reason for formation, and offers an indispensable opportunity to be coached and guided in developing their capacities to respond at the maximum level of competence. In addition, selection criteria for new faculty should include an individual's experience in and appreciation for parish life. The Catholic bishops have made it clear that the study of theology cannot be disengaged from its pastoral context. Achieving that outcome depends on well-chosen and well-developed faculty.

Third, expand the capacity of students to understand, critique, and work with the defining elements in American culture. It is all very well to assert that a priest is expected to be countercultural, but that devolves into naïveté about leadership if one equates the counterculture merely with circling the wagons. Warning of the dangers and temptations lurking within culture is only one level of response. Learning how to adapt certain aspects of culture as instruments of Christian formation enables pastoral leaders to move beyond reaction and to equip their parishioners to be critical participants in secular culture for the sake of the Gospel.

Certainly my list of recommendations could be greatly expanded as one considers the challenges of pastoral leadership mentioned in this essay alone. The pastorate is complex work, and work that we should never stop admiring when it is done well. And it is done well. We all know priests who have developed the knowledge, skill, and capacities to provide parish leadership that is based on vision driven by mission. They maintain a positive attitude despite a well-considered appraisal of the obstacles, for they are grounded in their faith, devoted to ongoing study of Scripture and theology, insightful about their own need to grow spiritually and personally, and reflective about their practice. They show little distress over losing their identity while the laity increasingly assume their own responsibilities for the Church's ministries. Those of us in seminary work need to learn from these priests and to give our students ample opportunities to learn from them, too. Together we can form a partnership that bridges outdated notions of ivory tower versus real life, theory versus practice, the Church as the domain of the clergy versus the Church as the possession of the laity. We are in this together. Our success depends on our ability to learn from each other.

Part II. Mission and Members of Theologate Communities

■   ■   ■   ■   ■   ■   ■   ■   ■

A. The Mission of Theologates

1. The Purpose and Function of Institutional Missions

Institutional leaders of all kinds—board members, administrators, and consultants—emphasize the importance of a mission statement for establishing the identity of an institution. These statements articulate the purposes of the institution and the foundational values that guide its operation. Theologate leaders are convinced of the benefits constituents will reap from reflecting on mission statements and embracing the values they promulgate. One rector's comment exemplifies this conviction: "A strong, defining mission statement promotes institutional stability when our very existence is precarious. At a time when personality and personal whim dictate so many choices, we need to be convinced about what, and clear about who, we are and not blow with the wind."

Every five to ten years, often in connection with accreditation visits, theologate boards, faculty, and students spend time discussing, debating, and thinking about the meaning of the school's mission. Although consequent changes to the statement are usually minor, the process of review serves to renew commitments and promote deeper understanding of the institution, especially among those who are new members. Even so, those involved in the daily life of the school can easily forget or disregard mission statements and think of them as mere window dressing required by sponsors and accrediting agencies. If a unified institutional purpose is to be maintained, however, theologate leaders must be explicit in linking the decisions they make on behalf of the institution with its mission.

Both *PDV* and the *PPF* address the matter of mission when they discuss the identity of theologates. In its section on "The Setting of Priestly Formation," *PDV* states that the seminary is "above all an educational community in progress." It continues, "The content and form of the educational work require that the seminary should have a precise program, a program of life characterized by its being organized and unified, by its being in harmony with one aim which justifies the existence of the seminary: preparation of future priests."[1] The document stipulates that particular norms concerning formation be drawn up by each bishops' conference. In the United States the NCCB has incorporated *PDV* in the *PPF,* and in line with *PDV* its approach to the mission statement is explicit: "The mission of the theologate is the proximate preparation of candidates for the priesthood." Subsequent paragraphs in the *PPF* state that the mission should

- incorporate "a brief summary of the Church's doctrinal understanding of the ministerial priesthood,"
- function "within the context of American higher education as a center of theological scholarship at the graduate level,"
- serve as a theological resource to its sponsors, and
- in preparing candidates for other ministries, retain the integrity of the program of priestly formation and not overextend its resources.[2]

Within these guidelines theologates have formulated their mission statements; careful analysis reveals a surprising richness and diversity in their expression. As each theologate articulates its mission, purpose, and vision, quite different images of Church, the nature of presbyteral ministry, and the place of other ministries within the Church emerge. Most of the forty-two theologates included in this research project have issued

---

[1] *PDV,* #60.
[2] In the *PPF,* #249–54 describe the mission.

their own mission statements, though a few of those attached to universities do not have a separate statement. When we analyze these statements, what do their content, order of presentation, and points of emphasis tell us about the institutions behind them?

2. Mission, Identity, and Foundational Values of Theologates

Most mission statements begin with a straightforward sentence declaring that the primary purpose of the institution is to prepare candidates for service as priests in the Roman Catholic Church. It is the presentation of other aspects of the mission that distinguishes the institutions. At one-third of theologates seminarians are enrolled in programs that for the most part exclude other students, while at two-thirds of them other students—lay and religious, women and men—join with seminarians in at least some programs and courses.

- Six theologates (14.3 percent) specify no other role for their institution than the preparation of seminarians for priesthood, though in practice several of them do admit lay students to classes or offer continuing education programs.
- Another eight theologates (19 percent) stipulate that their mission is "mainly for priestly formation," but they also offer programs or courses open to other students. Of these, four have almost totally separate and heavily subscribed programs for lay students; the other four mention, more or less as an afterthought, the possibility of lay students attending.
- Of the remaining twenty-eight theologates (66.7 percent), most indicate that their mission is to prepare candidates for priesthood (usually referred to as the primary mission) as well as for other ministries. Several, whose academic and pastoral programs are offered in a university setting, provide human and spiritual formation for seminarians at separate institutions. Their academic programs and courses include other students.

Compared with ten years ago, some shifts in mission that affect enrollment are apparent. Although the proportion of theologates enrolling lay students has remained virtually identical, the percentage of diocesan students enrolled in schools exclusively for seminarians has declined considerably—from 59.5 percent to 39.5 percent (see chart B). This change is due largely to the overall decline in total seminarian enrollment and the closing of seven seminaries since 1987.[3] Yet the decline in diocesan students enrolled in schools for seminarians only is surprising, since several diocesan seminaries that a decade ago were enthusiastically seeking lay students and extolling the values of a mixed student body have withdrawn publicly expressed support. In interviews, at least five rectors maintained that their seminarian enrollment would be negatively affected if they continued to advertise or even mention the presence of lay students. In fact, these schools do enroll lay students, and often in larger proportions than ten years ago, but their presence is downplayed. At the same time, a few schools that have never admitted lay students are seriously considering such a move, and several diocesan seminaries have transformed their institutions into significant theological resources for the whole diocese, developing extensive programs for lay ministry, the permanent diaconate, and ongoing ministerial formation. Most of them enroll moderate to small numbers of seminarians.

In the estimation of many theologate leaders, the appointment in recent years of decidedly more conservative bishops who prefer a single-purpose seminary has been responsible for changes in the stated missions of some diocesan seminaries. Meanwhile theologates operated by and for religious congregations not only continue to educate their own candidates but also have moved wholeheartedly into preparation of lay ministers. Ironically, most of the lay graduates of these programs will be working in diocesan ministries. It remains the task of further research to understand the effects on ministry, both ordained and lay, of these differing attitudes about enrollment policies based on the school's mission. The charts given below summarize the statistics to date:

[3] The seven theologates that closed since my previous study are DeSales School of Theology, Washington, D.C.; Oblate College, Washington, D.C.; Maryknoll School of Theology, N.Y.; St. Anthony-on-the-Hudson, N.Y.; St. Thomas Seminary, Colo.; Mary Immaculate Seminary, Pa.; and Mater Dei Institute, Wash. All were operated by religious congregations, but the last three were primarily for diocesan seminarians.

A. Profile of Enrollment in Theologates

	1967–1968	1975–1976	1985–1986	1996–1997
Diocesan Seminarians	4,761	3,109	2,672	2,268
Religious Order Seminarians	3,211	1,594	1,205	817
Unaffiliated Seminarians	—	16	31	—
Total Seminarians	7,972*	4,703	3,908	3,085
Other Students**	—	1,393	2,902	3,100
Total Enrollment in Theologates	7,972	6,096	6,810	6,185

*For every 100 seminarians in 1967–1968, there were
>   59 seminarians in 1975–1976
>   49 seminarians in 1985–1986
>   39 seminarians in 1996–1997

**Other students include lay and religious, women and men, permanent deacons, and diocesan priests in continuing studies. The proportion of full-time students in all categories was not available, but most part-time students are seeking degrees or certification. These statistics are based on CARA data, supplemented by data gathered from several schools that reported the enrollment of seminarians only.

B. Enrollment by Composition of Student Body*

	1986–1987		1996–1997	
	Number	Percent	Number	Percent
Diocesan Seminarians Enrolled in Academic Programs in Theologates for Seminarians Only	1,593	59.5	896	39.5
Religious Order Seminarians Enrolled in Academic Programs in Theologates for Seminarians Only	84	7.0	52	6.4
All Seminarians Enrolled in Academic Programs in Theologates for Seminarians Only	1,677	42.8	948	30.7

Diocesan Seminarians Enrolled in Academic Programs in Theologates with Other Students	1,084	40.5	1,372	60.5
Religious Order Seminarians Enrolled in Academic Programs in Theologates with Other Students	1,114	93.0	765	93.6
All Seminarians Enrolled in Academic Programs in Theologates with Other Students	2,240**	57.2	2,137	69.3
Total Seminarians	3,917		3,085	

*The same theologates are included in both sets of data, with the exception of those that have closed since 1986–1987. Sacred Heart Major Seminary, MI, replaces St. John's Regional Seminary, MI.

**This number includes 42 unaffiliated seminarians.

Mission statements do more than convey the institution's purposes. The four other elements that are typically included refer to

- the geographical region(s) being served and the types of students enrolled, such as older candidates for priesthood or lay students preparing for parish ministry;
- the documents, directives, and traditions that influence the mission;
- the principles that are promoted, sought after, or encouraged; and
- the institution's understanding of Church, priestly ministry, and other ministries.

a. The service focus of theologates. Ten of the diocesan schools are identified by their historical mission as "national" institutions, and they attempt to recruit students from all over the United States. Most of the remaining twenty-three diocesan schools are "regional" institutions with narrower or broader constituencies depending on reputation, location, and competition. According to many rectors, rapid turnover among bishops and vocation directors has resulted in too many changes in the use of a particular diocesan seminary. One rector expressed the sentiments of many when he said: "Territory has been transcended by ideological preferences, loyalty to a given seminary has been superseded by appeals to bishops to enroll their seminarians in a different seminary, long-term use has been abrogated by a new bishop's or vocation director's preference for their alma mater. The instability is exacerbated by bishops being moved from one part of the country to another. Planning is difficult when one cannot be sure of the allegiance of a diocese." Lay students enrolled at theologates operated by and for religious-order candidates usually come from many parts of the country, whereas the seminarians tend to be regionally based. The three Dominican theologates enroll students from Dominican provinces in the part of the country where they are located, as does the Franciscan School of Theology in Berkeley. The two Jesuit schools and the two Unions are national in scope, but location often determines the choice of school by an individual student or his province.

In addition to the geographical scope of the mission, some theologates serve a particular type of student or offer a specialized program. Three of them indicate that their primary purpose is to educate candidates of mature age, usually persons over thirty. Several other schools specify that their programs are oriented toward those who will minister in Hispanic settings or who are themselves of Hispanic background. One theologate has special programs for Polish students, and another for Asian (especially Vietnamese) students. Several other theologates with a sizable number of students from various ethnic backgrounds give them language training and other special services. The two-thirds of theologates that enroll a considerable number of lay students have designed formation programs for lay ministers. At least ten theologates have an organized continuing education program, and three or four educate candidates for the Permanent Diaconate. The variety of students gives a sense of the diversity among the schools.

b. Foundational documents, directives, and traditions. Virtually every mission statement or allied institutional narrative makes a point of noting that the school's programs are based on the Church's teaching regarding priestly formation. The two preeminent documents currently informing the mission, goals, and programs of theologates are *PDV* and the *PPF*. During interviews, *PDV* was universally acclaimed as an inspirational document, while the *PPF* was appreciated more as a practical guide. Other church documents, mostly from Vatican II and onward, also influence the philosophy informing the mission statements.[4] In addition to these documents, religious orders refer to their founding charisms and constitutions as motivating forces, for example, the Benedictine, Dominican, Sulpician, Jesuit, and Franciscan traditions,[5] with their particular emphases on liturgy, learning, preaching, or other charisms.

c. Operative principles. Foremost among principles promoted, sought after, or encouraged is a commitment to integrating the human, spiritual, intellectual, and pastoral programs, which is so universally embraced as to be part of the terminology of almost every school's mission statement. A commitment to collaboration, that is, to promoting creative interaction between ordained and lay ministers and cooperation with other agencies and groups is also evident. Most schools, especially in the Midwest and West, recognize that their graduates will be ministering in circumstances that require priests and lay ministers to work together and share responsibilities. Thus several statements mention the urgency of forming leaders who are able to coordinate the talents of people in many different roles. Another principle involves responding to the societal context in which theologates find themselves. The changing nature of contemporary culture, especially the growing reality of multiculturalism and religious pluralism, were seen as defining aspects of the context that call for attention in theologate programs. Concrete responses to these cultural phenomena include promoting ecumenical and interfaith dialogue and understanding, implementing programs for ministry in Hispanic communities, and supporting the ministries of justice and peace. Finally, the religious order schools in particular highlight commitment to research and scholarship.

d. Institutional understanding of Church, priestly ministry, and other ministries. Preparing candidates for the ministry

---

[4] From Vatican II, The Dogmatic Constitution on the Church (*Lumen gentium*) and The Pastoral Constitution on the Church (*Gaudium et spes*) were mentioned. Other foundational Roman documents regarding priestly formation are *Presbyterorum ordinis, Optatam totius, Ratio fundamentalis institutionis sacerdotalis*, and *Sapientia Christiana*. From the academic world, the standards of the Association of Theological Schools and of regional accrediting bodies were identified.

[5] See appendix A for the list of theologates, which designates the sponsoring dioceses and religious congregations.

of Word and sacrament, especially the Eucharist, is a dominant theme. Some statements express the school's commitment to ensuring that students learn to teach and preach the truths of the faith, and others also mention the hope that they will develop the courage to speak with a prophetic voice. "Liturgy," "prayer," "hospitality," and "community" are words used frequently to convey the nature of the Church's presence in parishes and other ministerial settings.

A few mission statements describe the priest as one sealed with a special character who stands apart, loyal to the pope and obedient to his bishop, demonstrating his love for the Church and her magisterium. These contrast with statements in which the priest is described as a person who, along with lay ministers, aims to build up the body of Christ through distinct but complementary roles, respecting and encouraging, facilitating and enabling the gifts of others. All priests are expected to exhibit attributes of both the conserving and the prophetic dimensions, but the focus of mission statements usually reflects similar perceptions about the nature of the Church, as is apparent from the varied terms used to describe the Church as "sacramental," "mystical," "hierarchical," or "communal." In their mission statements theologates generally welcome the challenges of a diverse membership and recognize that all Christians are called upon to work together in love for the sake of the Church and society, even though occasional phraseology suggests an image of the Church as standing over and against the culture, or separated from the world.

Importantly, the mission statements of religious-order theologates expand their understanding of priesthood and ministry beyond the parochial context. Depending on the particular charism of the religious-order sponsors, the emphasis may be on evangelizing, preaching, ministering to the sick, publishing, or conducting schools, retreat houses, and shrines. The mission statements underscore the differences between the "two traditions of priesthood" and these special ministries of religious.[6] Education of diocesan priests for scholarly futures—for example,

[6] See John W. O'Malley, S.J., "One Priesthood: Two Traditions," in *A Concert of Charisms: Ordained Ministry in Religious Life*, ed. Paul K. Hennessy, C.F.C. (New York: Paulist Press, 1997) 9–24. This chapter treats the relationship between the religious and diocesan priesthood and outlines the two traditions from Trent to Vatican II. Other chapters also reflect on the distinctiveness of religious priesthood.

as university faculty, writers, or editors—occurred more often in the past than it does now, so mission statements of diocesan theologates do not mention these forms of service but rather they concentrate on parochial ministry.

Summary analysis. In their mission statements theologates generally portray their institutions as places where spiritually and pastorally rich formation advances the ministry of the Church. Some theologates also project an image of a professionally rewarding and exciting environment dedicated to excellence in teaching and research. Several positive changes in mission since 1987 are evident from the published mission statements and from interviews. One change is toward greater integration of the various elements of the formation program, a concept now taken for granted. Rarely are departments allowed to work in isolation anymore, and students are urged to integrate learning and pastoral activity into their daily lives. While schools are still grappling with the problem of how to attain closer correlation between academic, pastoral, human, and spiritual formation, the necessity of achieving wholeness and unity of purpose in all elements is widely recognized.

A second, related change that ten years ago was considered by some students and faculty to be an unattainable, if not undesirable, goal is collaboration. Many mission statements seek to reflect the reality of the Church today by asserting that ordained and lay ministers must work cooperatively if the people of God are to be served and themselves brought into service. Not only is this principle frequently taught as the *modus operandi* of future ministry, but in the most effective theologates faculty and administrators model such cooperative behavior.

A third change concerns the necessity of preparing people for ministry in contemporary society. Even if the idea seems self-evident, the tension surrounding the understanding of culture should not be underestimated. *PDV* is eloquent in its insistence that the gospel message must be proclaimed through the cultural modes of the age,[7] and certainly most formation programs, if not mission statements, acknowledge this directive. Another aspect of this question is awareness of the Church's growing multicultural membership. Several schools make special mention of both their increasingly multicultural student

---

[7] *PDV,* #55.

bodies and the changing contexts in which their graduates will minister. Their mission to this varied population has caused them to develop programs that take into account their students as well as the Church's membership.

Among other shifts in attitude and emphasis at some schools is the apparent diminishment of support for a mixed student body, that is, of seminarians studying together with other students, whether laypeople, women religious, priests, or permanent deacons. This issue is still being debated, and arguments similar to those made ten years ago are repeated.[8] Those who support enrolling only seminarians believe that it is best if all formation is directed toward priesthood and all resources reserved exclusively for priestly formation programs. They contend that priestly identity is shaped most effectively in relative separation from other students. Added to these views is felt pressure to achieve higher seminarian enrollment and an attendant fear that the presence of lay students will deter some bishops from sending their candidates to the school. Those who support a mixed student body believe that the best formation environment will approximate future ministerial settings and be open to lay perspectives on Church issues. They hold that responsible stewardship of resources requires maximum utilization of facilities and personnel, especially faculty, who are becoming more difficult to hire.

Nevertheless, it is still the case that research delineating and demonstrating the benefits and drawbacks of the two models has not been done, despite the clear trend (see chart B) toward schools enrolling both seminarians and other students. Do seminarians who study theology with other students become better priests? Do lay students receive adequate formation and attention in contexts where many resources are set aside for seminarians? Each side has its advocates and opponents. Individuals on each side are baffled by the other side's failure to see the logic of the opposite position. Ten years ago this issue was also hotly debated, but now the two positions are more firmly entrenched. My research did not probe the outcomes of various modes of ministerial education, but such research is badly needed if schools are to make wise decisions regarding how best to use resources in preparing seminarians and lay students for the parts they will play in advancing the Church's mission.

---

[8] Schuth, *Reason for the Hope*, 52–53.

Another valuable source of reflection on the mission of theologates is the survey of rectors/presidents, mentioned in the introduction. A number of themes emerged in response to the question, "Consider the larger mission of seminary education at the theology level: What concerns do you have about it?"

- the quality of formation programs, especially as they are affected by the academic level of students;
- the effort to achieve correspondence between the needs of the Church and the content of school programs; and
- ideological differences at every level of the Church.

These interrelated themes recur in other chapters, but here the context is that of all theologate education rather than individual schools.

Concerns about academic excellence were raised by at least sixteen of the forty-two rectors/presidents. In a representative comment, one respondent doubted that academic work is "taken seriously enough. The sense of excellence in *scholarship* is too weak." Addressing the issue of students' prior education, another spoke of "the admission to theology of seminarians who, simply put, are in no way ready for the study of theology." Faculty interviews, reported on later, echo the same thoughts. In sum, many administrators and faculty are uneasy about the quality of academic achievement of graduates and the subsequent impact on their ability to minister to an increasingly well-educated and less docile Catholic population.

Correspondence between the needs of the Church and what the theologates are able to provide was another area of concern noted by rectors/presidents. More than half of them pointed to the difficulty posed by the immense scope of ministry required by the more than sixty million Catholics in the United States. Specifically cited problems included "inadequate attention given to preparation for ministry in the Hispanic community," "an incapacity to train flexible, resilient spiritual leaders who call forth and empower the gifts of diverse leaders in a community," and "lack of attention to lay ministry and preaching." More generally respondents wondered whether "seminaries are adequately preparing priests to serve in a rapidly changing Church," and indeed whether "seminaries will have any impact at all on the Church in the United States." Similar themes emerged in faculty interviews, especially the challenge of preparing seminarians and lay students for an uncertain future.

One-third of the rectors/presidents expressed concern about the strong ideological positions found among students and the polarization brought on by intense differences. For example, one respondent said, "I am concerned about the polarization in the Church seeping into the seminary and into the younger clergy." Another was troubled by the "changing theological climate of the Church reflected in the lack of openness to a broad spectrum of theological thought," and by "how to prepare students effectively for a Church of great diversity"; and yet another worried that "in some places the theological curriculum does not adequately or fully represent the full Catholic tradition, [for] in a secular society it will be important to 'give reasons for the faith that is in you.'" These three apprehensions about mission—lack of depth in academic studies, uncertainty about fulfilling the ministerial needs of the Church, and polarization—are serious. Obviously many strong programs are in place, and enormous efforts are being made to respond to the needs of a Church imbued with diversity, but in other cases much greater effectiveness in coping with these dynamics is demanded.

B. Students and Their Backgrounds: Religious, Intellectual, and Human

Introduction

Who will be our future priests? Who will be our future lay ministers? As the Catholic population in the United States grows beyond sixty million, these urgent questions are being asked more and more often. The profiles of students studying to be priests and lay ministers are of interest to Catholics everywhere, from bishops and priests to women and men in the twenty thousand parishes throughout the country. All are profoundly affected by their religious and personal commitment, their intellectual and pastoral abilities.

Diversity is the most obvious characteristic of persons preparing for ministry today. No longer are seminary students predominantly seminarians in their twenties from third-generation Irish, German, Polish, and Italian families who were raised in a dense Catholic culture. In some theologates they are as likely to come from Latin America, Europe, Asia, or Africa as from the United States, and they are more likely to be in their thirties or older. At other schools the student body includes not only seminarians, but also sizable numbers of lay women and men, and some women religious, who are seeking to become ecclesial ministers with responsibilities other than those reserved for the ordained. When both groups comprise the student body at a given school, lay students and their seminarian counterparts usually hold many parallel views of and perspectives on the Church, which often reflect the local ecclesiology. Where this situation prevails, relations between the two groups are usually amicable. At a few schools the views held by each group differ enough to create tensions that need to be worked through by the school.

Typically whether seminarian or lay, "many are relatively uninformed about Church teachings"; they "lack a vocabulary to help them form a Catholic identity and interpret their Catholic experiences."[9] So we find students from more ethnically varied backgrounds, who are older, less versed in Catholicism, and preparing in nearly equal numbers for lay ministry and for priesthood.

The present chapter begins with eight composite portraits of students, followed by a more detailed description according to three criteria. The representative profiles offer some sense of the range of persons who are studying in theologates these days. The second part of the chapter focuses on the seminarians, since they remain the majority of students enrolled full time in theologates, but it also provides information about lay students at these institutions. Both groups are important resources for the Church of the future, and in some theologates both are essential if the particular mission they have set out for themselves is to be fulfilled. The third part of the chapter addresses the challenges, hopes, and concerns that flow from working with students such as those whose backgrounds have been described. It discusses some of the issues that need to be addressed if effective ministry is to be assured.

---

[9] William V. D'Antonio et.al., *Laity American and Catholic: Transforming the Church* (Kansas City, Mo.: Sheed and Ward, 1996) 87–88. Chapter 5, "Post-Vatican II Catholics: Central Tendencies and Intergenerational Differences," describes characteristics that apply to the generation of most students currently enrolled in theologates. Other characteristics mentioned seem less likely, according to our interviews, to apply to seminarians than to lay students, e.g., they "place a higher priority on being good Christians than they do on being good Catholics," and they "tend to have a deinstitutionalized and democratic view of the Church" (84).

Portraits of Students

Many different religious and educational backgrounds, ethnic identities, and age groups are represented among theologate students, so it can be difficult to grasp just who they are. These eight composite portraits attempt to give a sense of some typical students.

Seminarians.

Dan entered the seminary at age twenty-four after completing a B.A. at a small Catholic liberal arts college and working for two years in an advertising agency. He took pride in his alma mater, which promoted its commitment to orthodox teaching of the Catholic faith. Because his family moved several times while he was in elementary and high school, Dan's religious education had been spotty; having passed through a number of parishes, he didn't know much about how any one of them functioned. But armed with the basics of his faith from college, he thought he could avoid the confusion of new ideas. When given a choice between two seminaries, he visited both and felt drawn to the one that reminded him of his college. On his campus tour with a third-year seminarian, he noticed that everyone—including first-year students—was wearing a Roman collar. He was further reassured when his tour guide told him that you never had to worry about the faculty; they stuck to the catechism and approved books.

Dan had been at the seminary for almost two years now. He found his classmates' beliefs compatible with his own. Many of his classmates were somewhat older, had more work experience, and surprisingly a few had even been married. The course work seemed quite easy compared with his undergraduate program. One just had to learn the basics from the lectures and assigned reading and repeat them on written exams. The rector's conferences about priesthood were inspiring—mostly about being a good and holy person willing to serve in the priestly role. Sometimes Dan worried about how he would do in a parish. Although he found the field education experience helpful, it was also puzzling at times. Not everyone accepted everything the priest said, and people tended to ask so many questions. In the large parish where he was placed, several lay people were working full time, and he wondered how he could blend his priestly service with their ministry.

Mark was thirty-five when he decided to look into priesthood, the first time it had occurred to him since he converted to

Catholicism two years before. On his own for ten years after earning his M.B.A., he had not been particularly active religiously. Having a good time was more important than thinking about the future. Then a Catholic work colleague began talking about the marriage preparation course he was taking at his church. After many conversations with his friend, Mark began to change his ideas about religion, and he decided to go through an RCIA program. Father Jamison, the priest who had given him instructions, mentioned the idea of seminary. It seemed out of the question at first, but he decided to look into it. Once he contacted the vocation director, everything was set in motion.

Mark's vocation director told him he would have to study some philosophy first, by enrolling in a pre-theology program designed for students whose academic backgrounds were deficient. He found the studies difficult after being away from school for so long, and all the Catholic terminology felt a bit strange. Even so, he got through the classes and, since he was a little older, his bishop wanted him to go straight into the theologate after only one year of pre-theology. Now in first-year theology, he was overwhelmed by all the demands of formation—human formation, spiritual exercises, courses, and pastoral work. He hardly knew anything about the Church, let alone the diocese where he lived, and he was already in a parish teaching a CCD class. As he got acquainted with other seminarians, he discovered that about half of them felt at ease with all the requirements, but plenty of them were like Mark—in over their heads. He was determined to tough it out, though, because of his strong sense of personal vocation.

Since college Rob had admired the men religious who ran his alma mater. Right after graduation he became involved in his teaching career, but five years later he still remembered the community spirit among the priests on campus, which seemed to have given them so much joy and enthusiasm. His own life and work had become rather routine, and when he went to Mass on Sundays he wondered if God wasn't asking something else of him. Though he considered diocesan priesthood, Rob decided to pursue religious life in order to continue teaching. The chances of doing that in his diocese were virtually nonexistent, given the shortage of priests. Finally he spoke with one of the priests from his college, and now in his third year of theology, seven years later, he suddenly had only one year left before ordination.

The theological school wasn't what he had ever imagined when he thought "seminary" years ago. Not only were a hundred or more men studying for priesthood, but an equal number of lay women and men were preparing for other ministries. He appreciated their perspectives in class; knowing that his future as a priest would be tied to working with lay colleagues, he was glad to forge good relations with them during theological studies. Occasionally he realized that his own religious congregation's formation put him in a different place from the lay students, but the school was working hard to develop a lay formation program that would level the playing field somewhat. Now Rob was looking forward to a teaching assignment, probably in one of the high schools run by his congregation. Even as he contemplated that future, however, he noticed that his provincial had just accepted responsibility for several parishes at the request of diocesan bishops. Maybe his teaching career was not so certain after all.

Carlos emigrated from Mexico to the United States about ten years ago at age sixteen, when his family moved so that his father could work. Three years later, after he finished high school, Carlos decided to enter the college seminary. He had long thought about becoming a priest, though his parents were not very encouraging. They wanted grandchildren, and his being an only son made the decision all the more unpopular. His older sisters would be getting married, but that wasn't quite the same as having a son's grandchildren. Nevertheless, Carlos determinedly proceeded right through his studies. Learning to speak English well enough to preach was difficult but, since many other seminarians likewise were not native speakers of English, both the college seminary and the theologate insisted that everyone learn a second language. It was comforting to see his Anglo classmates struggling with Spanish, and the Vietnamese students found learning English as challenging as he did.

Now that Carlos was a deacon, he could look back on the education he had received with great appreciation. The seminary made a concerted effort to prepare everyone for what it called a multicultural Church. More than being bilingual, this meant really understanding something about the variety of people he would be called upon to serve as a priest. He still found some of his Anglo classmates quite resistant to the idea of ministering in a largely Hispanic parish where they would have to speak fluent Spanish, but everyone in his diocese had to be prepared for a future that was sure to include ever more diversity. Though adapting to American culture was hard for Carlos, he lived in the midst of his new milieu, whereas some of his Anglo classmates stayed away from Hispanic parishes as much as they could. Since Carlos had always embraced opportunities to learn more from the faculty, who helped each individual discover what they needed to know, he felt prepared for a wide range of possibilities.

John was fifty when his mother died and he was finally able to think seriously about seminary again. He had taught before becoming a school principal about twenty years ago, around the same time that he was left with the care of his mother. As an only child he felt he couldn't leave her after his father died, but the idea of priesthood had always been in his mind. At last he was free to explore his lifelong dream, even if the idea of going back to school for four or more years was not a prospect he relished. He talked to his vocation director, who recommended a seminary for older candidates. John had no problem with the entrance requirements of the seminary he chose, since he had been a practicing Catholic all his life and came with good recommendations. He did find out, however, that some seminaries accepted people without doing much testing, and he heard about some older candidates at these schools who had been recently divorced or widowed struggling with different experiences of loss and change. John wondered how, for example, seminarians who were coming out of recent annulments and had quite negative attitudes toward women would fare in their ministries. He really appreciated the women who were in his classes, but he realized that not every male student did.

Because John did well in seminary—he had never been far from an academic environment—after two years his bishop asked him to condense his studies and finish in another year or so. He didn't really need the extra time after all, his vocation director told him. This development threw John into a temporary tailspin but, being a team player, he doubled up on his course work; despite his exhaustion from concentrated course work, he was going to make it. The seminary had concerns about accelerating his program, but they knew they had to accommodate his bishop if they expected to get other seminarians from his diocese.

Lay students.

Therese was forty-three and married; when her youngest entered college that year, she decided to enroll in the local seminary. After years of working part time as an office manager and many hours volunteering in her parish, Therese realized that she was free at last to pursue her dream of studying theology. The local seminary appeared to be the best place, she decided, after looking into its program along with those at other Catholic colleges in the city. She liked the supervised ministry and theological reflection offered there, and the pastoral studies program seemed best suited to her goal of working in parish ministry. For the most part it turned out that the other lay people in her classes had backgrounds similar to hers, except that many were already working in parishes full-time while studying part-time.

Therese enjoyed the late afternoon and evening classes now that she didn't have so many family responsibilities, but every now and then she took a course with the seminarians. Some of them were of her own age and quite welcoming. Others, often younger, eyed her with suspicion and would grimace at her questions that related the lecture to parish and family experiences. Therese was thrilled to learn about the Church she had always loved. She couldn't wait to start using her newfound knowledge—perhaps by working in adult education, or even coordinating religious education as a teacher of teachers.

Scott had planned to be a lawyer for as long as he could remember, so he was as surprised as anyone to be over thirty and studying theology. Right after college Scott entered law school, but in the middle of it he became disillusioned and went to work selling computers for a few years. Soon he found the routine tiresome and, even though he was married with two children, started thinking about studying theology. While he was working he took a few classes at the seminary located near his workplace. He knew he had found his calling and, in spite of the sacrifice of giving up his job and going into debt, he decided to prepare himself for a teaching career. His wife went back to nursing so that he could study full-time. After earning a two-year master's degree, Scott planned to pursue doctoral study and a Ph.D. in theology. Nothing would stop him now from reaching his goal of teaching theology.

Maria was twenty-six, just completing her commitment as a full-time volunteer for four years, when she started searching for a graduate theological school. She chose to enroll in a school that had a broad spectrum of students, including many young men from all over the world studying to be religious priests, lots of lay students—men and women—who wanted to go into ministry as soon as they finished, and a few intending to pursue doctorates in theology. The ministry choices were also wide ranging: Some students were thinking about campus ministry, others sponsored by a diocese had made a commitment to return there to work for three years in exchange for some help with tuition, and still others hoped to work in parishes. Her own path was as yet uncertain, but she relished the idea of studying with people of such varied interests. Maria knew that her background in philosophy was not as strong as the school had wished, but so far she had had no trouble with the classes she was taking. Her keen mind and hard work made up for any past academic courses she might have missed. Her greatest concern was with how to pay for all this education. She still had some college debt left over, since the volunteer corps paid very little; but with part-time work she hoped she could manage at least part-time study.

Description of Students

Introduction. One certainty about theologate students, as suggested by the foregoing portraits, is how difficult it is to generalize about them. Seminarians and lay students have some features in common, but in other ways they are quite dissimilar. Overall the diversity of students covers many areas: from religious background to academic competence, from age to racial and ethnic differences, and from spiritual attitudes to character traits. Some students are prepared religiously, academically, and psychologically to enter wholeheartedly into the formation process, whereas others exhibit one or more limitations that require special attention during their years of training for ministry. The descriptions that follow refer primarily to seminarians, who comprise by far the greater number of full-time students, but they often apply to lay students as well. Where the two groups differ significantly, the differences are noted.

In assessing the overall picture presented by seminarians today as compared with those of ten years ago, the most striking change is the increase in racial and ethnic diversity. In 1997, 23 percent of seminarians in theology were Latino, Asian, or black (most often from Africa), nearly double the percentage of "minority" students in 1987. Further, 33 percent of seminarians in college now represent these groups, which suggests that the proportion in theology is likely to grow accordingly. A large number, less easy to determine exactly, are coming for theological studies from Europe, especially Poland, Spain, and Italy, with the intention of being ordained for the Church in the United States. All of this presages an alteration in the face of American presbyterates over the next two decades.

Regardless of ethnic and racial composition, students in theology have distinctive religious, intellectual, and human profiles that increasingly set them apart from the faculty who advise and teach them. We shall look at each of these profiles in turn and then consider the challenges of formation associated with them.

1. Religious profiles. The religious backgrounds of students are extremely heterogeneous, though few studies have been done that provide exact statistical data.[10] However, almost all of the administrators and faculty interviewed commented about what they saw as the religious predilections of seminarians and other students in their schools. Students themselves indicated their preferences and ideals regarding religious practice. Four types emerged, which faculty tended to categorize as more or less favorable with respect to readiness for serious theological study. These types, with some variations, include (a) those who are deeply rooted in their faith, (b) those who come from a recent conversion or reconversion experience, and (c) those who have been formally identified as Catholic for a long time but have had a minimal connection with the Church. Cutting across these categories are (d) students who, for reasons of background or personality, have a quite rigid understanding of their faith, the Church, and their potential role in it. As we examine the characteristics of each of these types, it is important to bear in mind that, while a person may substantially belong to one particular group, he or she may exhibit behavior associated with the others, too.

a. Those deeply rooted in their faith. Many faculty and administrators described the religious background they have found most favorable for successful entrance into theological studies. Ideally students were raised in families where they practiced their faith consistently in a local parish, being involved on a regular basis beyond Sunday Mass attendance. Seminarians in this preferred group study for the diocese or religious congregation that was part of their earlier faith experience. They are

---

[10] Hemrick and Walsh, *Seminarians in the Nineties: A National Study of Seminarians in Theology.*

highly motivated and have done the discernment necessary to make an informed choice about priesthood. Lay students with a similar background would also adapt more easily to a ministerial position in a local church that was familiar to them. Both groups have a moderately good grasp of the Catholic tradition, some sense of the Church as universal, an adequate religious education, and a long-standing commitment to their faith. In the case of seminarians, their families were often acquainted with an exemplary priest, and so were at least accepting of, if not pleased with, the choice their son made to enter the seminary. These men are usually the most ready to embrace the routine of seminary life, with a realistic understanding of what their commitment will entail. Lay students of this type are also well qualified for theological studies by their backgrounds, which give them the basis for full entrance into the program. Most theologates would be delighted to find one-third or even one-fourth of all their students with this profile, a striking change from thirty years ago when virtually all seminarians would have belonged to this group.

b. Those recently converted. The background profile just detailed is the one that faculty and administrators prefer, but they find that most students exemplify another religious profile, offering greater challenges to those who work with them in formation programs. A large number, at least one-third, have recently undergone a conversion or reconversion experience. They may have converted from a different Christian denomination, but more typically the phenomenon is one of reconversion. Many of these students, though baptized Catholics at birth, have been away from the Church for a number of years. Among the factors precipitating their sense of vocational call was a significant prayer experience, for example, during a pilgrimage to Medjugorie or at a large religious gathering. In the case of seminarians, a charismatic person, typically a priest, may have asked them if they had ever considered priesthood, which they interpreted as a sign from God. Still others were impressed by an individual's commitment and dedication and wished to follow in his or her footsteps. Depending on the nature of the conversion experience and the convert's age at the time, the impact varies; the older the student or the more dramatic the conversion, the greater will be the obstacles to their religious development.

Because of the rather sudden shift in their life direction, these students have enjoyed only a short-term or sporadic association with a parish, and seminarians in this category especially lack familiarity with the diocese for which they plan to be ordained. Partly because of their religious history and partly because they grew up in a generation whose parents moved frequently, long-term identification with a specific diocese or parish was never a possibility for them. Many such seminarians sought out a diocese for affiliation other than the one in which they grew up or lived at the time when they identified their vocation to priesthood. They often reported in interviews that their eventual choice was made on the basis of personal preference for a particular bishop's style or ideology rather than their own rootedness in the local community.

The general insecurity that permeates American culture affects all students, but the consequences are particularly obvious with seminarians in this second category as they live together and mutually reinforce their previous experiences. One might expect that frequent transitions and moves would enhance flexibility and make change seem the order of the day. Instead, many faculty note, it can lead to a kind of rigidity born of a desire for security and stability. Their relative lack of religious background and knowledge of the Church's history can make them vulnerable, afraid of disturbing their new-found knowledge and losing the security they feel they have gained. One faculty adviser put it this way: "They don't want their perfect world disrupted. This attitude turns into perfectionism, a sense of having things exactly the way they see them and want them kept. As a formation adviser, I have to try to figure out what they are afraid of, what they are trying to defend, to hold on to." The concern of most faculty is not that these students are conservative, a characteristic common to many younger people, but rather that they tend to be rigid, overly scrupulous, and fearful.

c. Those with a minimal connection to the Church. The third group, who share certain characteristics with the first two groups and comprise about one-fifth of all students, have been formally identified as Catholic for a long time but have not practiced their faith consistently. Many did not attend Catholic schools, so that seminary may represent their first formal religious education. Their lack of regular practice means they have little sense of liturgy or experience in prayer. They have not yet developed a passion for being intimate with Christ. They want to be "good," but life for them thus far has not entailed any radical commitment to Christianity. Formation advisers find that people in this group are likely to go in one of two directions. Those who are caught up by Spirit and enter fully into the formation process are often the most convincing models for people in parishes. They have experienced what it is like to be indifferent to their faith, and they know how to appeal to parishioners who are struggling with the meaning of faith in their own lives. Others in this group never quite find their way and are apt to leave the seminary before ordination or before completing their education for a ministerial position.

d. Those who have a rigid understanding of their faith. The fourth group, whose membership may overlap with any of the previous three, constitutes the greatest challenge for faculty. Like most current students, they came of age after Vatican II concluded and have no lived memory of the Church before 1970. In fact, most have had the experience of living their entire lives to date during one single pontificate, a factor that is especially noticeable and significant in relation to seminarians and helps explain their unswerving devotion to the pope. Like their peers, they have been greatly affected by American cultural forms, especially the media, technology, and communications. After having sometimes been quite immersed in this culture, their response now is to withdraw and condemn the world as they see it. For some seminarians enormous fear is involved, fear of change and fear of the world; they regard seminaries as the last bastions of security. Although the secular culture touches other seminarians and lay students as well, not all of them respond by withdrawing; this pattern suggests that those who are rigid, while affected by the culture like the rest, also possess character traits that lead to withdrawal.

Administrators and faculty describe this fourth type of student quite vividly. External signs include an unhappy appearance, downcast eyes, tight body, and no sense of humor. They tend to express dissatisfaction with the seminary and to criticize it for lacking sufficient devotion or orthodoxy. This stance often results from their own inadequate experience of the Church and religious education. Without a larger perspective on the Church as a whole, they think of themselves as always right. In the words of a consulting psychologist, "They would rather be right than happy."

The attitude of these students toward learning is that any new insight is a threat, so they avoid critical thought. This type of seminarian expects faculty to conform to his own thinking rather than being open himself to the scholarly insights of faculty. Such men want only clear, distinct ideas that are aligned with their view of orthodoxy. One faculty member, addressing the inability among many seminarians to think critically, spoke about how this tendency contributes to other problems. She said that students seek only the "bottom line" answer because many cannot think through issues. As a result, they are drawn to defensive and fundamentalistic positions. Many students appear to grasp at easily memorized formulas because they cannot deal with sophisticated and nuanced thinking; thus they become suspicious of speculative thought simply because they cannot enter into it.

At their worst, these students exhibit signs of paranoia, suspicion, and constant vigilance in monitoring each other's motivation. Trust is absent. As one faculty member remarked, "A few, fortunately very few, students are Tridentine in their orientation and have no use for Vatican II; they are pinched and bitter, and their goal is to work against the changes Vatican II has brought; these are preconciliar students in a postconciliar Church. They manifest a kind of ecclesial arrogance, ready to criticize faculty and judge their orthodoxy and competency."

The number of students—seminarian or lay—represented by this extreme type is, I believe, quite small. However, the impact they have far outweighs their limited numerical presence. One rector commented that "a destructive element has created a defensive mode on the part of faculty. We have incidents of faculty being reported to authorities and to the general public—incidents of letters sent out widely about a particular professor being heretical—totally unfounded criticisms that nonetheless create an environment of guardedness. These students say, 'The Church is duped by liberals; we must provide the Catholic answer and save the Church and seminaries from these people.'"

Reviewing the types of religious backgrounds found among theologate students, we find some who are deeply rooted in their faith; some who have had less connection with the Church either because of recent conversion or reconversion, or because of minimal past association with the Church; and others burdened with a rigid understanding of their faith and the Church. Each group calls for specific formational responses if its members are to develop spiritually and psychologically into credible priests and lay ministers. The preponderance of students who are not knowledgeable about the Church requires that formation faculty assess and attend to the shortcomings exhibited by those preparing for ministry. New approaches to spiritual and intellectual development are required.

2. Intellectual profiles. The intellectual requirements for serving in the Church today are immense. A more educated Catholic population demands well-educated lay ministers and priests. Ethnic groups emigrating from many parts of the world necessitate greater understanding of foreign cultures and languages, and socioeconomic groups of enormous range require awareness of how the Gospel can be heard among them. These examples illustrate how much intelligence and knowledge will be needed to reach the great diversity within the Catholic Church. This section, more than the previous one, focuses on seminarians rather than lay students, because more data from interviews are available concerning them.

Given the fact that one of the key roles of the priest is to articulate and preach the faith convincingly, a man who is himself capable of learning and understanding the faith will be capable of fulfilling one of his chief priestly functions. Thus a holistic and honest discernment of vocation to the priesthood must include not only a consideration of his personal qualities and motivation but also whether he will succeed in apprehending the *res* of the Catholic tradition and then communicating it. What is said about intellectual formation in *Pastores dabo vobis (PDV)* applies to anyone working in the Church:

> The intellectual formation of candidates for the priesthood finds its specific justification in the very nature of the ordained ministry, and the challenge of the "new evangelization" to which our Lord is calling the church on the threshold of the third millennium shows just how important this formation is. "If we expect every Christian"—the synod fathers write—"to be prepared to make a defense of the faith and to account for the hope that is in us" (cf. 1 Pt. 3:15), then all the more should candidates for the priesthood and priests have diligent care of the quality of their intellectual formation in their education and pastoral activity.[11]

As with other qualities, intellectual achievement and ability vary considerably among students. A few candidates present

[11] *PDV,* #51.

themselves with doctoral degree in hand, whereas a few others enter after not much more than a high school education completed many years earlier. Most have earned a college degree, followed by intense study of philosophy for a year or so; and some, though a decreasing proportion, come from college seminaries where they usually majored in philosophy. Most are native English speakers, but for a growing number, perhaps 20 percent, English is their second language.

Apart from differences in prior educational experience, the intellectual ability of students also varies. While no in-depth statistical study of students' intelligence levels is available, faculty offered their own evaluations based on firsthand experience. Compared with ten years ago, most faculty report that they are teaching about the same small number of excellent students and the broad middle range of students also remains steady. The difference appears at the lower end of the spectrum; many faculty believe that the least gifted students are weaker now than ever before. After a semester or two, most theologate faculties dismiss students who they deem incapable of graduate study, but such students always seem to find their way into one or another school that prides itself on accepting those who could not make the grade elsewhere.[12]

---

[12] The practice of admitting seminarians who have been dismissed from another seminary—after not only academic failure but also personal and spiritual inadequacy—is challenged by a 1996 letter from the Sacred Congregation on Catholic Education, "Instruction on Admitting Candidates Coming from Other Seminaries or Religious Communities." Referring to canon 241 of the Code of Canon Law, which deals with the examination and selection of candidates for the priesthood, the Prefect of the Congregation, Pio Cardinal Laghi, speaks about the importance of holding to the prescriptions of the *ratio fundamentalis institutionis sacerdotalis* (chapter 8) regarding the examination and selection of candidates.

> Concerning the practical application of these norms, however, for some time now and from various parts of the world this dicastery has been notified of irregularities and omissions, together with the considerable harm which results for the life of the seminaries and for the spiritual good of the individual dioceses. In fact, the too-easy acceptance of ex-religious and ex-seminarians, made without thorough preliminary investigation, is usually the cause of unpleasant surprises and disappointments for "indulgent" bishops and at the same time a cause of discomfort for those local ordinaries who are rightly demanding in the selection of their candidates.

Another complicating factor related to academic achievement is the growing number of seminarians from other countries. Faculty find that the presence of these students affects their classes in contrasting ways: On the one hand they are enriched by experiences of different cultures, while on the other hand they may be impeded by these seminarians' inability to understand the nuances of American culture and the more technical aspects of theological language in English. In the first case, some international students, especially those with a European seminary background, arrive with a classical education that serves as an excellent starting point for theological studies. In the second case, either students who have a poor grasp of English are left behind, or the whole class must slow down to accommodate them.

As this overview suggests, grouping students according to intellectual achievement and ability is complicated, and many students show traits that cross categories, but several types are representative: (a) those with a first-rate classical education who are exceptionally talented students, (b) those with a good college degree and adequate intellectual ability, and (c) those who are less qualified because of one or more circumstances.

a. Most highly qualified students. A few have benefited from a first-rate classical education, during which they studied philosophy along with some Scripture and theology over at least three or four years. Realizing the importance of this background, they are determined to keep growing intellectually. They understand the relationship between learning and the capacity to minister with integrity. These students know how to use their time fruitfully, and they relish the opportunities available to them for study and application of their learning to ministerial settings. As one faculty member noted: "These students are mature and have no difficulty regulating their own time or coming to grips with the fact that the seminary is not a college dorm but a place of hard work and commitment. They ought to be raised to a new level of learning by the seminary curriculum, rather than having the seminary lower expectations to meet the needs of less qualified students." Some faculty expressed frustration at not being able to work enough with talented students because their numbers are small and attention must be directed to the students who need extra help just to get by.

b. Relatively qualified students. Those in the large second group, typical of most students, have reasonably good college degrees and adequate intellectual abilities. They want to learn what the Church teaches, and they are also looking for insights into the tradition. The challenge of integrating all aspects of their formation inspires many of them to spend hours in study, prayer, and pastoral placements. Some are well acquainted with the faith and life experiences of their peers and are able to translate the Church's teachings into language they understand. Their potential for growing into effective priests and lay ministers is obvious. Yet these students also have some deficits in their backgrounds that affect their ability to study theology. Many come with degrees in business, science, or technology, so they have had less exposure to the humanities. Even the brighter ones tend not to be readers, and they lack the broad cultural foundation afforded by study of the classics. Their appreciation of language and the imagination necessary to enter into the world of theology is underdeveloped, while they also lack the historical consciousness required for understanding the evolving Church. Faculty are faced with the task of inspiring these students to acquire a thirst for knowledge, to be more inquisitive and creative.

c. Insufficiently qualified students. The third and last group is made up of less qualified students who fall into several categories: (1) Some have weak educational backgrounds; (2) others have some kind of learning disability; (3) a third category—who may be very capable intellectually—has little or no background in English; and, finally, (4) some have been away from formal study for years and have simply lost their academic skills.

(1) Those with weak educational backgrounds. Of the first category, one academic dean said, "We are reaping the whirlwind of poor educational systems; we see the consequences in poor reading comprehension, poor writing skills, the inability to do research work, the lack of familiarity with library resources, and the inability to think logically and critically." A faculty member spoke passionately about the consequences of the problem:

> Many have a limited, linear view of religion: "In the beginning there was God, then the Jews, then Jesus and Christians, then us." We need either to teach a course in ancient civilization and the history of ideas or to establish it as a prerequisite. The students' lack of appreciation of poetry, narrative, and the power of language is lamentable, as is what appears to be a lack of imagination and creativity, all born of a narrow technological educa-

tion that prepared them for a job, but not for advanced theological studies.

(2) Those with learning disabilities. Those with learning disabilities pose an entirely different challenge. Seminarians with educational problems stemming from dyslexia or attention deficit disorder, for example, often have difficulty writing, suffer from short attention spans, and lack the ability to read advanced material with full concentration. Given the proper diagnosis and treatment, however, these students can achieve well; thus if theologates accept them, they are obliged to make a concerted effort to help them. Without proper assistance, learning-disabled students are often misunderstood and labeled as unintelligent, causing unnecessary anxiety and failure. This suggests the use of psychological counseling for learning-disabled students who develop negative self-images as a result of often years of poor academic performance.

(3) Those who lack English language preparation. The third category includes many seminarians from other countries who lack sufficient knowledge of English and of American cultural practices to be able to study here effectively at the graduate level. Often these candidates are intellectually capable but, for the sake of moving them quickly through their programs, they are not given the opportunity to study English over an extended period. Compounding the problem of language is the American educational system, which calls for active class participation along with written papers and exams. Time invested at the beginning with trained language instructors usually pays off in the long run, since few faculty are skilled in assisting these students.

(4) Those far removed from formal study. The last category of students includes some older candidates, men in their forties, fifties, or beyond, who have been away from academic study for many years or who may never have been interested in studying at all. When they arrive at midlife and decide to enter seminary, many bishops want them to get through the program as quickly as possible because of their age, whether or not they have adjusted to the seminary setting. Some have just completed a crammed year of studying philosophy, while others are admitted to theology without having completed a pre-theology program at all. The bottom line is that these men, as a result of external pressures or their own desires, are now expressing an urgency to get on with their priestly lives and want to push

through quickly. If one diocese requires two years of pre-theology, some will go to another diocese where requirements are relaxed. Descriptions of the plight of these students indicate that a growing number are struggling academically. The fallout from their struggles affects the entire academic program and other dimensions of formation as well.

Faculty comments about the learning styles and attitudes toward study of seminarians, regardless of their intellectual backgrounds, are informative. Faculty respondents noted that many seminarians, unlike most lay students, are reluctant to critique anything. According to one faculty member:

> Students can't make judgments or decisions; they find critical questions disquieting because they don't know logic or how to think through complexities, even about what is right and wrong with American culture. They haven't thought reflectively about their world in the light of the Gospel. This isn't about being traditional or progressive; they simply don't know how to make judgments on their own authority. They depend on the "official Church" to tell them about everything that is right or wrong. The problem is the official Church hasn't spoken on every individual matter that comes up in pastoral practice. They need to develop the ability to make distinctions, to have confidence in their own inner authority, to make decisions and render judgments in the midst of complicated pastoral settings.

Faculty may unwittingly contribute to the problem of students' failure to understand abstract concepts and to think critically if they engage critical thought using only one frame of reference. Others attributed the tendency of students to operate more on a feeling level, in the absence of cognitive richness, to the fact that their previous studies were career-oriented and did not provide the benefits of a liberal arts education. A concomitant tendency on the part of students is to champion "pastoral" over "academic," as if being pastoral and being intelligent were mutually exclusive.

Where do *lay students* fit into this picture? References throughout this description give some indication, but a few outstanding differences can be identified. First, since a greater proportion of lay students are from the United States and have lived here most of their lives, fewer must contend with learning a new language as they begin theological studies. They are also well acquainted with the culture, and many have worked in parishes before entering theology, which gives them an appreciation of the people they will serve. Because lay students normally pay their own tuition, they approach their studies very diligently, though the claims of jobs and families may curtail involvement with their course work. Both financial circumstances and other responsibilities lead most to enroll part-time; thus their average student career is longer. The advantage of spreading the degree over several additional years is that more time is available for assimilation and less pressure is felt to finish quickly. The disadvantages are that work sometimes proves to be a distraction, supersedes time for study, and causes discontinuity in progress toward a degree.

A weak background in philosophy is a major deficit that lay students themselves admit. Nevertheless, despite occasional complaints by seminarians to the contrary, almost no faculty feel that this lack has a negative impact on class progress. Another point of contrast is the previous religious formation that lay students have or haven't had. Some have grown up in a strong Catholic culture, but many are fairly new to religious influence. A few have proved to be sources of conflict and disruption for faculty who confront some of their preconceptions about theology. Theologates that enroll a large number of lay students are addressing these lacunae by developing all aspects of lay formation. In the final analysis, seminarians and lay students share many similarities in their intellectual backgrounds but also some differences, especially with respect to family origin, personal religious history, and the length of time they take to complete a degree.

3. Human profiles. A basic theological axiom of the Church is that grace builds on nature. When we have students who possess the components of a healthy personality and the intellectual capacity to complete an academic program successfully, then the building blocks are in place for effective formation. If in the past vocation directors and admissions committees tended to assume a level of maturity, commitment, and intelligence on the part of those seeking admission to theologates, they now want to assure that such a level is actual. Given the demanding roles that priests and lay ministers are asked to play, they must have the proper personal disposition and intellectual preparation necessary for managing and delegating, administering and guiding, in a collaborative Church.

a. Manifestation of positive qualities. The following excerpt from *PDV* emphasizes the fundamental importance of positive human qualities developed by means of human formation. Though written for those studying for priesthood, the qualities cited are suitable for everyone working in the Church:

> The whole work of priestly formation would be deprived of its necessary foundation if it lacked a suitable human formation. . . . Future priests should therefore cultivate a series of human qualities, not only out of proper and due growth and realization of self, but also with a view to the ministry. These qualities are needed for them to be balanced people, strong and free, capable of bearing the weight of pastoral responsibilities. They need to be educated to love the truth, to be loyal, to respect every person, to have a sense of justice, to be true to their word, to be genuinely compassionate, to be men of integrity and, especially, to be balanced in judgment and behavior.[13]

What proportion of students manifest these qualities, or at least have the potential to develop them? Most of those in a position to judge believe that, after the usual terminations occur (by virtue of student choice or dismissal) during the first two years of theology, a high proportion of students are at least minimally qualified to minister well. A concern of many faculty and administrators is that adequate tools are not available to help them evaluate those who are advancing toward priesthood or completing other ministerial programs. Further research on how effective various established programs have been in preparing candidates for ministry would help schools to revise their programs, but this research has not been done.

Despite inevitable doubts and questions, it is evident that, as students progress through their programs, more and more of them do reach acceptable levels of human development. Many possess positive qualities from the beginning, while others have obstacles and deficiencies to overcome. In reviewing faculty comments about students' human qualities, it should be noted that their concern is greater when deficiencies relate to character structure and internal disposition as opposed to circumstances of background and external factors. The effects of the former are more lasting and have a greater impact on the capacity of the student to do ministry.

Most seminarians enter theology physically and psychologically healthy, with sufficiently outgoing personalities to conduct

---

[13] Ibid., #43.

the public ministry required of the Church's ordained. Faculty describe most of them as earnest, pious, and committed. They enter consciously into a formation process that asks them to accept criticism and to change their behavior and attitudes in conformity with the expectations of priesthood. Earlier research suggested that this might be less true of older students,[14] but in general faculty had more positive views about older students now than they did ten years ago. They noted that these students are often more mature, educated, and responsible than their younger counterparts. At the same time they acknowledged that, if positive traits are not present in older candidates, it is more difficult to break negative patterns. Most faculty believe that "in terms of human development, what you see in older entering students is more or less what they will be like when they finish." A few are more optimistic about the power of the formation process to transform students who are notably deficient in positive human qualities. In either case, careful screening is essential.

b. Manifestation of shortcomings. Deficiencies come in many forms, some of which are amenable to change. Yet faculty are careful to recognize that certain deficiencies call for adaptation and acceptance rather than change. Among the latter are physical impairments, more common now than ten years ago because many students are older. Some students have severely impaired hearing and sight, and others chronic illnesses such as diabetes and Parkinson's disease. Faculty noted an increase in the number of those who are overweight, which can be more than a physical problem and is also a general trend in American society. Part of the formation task is to educate seminarians in the fundamentals of physical health so that they can maintain or improve their own well-being.

Relationship skills are essential for priests and lay ministers. Ministry today demands extensive collaboration, including skills in leading groups, running meetings, managing and delegating, and resolving conflicts. Those with a more extroverted personality tend to succeed in these roles, and many students preparing for ministry are able to respond well to these demands. A significant minority, however, is more introverted and passive by nature. In the view of one faculty member,

---

[14] Hemrick and Walsh, *Seminarians in the Nineties,* 30–35.

Too many seminarians have introverted personalities when they are entering a vocation, a career, that calls for extroversion. The shy, daily-Mass-in-the-corner type will encounter difficulties in parishes. We see the signs of this in their passive posture. It carries over to passive acceptance of formation; they need to cooperate more actively with God's love to find the inner openness that expresses itself in outer love for people.

One bishop complained that some of his newly ordained priests "tend to say Mass and retreat to the sacristy rather than greet the people, ask about their lives, and offer a word of encouragement. The more active nature of the calling is missing in too many of them." Human formation programs are designed to address these shortcomings, but an innate preference for introversion is highly resistant to change. Yet other faculty are less concerned about these personality traits; they believe that some priests who are more introverted are very effective in their ministry. It is perhaps priests who represent the extremes who are problematic. The exceedingly introverted person must learn how to be an external sign, a living presence, in the Church. The exceedingly extroverted person must learn the discipline of setting aside sufficient time for prayer and reflection. As formation programs are constructed, the reality of this diversity among students is almost always taken into account.

4. Cultural considerations. Among the factors that affect the way students understand themselves and relate to others, the cultural context is extremely important. To a greater or lesser degree, the positive and negative aspects of living in our culture shape their values. Certain traits have almost become bywords for defining the American character. On the negative side familiar terms include individualism, privatism, and materialism; more positively we speak of respect for the individual, a tradition of volunteerism, and a spirit of optimism. These tendencies affect the way seminarians and lay students construct their worldview.

Individualism is defined by Robert Bellah as an excessive insistence on self-interest and autonomy that destroys a sense of community and regard for institutions. It lends itself to insensitivity to others, inflexibility, and selfishness. Closely associated with this American phenomenon is privatism, which in a secular sense leads to indifference to the larger culture and a lack of concern for or involvement with others, alienation from others, and even simply a lack of courtesy. Religiously it is expressed in the primacy of and preference for personalized spirituality. In their responses, faculty associated the cultural milieu with the behaviors and attitudes of some seminarians regarding, for example, liturgy and social justice. They believe that seminarians should be encouraged to learn about the institutional Church as embodied in the local parish instead of suiting their own sensibilities and preferences in liturgical matters. Regarding prayer, private devotions have taken precedence over the liturgy of the Church and public worship in the minds of some students. Concerning social justice, one faculty member commented: "They tend to be a bit narcissistic, taking care of themselves first, saving time for themselves above all. It shows itself in other ways, too. The sign-up sheet for holy hours is always full, but it is hard to find anyone to serve a meal in a shelter."

Materialism is rampant in contemporary American society, and students are driven by the demands of this psychological orientation. The temptation to participate fully in our culture of elite affluence is especially strong for seminarians, who may strive to enjoy the best in restaurants, clothing, and other perquisites. Having many possessions is perceived as a sign of power and prestige. A faculty member at a seminary with many students from other cultures noted that

> American seminarians can be self-satisfied, unaware of how hard people have to work in other cultures just to support their families. Too many have a sense of entitlement and a lack of concern for the poor. The more affluent students have little awareness of the breadth of service the Church has given to the poor, how much this is part of our tradition.

Formational implications. Certain human psychological vulnerabilities carry serious formational implications. Many students are now survivors of what were once called "broken homes" but are now termed "dysfunctional families." The lack of stability in their early environments directly influences how much order, stability, and rigidity they expect in the seminary environment and what their ecclesial preconceptions are. Not finding order and stability in their microsocieties, they look to the institutional Church as the vehicle through which, in their view, these values can and should be established in the macrosociety. Seminarians, more than lay students, see themselves as working through the Church to establish such order. Confused and disoriented in their own personal lives, they expect the seminary experience to be an "ordering" experience and are dismayed when their expectations are not met.

Students who have personality disorders, suffer from substance abuse, or are victims of physical or psychological abuse cannot be formed in a few short years. Theologates were never intended as therapeutic centers and, if they were to assume that role, the program of formation would have to become even more highly individualized. The assumption that education for public ministry should be completed within four or five years would have to be dropped. The importance of careful screening and realistic expectations about how much the school can achieve in forming a person must be honored. As one formation adviser exclaimed: "In vain do we labor if the basic building blocks do not exist! The program must build on what is there; it cannot make up for some inadequacies, and our screening has to be carefully done so we don't overstep our competence."

Concerns about celibacy and sexuality have mounted in the past ten years, as theologates deal with the aftermath of sexual misconduct on the part of some priests. More is said in Part III, on formation, concerning how theologates are educating students about a range of sexual issues, but the topic is also germane to the issue of students' human qualities. A question frequently asked by outside observers is, how many seminarians are gay? The answer is not available for several reasons: A scientific survey has not been done on the question, not all seminarians have come to a point of clarity about their sexual identity, and the definition of what being gay means is subject to diverse interpretations. Pondering why the question is so dominant now, one rector commented, "My concern is that our men live a celibate life, a life that includes being intimate in ways appropriate to priesthood so that they can minister in a compassionate and caring way." Others see the matter from a different perspective, as expressed, for example, by this faculty member: "I have heard the concerns of spiritual directors with regard to the high number of seminarians who self-identify as homosexuals. I am troubled about the number of homosexual men and the imbalance that will result if we have a disproportionate number of homosexual clergy ministering to a largely heterosexual church population." Others—faculty, administrators, and seminarians—spoke about homophobic behavior that they found disturbing. "Discrimination manifests itself in many ways," one faculty member remarked.

Whatever the attitudes expressed, the past ten years have seen a great expansion of education about sexuality, and most seminarians are responding appreciatively to the added emphasis. One of them said: "For me celibacy is more than a question of legality. I truly want to understand and embrace it so that my life isn't cold and my ministry distant."

Concerns and Responses

Faculty relating to students. For faculties in Roman Catholic theologates, whose average age hovers around fifty, the demands of dealing with students who are considerably younger are great. Challenges present themselves on religious, intellectual, and human levels. The success or failure of the formation process is determined in part by how well students understand the goals faculty set for them. A common language and much patience are needed in working with students who differ increasingly from the older faculty members who teach them. At the same time, younger faculty members are more and more likely to share the same perspectives and experiences as students, so that the issue extends to the area of interfaculty relations. This added dimension is indicated by divisions beginning to show within faculties that have previously shared a common vision.

Referring to faculty-student divergence, one faculty member said: "We speak Vatican II language about renewal and commitment to the Church in ways they don't understand. We are trying to make priests like we were, and it doesn't work. The young in society as a whole are more traditional, more likely to have conservative leanings, so we shouldn't be surprised to find seminarians that way." Successful work with students requires faculty to enter into their ways of thinking so that the best of what faculty have to offer can be heard and, ideally, accepted by the students.

How faculty overcome the divergence in thinking between themselves and students is one of the critical issues that should be taken up in future faculty development programs. What are the sources of such different views? Older administrators and faculty tend to take for granted their own faith commitment and loyalty to the Church. Socialized into the Church from an early age, they assume, for example, that everyone understands the Church year, the role of liturgy, and the public dimension of ministry as part of the Christian heritage. They think of the Church as indestructible and have great confidence in its continuity, while also exploring new ideas and insights to keep it alive and growing.

The distinctive voice of young people in the Church was high-lighted for me during a recent Catholic Common Ground Initiative conference. Younger participants spoke of the multiplicity of changes in the Church during their lifetime that have made them fearful about the future. Although they grew up in a Church apparently in the throes of an identity crisis, they are "looking for the Church to be a rock, a fortress with a strong foundation." This mentality predominates among the students who are now enrolling in theologates. Despite varying ideas about how they expect the Church to evolve, their fundamental understanding of ecclesiology separates them from faculty and calls for responsive dialogue.

Because of such basic differences, the danger is that faculty will be seen by students as standing in opposition to them. This problem is heightened when it involves seminarians who are being evaluated regularly and often live in the same residence with priest faculty and administrators. Faculty may find themselves on the defensive when they criticize behavior that is inconsiderate or tactless, and students contend that the real object of criticism is their orthodoxy. Students may accuse faculty of not supporting their devotions or loving the Blessed Sacrament, to which faculty respond that they are simply asking students also to see Christ in others and serve accordingly. Faculty may depreciate students whom they consider theologically illiterate or too ready to question faculty orthodoxy. Or in another version, students may feel that faculty dislike them because they are "traditional," whereas faculty may regard students as unwilling to move toward a deeper understanding of their faith.

How to overcome the impasse is on the minds of many faculty. At a recent conference of Catholic theologate faculties, a Protestant observer expressed his concern about the way faculty sometimes talk about students with disdain rather than the Christian love that might encourage students to change. A fair assessment of the situation is that neither side is entirely at fault; both need to work together to discover how students can best be prepared for effective ministry in the present and future Church.

Summary analysis. One of the most striking changes of the past ten years is the increased racial and ethnic diversity of seminarians. What is not as clear is how that diversity affects seminary life and formation. How well do seminary faculty and administrators understand that diversity? How does formation take it into account? What are its implications for the presbyterates in which these men will serve? How are former seminarians from Asia, Africa, Europe, and Latin America doing now as priests? Many interviewees pointed out positive and negative consequences of diversity. Both can be further articulated as theologates attempt to move beyond the fact of diversity to the question of how to make positive use of it. The good will to do that is present, but the necessary skills need to be developed. For example, students can be racist, even non-Anglo ones; how can that be changed?

A second consideration: When we looked at the religious backgrounds of students at the beginning of this chapter, one of the concerns noted was the frequency with which they have moved, both with their families through young adulthood and on their own later on. A problem that admissions committees and vocation directors face is finding anyone who has known the candidate for more than a year or two. Some of these potential students have had little association with the Church at all; others have entered religious congregations or other seminaries from which they have been dismissed without the knowledge of the school now being approached. Since it can take several years to discern the real character of a person, such a history is problematic, even when that history is known. This problem has become so acute, as noted earlier, that an "Instruction" was issued from the Sacred Congregation on Catholic Education to deal with it.

When students are unfamiliar with their own diocese or with parish life, the school has an added task. For seminarians who are associating with a new diocese, the task is to facilitate their relationship with the chosen diocese, helping them learn about its people, direction, and goals. Parish experience is equally vital for anyone who expects to work in parish ministry. A year of parish internship in their own diocese introduces seminarians to both the diocese and parish life. For lay students who already struggle with financial responsibilities, an intense program like a full-time internship may be out of the question, but supervised ministerial experiences are a recommended means of orienting them to parish ministry.

The low academic quality of many candidates also has ramifications for the academic life of the seminary as a whole. Highly trained faculty say they are finding it necessary to "water down" or restrict course content, limit reading assignments, and even waste valuable class time in administering quizzes just to ensure that students do the assigned reading. Teachers are also finding themselves bogged down by long hours spent correcting the grammar, spelling, and logic of poorly written research papers. As a result, faculty have less time to devote to real scholarship. Indeed the low academic level of students can be a deterrent to more profound investigation on the part of teachers, since most already possess more knowledge than they could possibly impart to their audience. Thus faculty research is at risk. Likewise the few very good candidates (and they are the exception) can get lost in this shuffle and, given the fact that courses are watered down to accommodate the less-qualified students, the type of academic education an individual would need to pursue licentiate or doctoral studies is not being offered.

The implications of the many areas of diversity—religious backgrounds, academic capabilities, psychological differences, and cultural circumstances—require distinctive formation programs. Well-defined goals based on the traits of the students are foundational to the process. Faculty must be willing to practice a certain asceticism themselves if they are to successfully form students for ministry. Sometimes rather than engaging in an exchange of complex ideas about theological subjects, they will have to present material at a very basic level to students who have inadequate educational backgrounds or little experience and knowledge of the Church. At other times rather than engaging willing students in a process of conversion, they may need to overcome student resistance to new approaches and understandings of the Church in the modern world. Whatever the characteristics of students, faculty are obligated to understand them and reach out to them. Well-designed formation programs developed and deepened during the past decade contribute mightily to their efforts.

C. Board Members, Administrators, and Faculties

1. Governing Boards

Introduction. During the past decade governing boards of theologates have expanded their roles, developed their expertise, and grown in size. Rectors/presidents report that board members are indispensable resources for their schools; especially valuable is the advice they can offer about finances, investments, and fundraising. Boards have also improved planning processes, public relations, and connections with local communities and other constituencies. Good relationships with clerical members of boards are important both for financial support and for recruitment of seminarians. At least two-thirds of theologate boards have participated in one or more of the educational opportunities made available through the Association of Theological Schools and the Keystone Conferences for Boards.[15] On the whole, theologates have benefited significantly from the services rendered by board members, who are now more numerous than a decade ago, even though seven fewer theologates are operating.

Structure and function. Depending on the setting of the theologate—whether it is freestanding, collaborative, or university-related, and diocesan or religious—the structure of boards varies. Freestanding diocesan seminaries normally function with a single board of trustees. The local ordinary usually serves as chair of the board and, in accordance with canon law, is the ultimate governing authority of the school. When authority is shared with these boards of diocesan seminaries, they function much as any independent board does. Collaborative schools, where formation occurs at more than one institution, are usually sponsored by religious congregations. They are more likely to have two-tiered boards, the first tier consisting mainly or entirely of members of the sponsoring congregation, and the second comprising a mixed group of religious and lay members. Three of these schools have a third board whose role is purely advisory. University-related schools generally include a seminary board committee as part of their governing structure, but several of these theologates also have separate boards. While each of the forty-two schools has a board or board committee, eleven also have a second-level board, and three have a third-level board, making a total of fifty-six boards.

Most frequently, in thirty cases, this governing group is called the Board of Trustees; five or six each are called Board of Directors, Members of the Corporation, or Board Committee; and

---

[15] From 1989 to 1994, the Holy Name Province Franciscans and Lilly Endowment Inc. sponsored weeklong conferences for the rectors/presidents and up to five board members of some twenty-five schools. Through lectures and case studies, board members learned how to function more effectively and how to develop strategies addressing major problems at their schools.

two or three each are called Board of Regents, Board of Over-
seers, Board of Governors, or Advisory Council. Most boards meet
in full session three times a year for one day. If members live
nearby, separate dates are designated for committee meetings,
often as many as five or six times a year. But if members come
from greater distances, committee meetings are held shortly before the full board meeting. Local members offer the advantage
of being more available for involvement, whereas national members often provide a broader perspective and may be more representative of the school's constituencies. Many boards are fairly
simple in structure, consisting of just two committees, one for
financial matters and the other for programs. About ten boards
have as many as four or five committees, assigned to such areas
as finance, development, academic programs, spiritual formation, and board affairs.

The activity and complexity of boards are usually determined
by the interests of the rectors/presidents and the local ordinaries—bishops and religious superiors. Those with administrative
experience tend to be more skillful in organizing and involving
board members; if so, the school benefits enormously. The ordinaries also regulate the extent to which boards function with
full authority. Various forms of shared governance have been in
place for more than twenty years, and boards have made clear
progress in developing a significant role. In the few cases where
this has not happened, meetings are perfunctory and board
membership is seen as honorary rather than substantive. On
the whole, boards have assumed a justified importance and offer
meaningful counsel, which is seldom disregarded.

Membership, size, and status. Both the total number of
members and the size of boards have increased over the past
decade; their constituency has also changed. In 1997 there were
885 board members, of whom 518 (58.5 percent) were ordained
and 363 (41.5 percent) from other vocations. In 1987 there were
820 board members, of whom 533 (65 percent) were ordained
and 287 (35 percent) were from other vocations. The greatest
proportional increases can be noted in laymen and laywomen,
followed by bishops. Together these three groups have contributed nearly one hundred more members than in 1987 to theologate boards. The rationale offered for the increases is twofold:
More laymen and laywomen were selected to enhance the voice
of laity on boards and to increase their fundraising capabilities;
generally bishops were chosen to enhance their acquaintance

with the school and thus encourage them to begin sending or to continue sending seminarians there. The noticeable decrease among men religious is due largely to the closing of seven theologates, all sponsored by religious congregations. The following chart compares board membership from 1987 to 1997:

	1987		*1997*		*Change*	
	Number	*Percent*	*Number*	*Percent*	*Number*	*Percent*
Cardinals/bishops	98	12.0	123	13.9	+25	+1.9
Diocesan priests	157	19.1	154	17.4	-3	-1.7
Men religious	278	33.9	241	27.2	-37	-6.7
Women religious	30	3.7	37	4.2	+7	+0.5
Laymen	188	22.9	237	26.8	+49	+3.9
Laywomen	60	7.3	84	9.5	+24	+2.2
Other	9	1.1	9	1.0	—	-.1
Total	820[16]	100.0	885	100.0	+65	—

Boards range in size from seven to thirty-five members. During the past decade the average membership has increased from thirteen to sixteen members. Similarly, 46 percent of boards were comprised of fifteen or more members in 1987, whereas now 63 percent are comprised of fifteen or more members. Among the advantages of having a larger board, according to rectors/presidents, is the access afforded to a wider range of viewpoints and expertise, the engagement of more people to support the school, and the greater feasibility of staffing the increased number of committees. The most dramatic change is the drop in the number of boards with fewer than ten members, which is now six compared with seventeen a decade ago. Small boards are less favored because the absence of even one or two members negatively affects the conduct of a meeting. Although boards with over twenty-five members (of which there are five) can be unwieldy,

---

[16] In 1987 the data included all boards except those of the North American College in Rome and the American College in Louvain; thus for the sake of consistency the same pattern is followed for the 1997 data. Each of the boards is composed of one representative from the thirteen regions designated by the NCCB. If those members were included for both years, the statistics would be 124 cardinals and bishops out of 846 board members (14.7 percent) in 1987 and 149 cardinals and bishops out of 911 board members (16.4 percent) in 1997.

some of the larger institutions feel that they need more board members to ensure representation of many constituencies. The size distribution of boards is as follows:

< 10 = 6 boards	(5 first-level, 1 second-level)
10 - 14 = 15 boards	(13 first-level, 1 second-level, 1 third-level)
15 - 19 = 19 boards	(14 first-level, 4 second-level, 1 third-level)
20 + = 16 boards	(10 first-level, 5 second-level, 1 third-level)

Theologate boards have made many advances over the past decade: Long-term members have become more familiar with their role and are therefore able to participate more fully in the governance of the schools; ordinaries almost without exception seek and follow the advice offered by boards (though theoretically they are not obliged to do so), which means that board members are deeply committed to the welfare of the schools they help to govern; and faculties are more comfortable with the reality of an external body helping to direct the operation of the school.

Several areas calling for growth remain: Many schools are seeking advice about all aspects of formation but, except for the few board members with experience in educational processes, the majority are reluctant to offer what they consider to be non-professional opinions about complex matters; while both orientation and education of board members has improved, there is room for further improvement; and procedurally some boards function less effectively than others, for example, if the chair or rector/president is unable to elicit the expertise of members who then become frustrated with a purely passive role such as merely listening to reports.

Ten years ago the two foremost issues concerning boards were the need for integration of lay members with clerics, and board education. Most boards have made considerable progress in these areas. The best way of determining whether a board is functioning effectively is to conduct periodic evaluations. Boards that have regularly assessed their performance usually improve their operation by engaging their members more fully. Evaluations take various forms, some involving elaborate written surveys and oral interviews, and others a simple statement about the meeting just concluded. Regardless of the form, proper assessment of board progress is the most important tool for continued upgrading of board performance.

2. Administrators

Introduction. The rectors/presidents are the chief administrators of theologates, with various others assisting them in either
a full-time or a part-time capacity. At some theologates, where the
academic program is given in the context of a university, the chief
administrator is the dean or chair of the department of theology
and a rector leads the associated formation program.[17] In order to
include all types of chief administrators in the following analysis,
the designation used here is chief executive officer (CEO). The
analysis is based on the responses of CEOs to an extensive written
survey,[18] as well as individual interviews with almost all of them.
Because academic deans at most theologates hold an influential
position, they are also considered. Pertinent information is drawn
both from interviews with deans and from a comprehensive study
of deans by Jeanne P. McLean.[19] A briefer analysis of other administrative positions concludes the discussion.

a. Chief executive officers (CEOs). Several studies have analyzed the role of rectors/presidents of seminaries and schools of

[17] The five schools employing a dean or chair of the theology department and a rector in an associated institution are The Catholic University of America and Theological College, the University of Notre Dame
and Moreau Seminary, St. John's University and St. John's Seminary,
Oblate School of Theology and Assumption Seminary, and the University of St. Thomas in Houston and St. Mary's Seminary.

[18] All rectors/presidents except one, who was new to his position and
did not feel adequately informed, responded to the questionnaire. The
total number of respondents is forty-two, including the rectors/presi-
dents of all thirty-three theologates whose primary mission is the formation of diocesan seminarians and those of nine theologates whose
primary mission is the formation of religious-order seminarians, among
the latter one president from a school that closed at the end of the
1997–1998 academic year.

[19] Jeanne P. McLean conducted a study of chief academic officers in
North American theological schools from 1993 to 1995. Four mono-
graphs report her findings: "Leading from the Center: The Role of the
Chief Academic Officer" (vol. 1) by McLean, "Challenges of Academic
Administration: Rewards and Stresses in the Role of the Chief Aca-
demic Officer" (vol. 2) by Karen M. Ristau, "Career Paths and Hiring
Practices of Chief Academic Officers Theological Schools" (vol. 3) by
Mary Abdul-Rahman, and "Professional Development for Chief Aca-
demic Officers" (vol. 4) by McLean. All four are published by the University of St. Thomas in St. Paul, Minnesota (1996).

theology.[20] All of them report that the position has changed: Formerly rather simple and internally oriented, it has expanded to encompass external responsibilities and far more complicated internal structures. The role of the rector/president varies depending on the extent to which a school is either self-contained or interconnected with other institutions. The CEOs of self-contained schools tend to emphasize spiritual leadership within the seminary, guidance of other administrators and faculty, and frequent interaction with students. The CEOs of theologates that focus on connections with people and organizations outside the school devote more time to Board development, fundraising, and participation in professional organizations such as the NCEA Seminary Division and the Association of Theological Schools. All rectors/presidents make a point of building and maintaining good relationships with their constituents, especially with those who send students or provide personnel and financial support. Almost all CEOs at schools for diocesan seminarians devote considerable time to visiting bishops and vocation directors with the aim of persuading them to send or continue sending seminarians. The combination of these varied and complex tasks proves to be a source of distress for many CEOs, who find their attention divided among them.

The titles of CEOs include some form of "rector" and/or "president," unless the position is that of dean or chair of the theology department. At the diocesan schools, seventeen use some pairing of rector and president, one is a rector/dean, another rector/vice-president, and ten are simply called rector. At the religious-order schools, all CEOs are called president. Often the title of rector implies an internal pastoral focus, and that of president an external managerial focus. However, holders of all titles have some responsibilities in both arenas.

Who are the CEOs? The present group comprises twenty-two diocesan priests (52.4 percent) and twenty religious-order priests (47.6 percent). Ten years ago there were twenty-two diocesan

---

[20] Neely Dixon McCarter, *The President As Educator: A Study of the Seminary Presidency* (Atlanta: Scholars Press, 1996); Schuth, *Reason for the Hope: The Futures of Roman Catholic Theologates*, 83-90; Robert Wister, "The Study of the Seminary Presidency in Catholic Theological Seminaries," in *Theological Education*, vol. XXXII, supplement I (Pittsburgh: The Association of Theological Schools, 1995).

priests (44.9 percent) and twenty-seven religious order priests (55.1 percent). The proportion of diocesan priests has increased by 7.3 percent, while the proportion of religious-order priests has declined by the same number. Two-thirds of these leaders come from the ranks of the faculty or from another administrative position within the school, and the remainder have usually served as diocesan or religious-order administrators. Finding priests who are qualified to serve as rectors/presidents is a significant concern, as it was a decade ago. Although some of the negative attitudes about the position that were prevalent in the past have abated, there is a decreasing supply of priests and an increasing demand for priests who are willing to give up parochial ministry or teaching to become administrators.

The academic credentials of the present CEOs are almost the same as they were ten years ago, when 74.4 percent had doctoral degrees and 28.6 percent had master's degrees. Twenty-four rectors/presidents (57.1 percent) now hold pontifical degrees, as compared with 51.2 percent ten years ago. The current credentials are distributed as follows:

Degree	Number	
Ph.D.	15	
S.T.D./J.C.D. (1)	11	71.4 percent
J.D.	2	
D.Min.	2	
S.T.L.	2	
Both J.C.D. and S.T.L.	2	28.6 percent
Master's	8	

The fields of study represented by rectors/presidents cut across disciplines, as they did ten years ago, though now with a slightly higher proportion prepared in systematic and moral theology, and fewer in pastoral theology. Here is a list of the academic fields of CEOs:

Field	Number
Systematic Theology	8
Pastoral Theology	7
Moral Theology	6
Theology (field not specified)	5
Scripture	4
Other (Psychology 2, Law 2, Education 3)	7
Not specified	5

The CEOs' length of time in office is a concern for governing boards, bishops, and religious superiors. Even if an ideal term has not been established, stability is preferred to frequent turnover, and many rectors/presidents regard a period of at least six to ten years as advisable. In fact, longer-term CEOs have often provided highly effective leadership not only at their own institutions, but also in theological education more broadly. However, if CEOs stay in office for too long a period, the school may stagnate from lack of a fresh perspective and direction. At the same time, too short a term prevents CEOs from gaining confidence, developing plans, and realizing a vision.

When changes in leadership occur, the institution often experiences a period of instability brought on by uncertainty about the direction the new leader will take. During such a transition, established networks are disrupted. For example, bishops and religious superiors may decide to send their seminarians elsewhere and thus affect enrollment, and benefactors whose primary loyalty was to the previous CEO may discontinue financial support; or internally faculty and other administrators may reconsider whether they want to remain in their positions and thus precipitate further disorientation. Each situation requires careful analysis to determine the appropriate length of term, but the preferred minimum seems to be six years.

How well does the reality match the preferred term? Generally CEOs have served for slightly shorter periods than the minimum recommended length. Over the past thirty years, from 1968 to 1998, CEOs were in office for an average period of 5.5 years, with 5.6 being the average number of CEOs who have served at each institution since 1968. A widely held assumption is that in recent years the length of service of CEOs has decreased. In fact, the opposite is true. The terms of those currently in office average 5.8 years, an increase of one year since 1988, when it was 4.8 years, and since 1978, when it was 4.9 years. The completed terms of the immediate predecessors of current CEOs averaged 6.3 years, and those of their predecessors 5.9 years. These figures suggest that, by the time the present CEOs finish their terms, they will have served for longer than their predecessors, a positive turn of events.

The viability of their institutions is a major concern for rectors/presidents. Enrolling an adequate number of qualified students was a top priority at almost every school. To achieve this goal, CEOs recognized the importance of mounting an extensive recruitment campaign and judiciously screening all candidates. Apart from the interest of prospective students, the support of primary constituents—bishops, clergy, boards, and religious congregations—is considered a prerequisite for adequate enrollment. Unless the school is understood and accepted by these constituents, they will neither send students there nor provide the financial base needed for successful operation. Well-qualified faculty with a positive and enthusiastic attitude toward ministry and the Church also contribute greatly to the viability of a school, since they have major responsibility for teaching courses and advising students.

What obstacles do rectors/presidents encounter that hinder their effectiveness? Role expectations and time constraints stand out above all others. As one rector/president lamented: "It is not just a matter of being busy, but the multiplicity of demands. We are expected to do so many *different* kinds of things. Everything receives a lick and a promise. I miss the satisfaction of being able to do a few things well." In the same vein, others commented that they may have experience pertinent to some areas of responsibility, for example, the formation of students as part of the school's internal operation, but know little about such areas as fundraising or recruitment.

Indeed rectors/presidents name as other obstacles the challenges of securing enough students and resources for the school. Almost all theologate leaders are engaged in the quest for more students and more dependable sources of students. But there is a contradiction here: Although most rectors/presidents of schools that are primarily for diocesan students complain about dioceses frequently changing seminaries, they themselves actively and vigorously recruit in any and every diocese where they might possibly find a candidate. Competition for students is strong, and the constant recruitment activity of rectors/presidents exacerbates their feeling of being overburdened with work.

Administrative and personnel issues can also hinder effectiveness. Even small schools, by far the majority, sponsor numerous programs requiring administrative oversight. Students may be few in number, but their diverse backgrounds call for much individual attention. Thus the problem of finding faculty who can minister to these formation needs becomes acute. Moreover, faculty in certain academic fields are practically unavailable, so that schools may function for several years with part-time faculty in foundational disciplines. Another perceived inadequacy of rectors/presidents lies with the problem of handling difficult colleagues, many of whom were formerly their peers. Finally polarization in the larger Church manifests itself in many ways at their institutions: Faculty morale is negatively affected by students who confront them about their orthodoxy or their evaluation of students. Negotiating differences between faculty and students can absorb considerable time and emotional energy. But once they have gained some experience, CEOs feel more comfortable; they also value interaction with peers at orientation seminars and regional meetings sponsored by the ATS or NCEA.

When asked what advice they would give their successors, CEOs referred to five broad areas: (1) care for themselves as professionals, (2) leadership practices, (3) mission and program tasks, (4) work related to faculty, staff, and students, and (5) external relations.

(1) Many underscored the importance of maintaining one's spiritual, physical, and mental health—taking time to read, write, think, and keep connected with colleagues in theological education. To that end they appreciated occasions that brought them together with colleagues, even if in prospect the meeting or conference had seemed like yet another obligation.

(2) Most of the advice under this heading favored the leadership style that worked best for individual respondents. They found it helpful to stay in touch with constituents by consulting, listening to new ideas, being open to change, and communicating regularly and often. They also advised delegating and collaborating, but ultimately facing the hard decisions that take courage to make. For many focusing energy on a positive vision, thinking ahead, and keeping the big picture in mind were essential. Several "don'ts" were specified: Don't defend the indefensible, don't try to respond to every crisis, and don't overlook the pastoral role that is integral to being a rector/president.

(3) Respondents stressed the importance of remaining faithful to the mission and the vision it espouses while reminding others that this is what drives decisions. Thus schools should attend first to providing an excellent educational and formational experience that will serve the Church of the next generation. Developing faculty awareness about the scope of the task and engaging students in the total formation experience are crucial to the implementation of the mission. Second, at a

time when enrollment is a major concern, schools are tempted to initiate too many new programs for the sake of enrolling a few more students, thus excessively diffusing the mission and vision. Some CEOs also cautioned against getting bogged down in routine daily tasks at the expense of realizing the Church's mission.

(4) CEOs identified good recruitment and good relationships as the core of faculty, staff, and student work. The task is to gather competent people and then let them apply their talents. Faculty and staff must be selected with care, considering not only their credentials but also their compatibility with the institution. Once faculty and staff are on board, their development needs to become a priority if exciting, effective, and qualified people are to be retained. CEOs remarked that productive relationships with faculty, staff, and students are best fostered by listening to their input, trusting them, and supporting their efforts with resources and words of praise. More difficult but even more vital is the task of including in evaluations constructive criticism of faculty, staff, and students, which is often poorly done, according to many respondents.

(5) External relations claim the lion's share of some CEOs' time; for the others, good external connections are still critical if less time-consuming. Developing the confidence of bishops and religious superiors, maintaining cordial relations with benefactors, and informing the local presbyterate as well as lay leaders of the school's role and particular contribution are all part of the agenda.

Altogether this advice of CEOs is based on the premise that patience and good humor can go a long way toward producing a successful leader of a theologate. CEOs also acknowledged that the cooperation of other administrators makes it possible for them to do their own jobs better. Chief among these other administrators are academic deans.

b. Academic deans. Like rectors/presidents, academic deans of seminaries and schools of theology have multiple responsibilities, but in almost all cases their work is internally focused. The role of academic dean is shaped by the size of the school, the complexity of the programs, the leadership style of the rector/president, and the personal skills and preferences of the dean. According to the McLean study of deans, "They viewed themselves as functioning in two predominant modes, as managers and leaders."[21] Besides supervising the academic programs of the school, deans may also teach, advise, and fulfill pastoral functions. The combination of these responsibilities is usually manifest in one of three patterns:

1) As faculty leaders, most academic deans teach one or two courses a year, lead faculty development efforts, develop curriculum, work with academic advisers and students in special situations, and serve on numerous committees;
2) As managers, a few academic deans teach a great deal, oversee schedules and registration, and advise individual students;
3) As all-school leaders, a few academic deans play a significant role in shaping the school's mission and purpose; they teach one course every year or two, hire and develop faculty, provide curricular and academic oversight, and help implement the overall vision for the school.

All academic deans devote time to building and maintaining good relationships within the schools, but the extent of their influence depends on the institutional context, the length of their term in office, and the quality of their leadership.

The titles of academic deans are almost always one of four: Twenty-two are called academic dean, one of whom is also registrar; eight use the simple title dean, one of whom is also director of the M.Div. program; five serve as vice-rector and dean, all in diocesan seminaries; five others serve as vice-president and academic dean, all in religious-order schools. Two other variant titles are found in university settings, one being associate dean and the other academic adviser. In this study the title academic dean is used to distinguish its holders from other deans, for example, of formation or spiritual life. To a great extent the particular title reflects the respective range of responsibilities. Vice-rectors and deans usually substitute for rectors in their absence and have other administrative duties beyond the academic arena. Similarly, vice-presidents and deans are considered senior administrators with overall responsibility for the operation of the school.

Who are the academic deans? The vocational status of the present group compared with that of ten years ago is detailed here:

---

[21] McLean, "Leading from the Center: The Role of the Chief Academic Officer," vol. 1:8.

	1987–1988		1997–1998	
	Number	*Percent*	*Number*	*Percent*
Diocesan priests	24	49.0	15	37.5
Men religious*	21	42.9	18	45.0
Laymen	3	6.1	4	10.0
Women religious	1	2.0	3	7.5

*All are priests except one who is a brother.

The proportion of diocesan priests serving in the office of academic dean has decreased by 11.5 percent, while the proportion for each of the other three groups has increased slightly. Almost all of these leaders derived from the ranks of the faculty at their own theologate, with the remaining few coming from another educational institution.

The academic credentials of academic deans are impressive, with 97.5 percent (all but one) holding a doctoral degree or the equivalent. This compares with 81.6 percent holding doctoral degrees ten years ago. Twenty-four academic deans (60 percent) hold pontifical degrees, compared with 40.8 percent ten years ago. The credentials of current deans are listed below:

Degree	*Number*
Ph.D. (+S.T.D. 1)	15
S.T.D./J.C.D. (1)	12
Ed.D.	2
D.Min.	2
Other doctorates (Dr.T.,H.E.D.,T.D.,D.Phil.)	6
S.S.L.	2
J.C.L.	1

The fields of study represented by academic deans cover a range of disciplines, as they did ten years ago. The academic fields are as follows:

Field	*Number*
Systematic Theology	10
Scripture	7
Pastoral Theology	6
Moral Theology	4
Theology (field not specified)	3
Church History	3
Other (Psychology 2, Education 1)	3
Church/Canon Law	2
Not specified	4

The academic rank of academic deans reflects their time of service both at their present institution and at other educational institutions. Compared with a decade ago, the ranks held by academic deans are slightly lower, related in part to the turnover rate of deans at many schools. The most striking difference is the large number of schools that assign rank compared with the situation ten years ago. All but six theologates assign rank now, compared with seventeen ten years ago; all but seven deans hold rank. The ranks held by academic deans are as follows:

Rank	Number
Professor	9
Associate Professor	15
Assistant Professor	9
Others ranked, but not the dean	1
Rank not given by the school	6

The length of time in office for academic deans has increased over the past thirty years, though a few schools still suffer from rapid turnover and lack of continuity in academic leadership. From 1968 to 1998, 4.3 years was the average term in office for deans, and an average of 7.2 deans served at each institution during this period. The averages hide some exceptional cases, however: Seven schools have had ten or eleven deans, and three schools have had only three or four deans. Regarding their ideal length of service, as with rectors/presidents, too short a term usually disrupts the direction being set for the school and ordinary follow-up on faculty and student progress suffers. The consensus is that generally deans are in office for too short a time.

Nevertheless, an encouraging shift is occurring. The terms of deans currently in office now average 5.3 years, an increase of more than one year compared with the average of those who were in office in 1988, when that figure was 3.9 years, and in 1978, when it was 3.8 years. The completed term of the immediate predecessors of current academic deans averaged 5.5 years, and that of their predecessors 5.0 years. By the time the present deans finish their terms, they will have served for a longer time than their predecessors, a positive change that should contribute to more accountability and continuity in academic leadership.

What obstacles do academic deans encounter that hinder their effectiveness? Like their counterparts a decade ago, they find that preparation for the job is lacking and that the multiple responsibilities usually associated with it create stress.[22] Although some take advantage of regional deans' meetings and other national programs, the timeliness of these opportunities is a concern. Most academic deans are appointed without adequate preparation or prior experience and, even if developmental conferences are helpful, they may come too late. Nonetheless, whenever deans have the chance to interact with their peers, they benefit from the exchange.

Stress can also hinder effectiveness. As reported in the Ristau study,[23] some deans find the workload overwhelming, and others object to putting their scholarly activities on the back burner. Still others manage the inevitable conflicts that arise with difficulty and miss the companionship of faculty, with whom they are no longer on an entirely equal footing. The pressures that result from the fragile position of many institutions only add to their distress. Although 73 percent of deans report that their jobs become more manageable the longer they serve,[24] most deans are in office for a relatively short time and do not benefit from longevity.

Despite these formidable obstacles and their reluctance to accept the position, the majority of deans appreciate the significance of their role. During interviews they expressed how gratified they were by the dedication of their colleagues, which they understood in new ways. Many of them realized the influence they could have on the direction of the school and on the lives of individual faculty and students. They saw their work as serving the mission of the school in a unique way within their larger call to prepare men and women for ministry.

c. Other administrators. Since the mid-1980s, a substantial number of new programs have been introduced at theologates. Almost every diocesan school has inaugurated a two-year pre-theology program, many schools have added master's degree programs, and others (especially religious-order schools) have augmented lay formation programs. All of these changes,

[22] See the McLean series on academic deans. Ristau, "Challenges of Academic Administration: Rewards and Stresses in the Role of the Chief Academic Officer" (vol. 2); and McLean, "Professional Development for Chief Academic Officers" (vol. 4).

[23] Ristau, "Challenges of Academic Administration," 3–6.

[24] Ibid., 2.

along with more fundraising and recruiting activities, have resulted in an increased number of administrative positions.
Besides rectors/presidents and academic deans, theologates
average about eight other administrators. The following officers
are typically named:

- vice-rector at twenty-eight schools, all diocesan;
- dean of students at twenty-two schools;
- dean/director of spiritual formation at thirty-five schools;
- director of pastoral formation/field education at all forty-
  two schools;
- director of development/institutional advancement at twenty-
  two schools;
- business officer at thirty-three schools;
- registrar at thirty-three schools.

About ten schools each name one or more of the following: director of admissions/recruitment, director of financial aid, director of personal formation, director of lay ministry, and director of
continuing education. Another ten schools list a director of worship (or liturgy) and/or music, but almost all schools appoint a
faculty member to that position even if he or she is not identified
as an administrator. Two further positions mentioned by a few
schools are director of planning and director of multicultural
studies.

Apart from these named positions, most schools employ a
head librarian and library staff as well as several academic program directors. Head librarians and most of the academic administrators hold faculty status. Schools also employ various
administrative assistants, secretaries, facilities managers, com-
puter managers, and other organizational personnel. The ratio
of clerical and other assistants to administrators is usually more
than one-to-one, so that typically a school with ten administrators employs at least fifteen assistants. Faculty at several schools
complained about these high numbers, and leaders are indeed
concerned that the growing complexity of their institutions will
divert energy and resources to administration and away from
the vital tasks of teaching, learning, and scholarship. Yet at virtually every school, faculty and administrators acknowledged
that the work of various assistants is indispensable. Many of
these assistants are women who have been employed by the
schools for many years, carrying institutional memory longer
than anyone else. The tension over numbers means that one of

the most difficult tasks of chief administrators is to make appropriate personnel decisions.

3. Faculty

Introduction. Through their teaching, speaking, writing, and overall influence on students, theologate faculty play a determinative role in shaping the Church's future ministry. Therefore it is important to know who they are, what they do, and how they view their work. To acquire this information, I compiled a list of theologate faculty along with their positions and credentials. Along with colleagues, I also conducted a survey of a random sample of over two hundred faculty and interviewed about four hundred more. Their views and attitudes are reflected throughout this book, but in the present chapter special attention is accorded to faculty composition, the multiple roles faculty perform, and the major sources of satisfaction and frustration that they experience in their work.

a. Faculty composition. Who are the faculty now, and how have their numbers and composition changed over ten years? According to the schools' catalogs, the total number of faculty was lower in 1995–1997 (at 741) than it was in 1985–1987 (at 898). Given the fact that seven theologates have closed during the past ten years, the decrease of 157 is to be expected. Moreover, the number of theology-level seminarians has declined by about eight hundred; at the same time, however, about five hundred more lay students—many of them part-time—have enrolled in theologates. The proportion of faculty to students is therefore quite low, both because ministerial education is labor-intensive and because a relatively large percentage of priests listed as full-time are actually serving the school only part-time while holding other positions outside the school. Some of them work at diocesan offices or parishes, and others serve in administrative or formation roles for their religious congregations. Although some priests worked in dual positions in previous years, the proportion has increased sharply from about 10 percent to more than 30 percent, largely because of the diminishing supply of priests altogether. Thus theologates continue to employ a large number of faculty, about a third of whom are available only on a limited basis because of other responsibilities. Another factor contributing to the high faculty count is the addition of many programs, in particular about twenty-five in pre-theology, about fifteen for Hispanic ministry, and an equal number for fully developed lay ministry.

• Vocational status. The vocational status of faculty continues to shift away from the situation in the early 1960s when virtually all faculty were priests. By 1985–1987, 75 percent of faculty were priests and 25 percent women religious, laywomen, and laymen. By 1995–1997, 66 percent of faculty were priests and 34 percent women religious, laywomen, and laymen, a decrease in priests of about 1 percent per year. Changes since a decade ago include the following: the number of diocesan priests has dropped from 292 to 246, 46 fewer; the number of religious priests has dropped from 392 to 243, 149 fewer; women religious are nearly stable at 95 compared with 93 ten years ago; laymen have increased by 20 from 88 to 108; and lay women have increased by 16 from 33 to 49.

• Credentials. The academic preparation required of faculty members in theologates is specified in the *PPF:* "The professors should have advanced, preferably terminal, degrees in their teaching areas. Professors in the sacred sciences, including philosophy, should possess a doctorate or licentiate from a university or institution recognized by the Holy See. Priest faculty members should have appropriate experience in pastoral ministry."[25] Considerable progress toward this goal was made during the past decade (see table 1). The number of current faculty with doctoral degrees is 553 (74.6 percent) compared with 605 (67.4 percent) a decade ago. Every category of faculty by vocational status have improved credentials, but especially notable is the increased proportion of those who hold doctorates: women religious (from 53.8 to 66.3 percent), laywomen (from 54.5 to 71.4 percent), and laymen (from 67.0 percent to 86.1 percent, the highest of any group). Men religious moved from 77.6 to 84.8, percent and diocesan priests from 59.6 to 63.4 percent.

Table 1   *Faculty: Degrees and Vocational Status*

	Diocesan	*Men Rel.*	*Women Rel.*	*Laymen*	*Laywomen*	*Total*
Doctorate						
Ph.D.	52	90	43	80	27	292
S.T.D.	66	73	9	4	3	155
Dr.Sc.Re.et al.	7	16	6	8	2	39
J.C.D.	15	10	1	1	1	28
D.Min	6	6	3	—	2	17
Total	146	195	62	93	35	531
Percent	(59.3)	(80.2)	(65.3)	(86.1)	(71.4)	(71.7)

[25] *PPF,* #486.

	Diocesan	Men Rel.	Women Rel.	Laymen	Laywomen	Total
Doctorate						
S.S.L.*	10 (4.1%)	11 (4.5%)	1	—	—	22 (3.0%)
S.S.L. &						
Doctorate	156	206	63	93	35	553
Percent	(63.4)	(84.8)	(66.3)	(86.1)	(71.4)	(74.6)
Licentiate, Master's, Bachelor's						
S.T.L.	24	13	—	1	1	39
J.C.L.	8	—	—	—	—	8
M.Div./M.A.	57	24	32	12	13	138
B.A.	1	—	—	2	—	3
Total	90	37	32	15	14	188
Percent	(36.6)	(15.2)	(33.7)	(13.9)	(28.6)	(25.4)
Vocational Status:						
By number	246	243	95	108	49	741
By percent	(33.2)	(32.8)	(12.8)	(14.6)	(6.6)	(100.0)

*s.s.l. degrees are considered terminal teaching degrees by accrediting agencies and so are separately identified.

• Sources of Degrees. Faculty have earned degrees from a variety of universities. At a few schools a large percentage of faculty members have pontifical degrees, whereas at most schools there is more variety. Changes in schools where degrees were earned are relatively small; most notable is a drop (from 40.5 to 32.6 percent) in European universities. The chart below gives figures for all current faculty members compared with those of a decade ago:

Source of Degrees	1985–1987	1995–1997
	(%)	(%)
Roman Pontifical Degrees	25.7	23.2
University of Louvain Degrees	5.1	2.5
Other European University Degrees	9.7	6.9
Catholic University of America Degrees	11.6	12.4
Other American Catholic University Degrees	30.0	33.7
Non-Catholic American University Degrees	18.0	21.3

• Hiring and Retention. The avenues leading to a position on a theologate faculty are gradually changing. In the past it was the leaders of the dioceses and religious orders sponsoring a theologate who selected, prepared, and assigned priests to teaching and administrative positions. Another significant factor affecting the proportion of priests on faculties was the founding of two unions—the Washington Theological Union and the Catholic Theological Union in Chicago—about thirty years ago. To that end some fifty men's religious congregations decided to close their small seminaries and combine their resources, including faculty. A large number of priest faculty could not be employed by the two unions and so became available to teach at other schools. Many of those who were hired by diocesan seminaries then have now reached retirement age, and other priests from religious orders are not available to replace them. The problem is exacerbated by the reduced number of younger priests undertaking graduate studies. As a result, schools must look elsewhere to fill faculty positions, which means hiring women religious, laymen, and laywomen; yet because of the specialized roles of faculty, theologates still attempt to maintain a majority of priests. Commenting on the problem, a dean at one diocesan seminary said:

> We need a coordinated approach to the selection, preparation, and assignment of priests to the faculty. Individual dioceses operating seminaries can no longer take responsibility for supplying all the priests. We need planned collaboration with dioceses that use our school, but they are reluctant to assign their best men to studies, only to have them work outside the diocese.

Hiring faculty who are not priests is made more difficult by the relatively low salaries and, in some cases, the limited size of the student body and scope of the theologate's mission.

An alternative strategy is to retain present faculty—both priests and others—by awarding whatever benefits can be afforded and by making the work situation as congenial as possible. Some schools have been successful in retaining most of their faculty until retirement, but others are plagued by continual turnover. The lack of continuity at the latter schools affects enrollment and contributes to a downward spiral in the student body and therefore in the faculty. Rectors/presidents and academic deans have employed several strategies to ensure long-term stability among faculty, including a concerted effort at faculty development—providing opportunities for faculty to improve their teaching ability and their capacity to perform other functions in administration and formation, offering sabbaticals, and increasing salaries and benefits as much as possible. Mentoring programs for new faculty members also contribute to their success and satisfaction, and thus to their long-term retention.

In what fields is it most difficult to recruit faculty? Deans report a shortage of people who are trained to teach moral theology (ethics) and several of the pastoral disciplines, for example, preaching and pastoral counseling. Until recently faculty trained in Scripture and liturgy were readily available, but now they too are in short supply. Individuals with knowledge of Hispanic ministry, particularly those of Hispanic heritage, are almost entirely unavailable. More frequently schools are hiring part-time faculty to fill these positions, a practice that puts additional strain on the full-time faculty, who then have more responsibility for formation and administrative tasks. Without long-range planning and a coordinated effort to educate future faculty—especially priests—this already-serious situation will become acute in another five to ten years.

b. The multiple roles of faculty. The roles of faculty are comprehensive and time-consuming. Most schools, in particular freestanding, self-contained diocesan seminaries, expect faculty to function both academically and in other formation roles—human, spiritual, and pastoral. Besides teaching, faculty are expected to assist with program and curriculum development and to perform certain administrative tasks, including multiple committee assignments and program direction. Most people find it difficult to combine these tasks, especially since formation work is increasingly specialized and appropriate professional training is expected. In addition, faculty are often involved outside the school with service to parishes and religious communities. Such involvement can take the form of speaking, teaching, or direct pastoral service.

Given all these duties, what happens to research and publishing? For at least half the faculty, little energy remains for scholarship, and motivation for publishing and research is often low. At many schools funding for sabbaticals is limited, and there may be no possibility of taking time off in any case. Those who have little time for research worry that their teaching will also suffer because they lack the time to delve deeply into their discipline. One rector troubled about the many obligations weighing on his faculty asked: "How do faculty feel about their discipline, about contributing to it by publication and professional meetings, when they are torn in so many directions? Are they intrinsically interested in it and excited about it? Will they maintain quality teaching if they are not themselves engaged in scholarship?" By contrast, several schools ensure that faculty do have the time to write and the funds to support them. The deans at these schools regard their faculty publications as equal in both quality and quantity to those of any university professor.

Being a faculty member at a theologate involves more than simply performing a plethora of assigned tasks. The vocation of a seminary faculty has an enhanced communal dimension in comparison with those at other institutions. Community is intentional and requires that faculty be concerned about the professional, spiritual, and personal welfare of colleagues. A document published by the Roman Congregation for Education in 1994, "Directives concerning the Preparation of Seminary Educators," further reinforces this communal notion. Many of the qualities required of faculty relate to community, the spirit of communion among them, and their capacity for communication with each other and with students. Most schools are so small that everyone must work cooperatively at designated tasks to achieve success. A graduate degree in theology may ensure academic competence, but beyond that a willingness to work in a collaborative manner is needed.

c. Faculty attitudes and views. The principal instruments used to discern faculty attitudes and views were a written survey and many interviews. The survey involved a random sample of 216 Roman Catholic theologate faculty from all schools accredited by the Association of Theological Schools.[26] It yielded specific data about several key topics related to the school and its programs. On the whole, faculty were quite positive about their situations, indicating only a few areas of discontent, as described below. Interviews were conducted with some four hundred faculty on site at thirty-five theologates, one Catholic university's ministry division, and about twenty faculty from the seven other theologates. The interview format allowed respondents to present and nuance their views about every aspect of their work. While faculty substantiated many of the positive responses suggested by the survey, they also raised issues of concern and frustration that undermined their morale.

The written survey contained sixty-three statements in two categories: students, faculty, and administrators; and teaching, scholarship, and working conditions at the schools. Faculty were asked to gauge their agreement with a series of positive as-

---

[26] This survey was conducted by the Auburn Center for the Study of Theological Education in 1994 as part of the Project on the Future of Theological Faculty. Answering the same survey were 790 faculty at Protestant theological schools.

sertions, using a scale of 4 (strong agreement) to 1 (strong disagreement).[27] From these data it was possible to ascertain the sources of greatest satisfaction and discontent. The response to one-fourth of the items was above 3.5 (highly positive); on only two items did faculty responses fall below the median of 2.5 (more negative than positive). For the sake of analysis, another twelve of the low responses (with an average score under 3.00), are reviewed. Even those twelve are more positive than negative, but they do point to areas where the schools might improve their effectiveness. Open-ended interview questions on similar topics allowed faculty to elaborate on major sources of satisfaction and frustration. Their interpretations complement and explain the written survey responses.

1. Faculty satisfaction. What gives faculty the greatest satisfaction? According to the survey results, four answers stand out: teaching, working with students in other ways, general working conditions, and aspects of tolerance versus prejudice.

• Teaching. The survey shows that faculty believe they are good at teaching and that their institutions support their endeavors. A very high proportion strongly agree with the statement, "I regard myself as an effective teacher" (3.62). Furthermore they say "I feel prepared to teach students of different ages" (3.52). They acknowledge administrative backing: "The school in which I teach values good teaching" (3.62), and "Library resources are adequate to support my teaching" (3.54).

• Working with Students. Essentially the responses to these statements show that faculty feel that they fulfill their responsibilities toward students effectively. They agree that "faculty should help students strengthen their faith and moral character" (3.77), and that "a school like ours should play a role in judging the fitness of students for ministry" (3.68). In the same vein, they concur with the statement that "faculty are interested in students' personal problems" (3.53). Most faculty would say, "I have excellent relationships with students" (3.57).

• General Working Conditions. Faculty strongly appreciate their relationships with colleagues. One indication of this

[27] Detailed results are reported in an article by Katarina Schuth, "Theological Education in Seminaries," in *Theological Education in the Catholic Tradition,* ed. Patrick W. Carey and Earl C. Muller, S.J. (New York: Crossroad, 1997).

appreciation is their affirmation that "Faculty are committed to the welfare of this institution" (3.71). The statements, "I am satisfied with the competency of my colleagues at my job" (3.57), and "I have excellent relationships with my faculty colleagues" (3.50) also win their agreement. About the job itself they report, "I am satisfied with the autonomy and independence at my job" (3.54). A related finding that may surprise some observers is the positive response to "the school in which I teach offers sufficient academic freedom for faculty members to do their work" (3.43).

• Tolerance versus Prejudice. According to the survey results, theologates are places where tolerance is high and discrimination minimal. Respondents indicate that in their school they find "little discrimination on the basis of race" (3.84), "little racial conflict" (3.69), and "little discrimination on the basis of gender" (3.66). Moreover, faculty believe that "diversity and pluralism have not undermined the collegiality of our campus community" (3.50). Since most faculty are non-Latino white males, these findings are not surprising. Overall only 4.3 percent of faculty are members of racial and ethnic minorities and, although women are more numerous, they still comprise only 18 percent all faculties. Thus it is understandable that women differ significantly from men on the question of gender discrimination (3.28 compared with 3.86). Although the environment is judged to be less favorable by women, even they agree that gender discrimination is not pervasive.

• While the supplementary interpretations tended to corroborate the survey findings, they also introduced some considerations not mentioned in the survey. First, about teaching itself one sacramental theologian commented: "Being able to walk someone through the reasoning process, play with ideas, get others excited about learning—all of this makes teaching enjoyable. I consider it a real honor to be doing this work." A church historian added, "To see students come alive and to see them make connections, get into their tradition—be critical of it but appreciative of it as a means of giving focus to their lives—this is what makes teaching worthwhile." Working with students in other ways than in the classroom is satisfying to many faculty. As one priest put it: "I enjoy the variety that is part of being on the faculty here. Teaching is great, but I like the formation advising I do, too. It gives me a chance to let seminarians know how much the priesthood means to me, what a privilege it is to serve people in the ordinary and extraordinary moments of their lives."

Another factor mentioned in the interviews, but not in the surveys, was the gratification faculty feel because of the importance of the work they are doing. Making a representative observation, one said: "What we teach and the way we teach has an impact on students' lives, on their future as ministers for the Church. I feel that I am not just peddling academic truths, but that I am preparing people who will touch the lives of thousands of others. They will represent the Church as pastoral leaders, teachers, preachers, and sacramental ministers." A faculty member teaching at a theologate that specializes in educating older candidates for the priesthood remarked: "Seeing people at an older age getting enthused about priesthood is rewarding. Their maturity can be a real asset; they often bring experience that helps them make connections and assimilate what they are studying. So many of our graduates have served well in many ministry settings."

2. Faculty frustration. At the other end of the spectrum, what is of greatest concern to faculty or causes them the most frustration? Since only two survey items of the sixty-three fall below 2.50 (the negative side of the median), other items that rank toward the low end of the spectrum are also considered here. Sources of frustration, or at least lower satisfaction, fall into four categories: workload and lack of time, the quality of students and working with certain groups of them, some dimensions of teaching and curriculum, and salary and benefits.

• Workload and Lack of Time. The strongest negative responses relate to heavy faculty workloads, including the most negative of all: "My workload is increasing significantly" (2.20). The constraint of a heavy workload means that faculty do not have enough time to do some things they would like to do. They tend not to believe that "faculty here are given sufficient time to produce research for publication" (2.50), nor are they satisfied "with the time available for keeping current in my field" (2.56). A related source of dissatisfaction is that they are required to do some things they would rather not do. They believe, for example, that "too much faculty time is spent on governance and administrative activities" (2.53). One faculty member wondered if the problem of overwork was part of the "I just can't say no" syndrome. "The problem," he reflected, "could be complicated by weak boundaries. Our many tasks, especially student-related, contribute to being enmeshed in multiple and overlapping relationships. How many boundary issues lurk beneath the surface?"

The sense of being overwhelmed with work may account for an otherwise puzzlingly low response concerning faculty morale (2.91). Several faculty explained the phenomenon in this way: Although they enjoy their work, colleagues, students, and the atmosphere at the institution itself, they still feel uneasy about how their part fits into the whole scheme of things—within their dioceses and the universal Church. Confusion about where the Church is going, plus an incongruence between personal beliefs and the requirements of the position, create tensions that sap energy. Believing that their efforts are minuscule in the face of all that needs to be done by the Church, some are filled with disquiet and malaise.

• Students. Faculty identified two problems relating to students. First, the majority concur with the statement, "The quality of students here has declined significantly in recent years" (2.90). Amplification of this response shows that faculty hold antithetical opinions about the quality of students, basing their perceptions on students' academic ability, pastoral awareness, and religious and educational backgrounds. Some maintain that the quality of students has declined, whereas others judge current students to be as good as they have ever been. Sometimes faculty at the same school hold opposite views, and from one school to another attitudes vary considerably. These differences become more evident during annual evaluation sessions, contributing to disagreements about what criteria should be used to assess candidates for priesthood and other ministries. Chapter II B treats these topics more fully.

The other problem concerns the experience of faculty teaching students rather than the students themselves. Faculty believe that they are not fully prepared to teach certain types of students, namely, those "from a variety of religious backgrounds" (2.97) and those "from a variety of ethnic backgrounds" (3.00). Interviews shed light on the difficulties faculty encounter in teaching students from backgrounds other than their own. Most current faculty, who have been well schooled in their faith throughout their lives, interpret the differences in religious background in one of two ways: For some the critical factor is that students have little academic or experiential knowledge of the faith; for others it is that students may have been practicing their Catholic faith for only a short time, either because they are converts or because they stopped attending church as teenagers or young adults. After a conversion experience of one kind or another, these students are bursting with an enthusiasm that is often neither deeply rooted nor informed by a knowledge of the tradition of the Church. Faculty prefer not to teach students whose backgrounds seem to prohibit them from developing into high-quality ministers.

The reason for hesitation toward working with students from a variety of cultural backgrounds is straightforward: Most faculty are of white, Anglo heritage in contrast to the growing number of students who come from Hispanic, Vietnamese, Filipino, and other cultures. Only a small percentage of faculty have worked with or lived in ethnic and racial communities other than their own. One rector insightfully commented:

> Students in seminaries are ethnically and racially more diverse than at any other point in the history of seminaries. I wonder how well faculty in fact understand and appreciate the wide cultural diversity. The faculty's perceived absence of discrimination and sensitivity to difference seems higher than I would guess actually exists. There is little or no overt discrimination, but most faculty come from a common cultural background different from that of most students. I find a sense among faculty that they need to stretch more to meet the needs of the diverse student community. Where can we find the resources to assist them?

• Curriculum and Teaching. Faculty also expressed discontent with aspects of curriculum and teaching, partly in relation to the issue of student diversity. According to the second lowest and only other truly negative response (the lowest being excessive workload), they do not believe that "many courses include minority group perspectives" (2.48), or that "recent social movements such as feminism have made a difference in our curricular offerings" (2.91). These two responses, combined with expressed concern about teaching students from varying ethnic and racial backgrounds, suggest a possibly serious lacuna in the preparation of ministers to serve an increasingly diverse Catholic population.

The other set of responses in this category deals with faculty being prepared to teach when they begin their jobs, and then as their careers progress having opportunities to upgrade their skills. Faculty disagree that "graduate study prepared me to be an effective teacher" (2.79), or that "the school provides adequately for faculty development" (2.94). Interviews with deans and faculty indicate that faculty development for teaching is not the highest priority at most theologates. Faculty may struggle for years trying to find successful ways to teach; they do not always seek, nor are they offered, assistance that could help them overcome difficulties.

• Salary and Benefits. As might be expected, faculty are not pleased with the compensation they receive. They are not totally satisfied "with my benefits, generally" (2.93), and even less satisfied "with my salary" (2.68). Laymen and laywomen are most affected by the relatively low salaries and modest benefit packages offered at theologates, but diocesan priests as well as women and men religious are also affected. Diocesan priests need to set aside funds to provide for their retirement, and religious feel obligated to support the aging members of their congregations. Administrators face the strain of working without sufficient resources to hire, retain, and develop a strong core of faculty.

Summary analysis. The faculty who are teaching, writing, advising, and administering constitute an irreplaceable resource enabling theologates to accomplish their missions. The total number of faculty has diminished minimally in recent years, but the number of priests continues to decline as the number of women religious, laymen, and laywomen on faculties rises. Yet the perceived nature of ministerial education, especially the education of seminarians, leads most rectors/presidents to insist that priests should constitute the majority on theologate faculties. However, the process of recruiting and retaining priest faculty poses a special problem in light of the increase in retirements and decrease in the number of young priests being prepared for seminary work. Careful mentoring and improved working conditions at theologates are ways to enhance the potential for high retention, especially critical in fields like Scripture, moral theology, and several pastoral disciplines in which few people are prepared or willing to teach.

The special nature of the vocation of a theologate faculty member makes these positions both rewarding and burdensome. Faculty are both encouraged by the important influence they have on future Church ministry, and discouraged by the enormity of the task and the seemingly insignificant contribution each one can make toward the desirable goal of preparing ministers to serve so many American Catholics. While feelings of satisfaction arise from experiences of teaching, working with students, and general working conditions, including congenial colleagues and a positive environment, feelings of discontent stem from equally important sources—excessive workloads and lack of time, the quality of students, working with certain groups of them, some dimensions of teaching and curriculum, and salary and benefits.

Thus although much that is positive recommends the present situation for faculty, beneath the surface of the surveys and interviews a sense of unrest and uncertainty is evident. Resident faculty, mostly priests, feel especially burdened by their workload and the requirement of constant presence. Some resent those who are not always present but seem to enjoy the same benefits. Some women religious, laymen, and laywomen feel excluded from the decision making and community life that they perceive as reserved for resident faculty. Divisions between older and younger members of the faculty, women and men, can also occur for other reasons. When these problems, and others like them, are openly discussed and resolved, the faculty tend to be quite satisfied; but when they are allowed to simmer beneath the surface, faculty may become restless and disengaged. Theologate leadership is crucial to creating an environment that fosters an open community with a view to retaining the faculties whose presence is essential to the success of the schools.

Part III. Formation Programs

■　　■　　■　　■　　■　　■　　■　　■　　■

A. Evolution and Development of Formation Programs

Introduction

As it is understood by those who prepare seminarians and lay students for ecclesial ministry, the meaning of "formation" has evolved and expanded over the past ten years. A decade ago, "formation" usually denoted spiritual formation, including the dimension of personal growth. More recently, the understanding of the term has been extended to embrace all aspects of formation—human, spiritual, intellectual, and pastoral—and this part of the book is concerned with all four of these.

The first section gives an account of why and how programs have changed in recent years, a description of the settings where formation is provided, and an overview of the goals of the programs. The second section deals with human and spiritual formation structures and personnel, including an explanation of the role of internal and external forum advisers, the third section discusses intellectual formation, and the fourth section deals with pastoral field education. The concluding section examines the tasks of integration and evaluation in light of the Church's need for various forms of ministry.

Rationale for program changes. Why were changes made in formation programs? Several precipitating circumstances are notable, including positive developments like the publication of *Pastores dabo vobis,* urging augmentation of human formation programs and development of other formational areas, and the fourth edition of the *Program of Priestly Formation*, which followed suit. Further, lay students by then had been enrolling in theologates for about twenty years and felt the need to supplement their academic and pastoral preparation with a more complete human and spiritual formation program. Specific guidelines for lay ministry preparation have not been issued to address the formational needs of those students, but several schools have developed effective programs in cooperation with students and graduates already working in ministerial settings.

On the negative side, changes were prompted by the sexual abuse and pedophilia charges against clergy that came to light during this period. As a result theologate staffs recognized their obligation to reinforce and specify more than previously guidelines for appropriate professional conduct. A more neutral catalyst was the changing pool of students with their increasing ethnic and cultural diversity, their often minimal religious education, and the greater insecurity of their family backgrounds. At the same time, the number of seminarians has dropped and the need for fully prepared lay ministers correspondingly intensified. The preceding chapter describes the types of students who are currently enrolled in theologates; it underscores the importance of having a more developed formation program to address the altered student profiles, emphasizing the talents and minimizing the weaknesses students bring with them when they enroll in professional ministry programs.

In response to these factors, formation personnel restructured their programs. Details of the implemented changes depended on the enrollment patterns and organization of theologates. In twenty-eight out of thirty-three diocesan seminaries, the same institution is responsible for all aspects of formation.[1] At the other five, students attend a related university or school of theology for their academic courses. These thirty-three theologates, designed mainly for diocesan candidates, are highlighted in the following section B. The other nine theologates are operated by religious orders for their own candidates. These men usually receive human and spiritual formation in their own formation houses and, although the content of their programs is similar to the diocesan programs in many ways, the schools where students take courses do not provide it. In all cases where lay students enroll

---

[1] The exceptions are Assumption Seminary, Texas, St. Mary's Seminary, Texas, Theological College, D.C., the North American College, Rome, and the American College, Louvain.

and participate in human and spiritual formation programs, the academic institution, whether diocesan or religious in focus, sponsors the programs. In addition to the schools referred to above, two Roman Catholic universities offer master of divinity programs for lay students only, with some of the best-developed lay formation available. These programs are discussed in each section as they apply, but much of the discussion following concerns formation for diocesan seminarians.

1. Goals of Formation for Ministry

Although each of the four dimensions of formation has its own goals, all areas are interrelated as well. Seminarians are being prepared for priestly service in the Church, and lay women and men for a growing number of positions related to parishes, dioceses, and other Church-related entities. At the end of the formation period, rectors in diocesan seminaries and formation directors in religious congregations should be confident that they are recommending worthy candidates for ordination. Future priests must be capable of embracing a lifestyle of obedience, celibacy, and simplicity. Further, they cannot function without a firm grounding in the Catholic tradition in all its manifestations, a thorough knowledge of theology. As the Church's future pastors, these men should be holy and mature; ready to live among God's people and serve them; prepared to preach, teach, and celebrate God's Word. A lifetime of servant leadership awaits them; thus from the formation program they need an adequate background to get started.

Lay students are preparing for equally demanding roles in the Church, with less structure to support them. Their ministries have a shorter history, which means that they will work in situations where they are pioneers, forging the direction and setting the tone for new ministries. Because their places are less secure, all the more do they need to develop personal holiness and maturity, knowledge of the tradition, and creative approaches to the rendering of pastoral services. In light of the recent growth in lay ministry, schools enrolling lay students are investigating ways to construct programs that satisfy the needs of these students.

The range of program goals reflects assumptions about the varied backgrounds of seminarians and lay students and the ministries they will undertake. Human and spiritual formation focus on the internal life of the individual, while nevertheless subordinating personal and spiritual development to the goal of transformation for the sake of service to the Church. More specifically, human formation is concerned with discernment of vocation and developmental growth in qualities necessary for effective ministry. Spiritual formation concentrates on relationship with God—prayer life, personal faith, and spiritual growth in general. The closely related academic and pastoral areas seek to educate seminarians for priestly service and to form pastors.

The overall goals of lay formation are similar, but the emphasis is slightly different, depending on the type of ministerial service the individual is preparing to enter. In all cases, the major consideration in determining the content of formation programs is to honor the expectations that the Church has of its priests and other ecclesial ministers. Bishops, religious superiors, and vocation directors choose theologates for their students based on how well they believe their expectations will be met, so faculty and administrators attempt to adapt their programs with reference to these expectations.

2. Context: Desirable Characteristics of Settings for Theological Education and Formation for Ministry

The vision of what is an appropriate institutional context, or environment, for theology-level education varies considerably from one school to another. Models range from the more or less self-contained to the more or less interconnected. Common to all models is the intention to promote authentic discipleship, healthy community life, and leadership potential. All models try to encourage contemplation in action, that is, to be places that promote an atmosphere for self-reflection, prayer, and meditation that will lead to effective service of the Church in the world. No seminary describes itself as exclusively exemplifying one model or the other, but different proclivities are evident. The two prototypes are outlined below, with the understanding that in any given theologate some aspects of each are present.

The context for the *self-contained model* is described as a place set apart where energies and resources are focused on priestly formation and identity and, with a few exceptions, only candidates for the priesthood are enrolled. This model emphasizes formation at the seminary site through courses and lectures, which are the main methods used to foster a vision of the Church. Contacts with the world beyond the seminary are kept to a minimum, with pastoral placements being carefully constructed and restricted. Seminarians learn from each other and from the faculty, especially priests, who stand as personal models for their future ministry.

The context for the *interconnected model* is described as a place that provides a formational climate closely reflecting the reality of contemporary ministry. It develops faith partnerships with members of the larger community and promotes collaboration. It fosters a vision of the Church by having students interact in parishes and other ministry settings. In their programs, the schools that follow this model educate seminarians and lay students who will be ministering together after they complete their courses. Here students learn from each other and from a broad spectrum of people both inside and outside the seminary. In many cases they are encouraged or expected to take courses at another seminary or university to broaden their perspective.

The differences between the two contexts are many, but one major factor that distinguishes the two is whether or not lay students are present in significant numbers. Attitudes about how their presence is regarded has undergone several alterations since the mid-1980s. A number of seminaries that were working hard ten years ago to develop lay programs so as to attract a wider range of students have shifted their focus almost exclusively to seminarians. The rector of one such seminary told me:

> We have put the recruitment and enrollment of lay students on the back burner. Some of our sending dioceses changed bishops, and they were concerned that the mission of our seminary was too broad. By limiting lay student enrollment to a few part-timers, we have picked up seminarians from some new dioceses. Preferences of bishops are important in maintaining our enrollment.

Several rectors whose schools continue to enroll lay students said that they are cautious about the way they advertise their schools. By keeping a low profile on their lay programs, they feel that they can attract more seminarians. At least ten seminaries fit one of these two patterns, with diminished lay enrollment as a consequence.

Shifts in the other direction are also occurring. The nine theologates sponsored by religious congregations have largely intensified their efforts to enroll and educate lay students. Most of the nine have enhanced their recruiting strategies and developed programs more compatible with the needs of those studying to be lay ministers. They have done everything possible from establishing scholarship funds to helping graduates find suitable placements. Two or three diocesan seminaries that have never enrolled lay students are also exploring this possibility, and at least six schools have put new energy into developing lay ministry programs for their own dioceses. These programs for lay students have become important resources for the local churches and are regarded as central to the future of diocesan ministry.

What do these changes mean for the future of the Church? They may be harbingers of the style of ministry that will prevail in particular dioceses depending on the choice of theologate. The nature of these models is critical, since the environment created in the school *here and now* is what students experience as good community spirit and they are likely to replicate that experience in future ministry. All agree that the environment is formative. What is the proper balance between the two theologate models? What are the effects of separating or integrating priesthood and lay ministry candidates? Some schools have enrolled lay students for a long time, others have maintained enrollment primarily of seminarians. Research is needed to determine the patterns and styles of ministry engendered by the divergent models. Which models match the expectations and needs of the Church?

Ten or more years of experience have brought little clarity in answer to these questions, partly because a thorough study of the effectiveness of pastors, associates, and lay ministers formed in different settings has not been done. One faculty member in a diocesan seminary queried: "Is it possible that behind the questions is the notion that 'we are not turning out the right kind of priests'? We have a lot of theories about what generates priestly identity, but not much research to back it up." In general, we find that those who were strong advocates of one pattern or the other ten years ago have maintained the same viewpoint. Yet pressures for enrollment have altered some of the practices associated with the two main models identified here.

Especially at diocesan seminaries, faculty and administrators are asking how to discern which is better given the structures and personnel their graduates will find in local parishes. It is possible that the self-contained and the interconnected models both work, that each model has its strong points and its shortcomings. By exploring some of the concerns of those who prefer one model over the other, we may be able to shed more light on the subject.

Bishops, religious superiors, and vocation directors are all intensely committed to formation that promotes a realistic and distinct priestly identity. For a few, particularly in diocesan settings, this means (as it were) returning to an earlier era when formation for clerical culture was the goal. Some worthy intentions of such a model are indisputable: creating a strong sense of brotherhood among future priests, enhancing education about the specific tasks associated with the role of priest, and deepening the spirituality characteristic of diocesan priesthood. Critics, however, argue that this style of formation is based largely on an "isolation-clan" model and cannot be sustained now that collaborative ministry is becoming the norm in all but a few parts of the country. Human and spiritual formation, they say, can easily be supplied separately for seminarians and, if some classes should focus exclusively on priestly ministry, they too can be offered for seminarians only.

Those favoring an interconnected model, according to which both lay students and seminarians are enrolled in the same school, contend that priestly identity can be forged only through interaction with the other. In their view a mix of students anticipates a future of collaborative ministerial service. Lay students, especially those with families, they feel, ask questions and express perceptions that are more relevant to interests of parishioners; raising these issues in an academic setting enlivens the subject matter and prepares students more effectively for modern ministry. Critics would counter that the diminished focus on priesthood makes it more difficult for seminarians to grasp the distinctive aspects of their role. As one rector said: "We fear seminarians won't 'get identity'; they won't know what it means to be a priest if they are formed in a mix of students." Administrators who are critical also believe that the efforts of faculty in interactive settings are diffused and the time available for seminarians thereby reduced.

The overall trend or wave of the future regarding the self-contained model versus the interconnected model is difficult to discern, partly because schools are moving in opposite directions. The clearest difference is between religious-order schools and the majority of diocesan seminaries, where the former are moving whole-heartedly toward incorporating lay students and thus, in their view, strengthening priestly identity, while the latter are downplaying their presence or eliminating lay students from their programs. However, at least a half-dozen seminaries operated by an individual diocese have made a full commitment to the education of all ministers—lay and ordained—for their diocese. Their decision is perhaps indicative of the trend on a broader scale—these seminaries have lost enrollment of seminarians and usually have only a few seminarians from dioceses other than their own. Determining factors are assumptions about what leads to priestly identity and how well bishops believe their expectations for formation are being met.

B. Human and Spiritual Formation in Theologates

1. Personnel and Organization

In comparing the human and spiritual formation programs of the mid-1980s with the mid-1990s, we find that ten years ago structures were less complex and content less comprehensive. To illustrate, in 1986–1987 formation deans, directors of formation, or directors of spiritual formation were listed for fourteen schools; another fourteen listed a spiritual director only; and five had formation teams. By 1996–1997 all but three schools listed a formation dean, director of formation, or director of spiritual formation; three listed a spiritual director only; and eleven had formation teams. An individual school often had more than one dean or director to lead different parts of the program. The number of faculty staffing human and spiritual formation programs grew from about eighty to over two hundred.

In effect the concept of formation has broadened, with human formation being named as a distinct component of formation for the first time about five years ago. Significant content was added in the areas of personal growth and celibacy formation. These changes led to the creation of new structures that incorporated human and spiritual formation and also included assessment of some dimensions of academic and pastoral formation. Classroom contact alone was judged to be an inadequate basis for making accurate assessments of students' readiness for ministry. Subsequently faculty were recruited and trained as formation directors, who would be required to review all aspects of the candidate's life in the external forum.

The growth in human formation programs is ongoing, and the types of structures being used are still very much in flux. Most schools combine administration of human and spiritual formation in one department, although conceptually the content is somewhat divergent. At several schools separate departments, each with its own personnel, administer the programs, but even in these cases the connection between the two is close.

In the earlier period, most aspects of formation were dealt with under the heading of "spiritual formation." Programs featured group conferences with the rector and/or spiritual director, as well as individual spiritual direction. The major criticism of this arrangement was that too much information about seminarians was being held in the internal forum, that is, as privileged information between the seminarian and his spiritual director. Theologate personnel felt that students could conceal details of their lives and backgrounds that might call into question their suitability for priesthood. This problem led seminaries to reexamine the function of the internal forum and limit its role to spiritual direction as well as, of course, the sacrament of reconciliation. At the same time formation teams were expanded to include faculty advisers who related to students in the external forum, where they held seminarians accountable for human and spiritual growth, as well as academic and pastoral development. These adjustments ensured that appropriate knowledge about a person who would eventually be serving in a public ministerial position would come to light in the external forum. With those changes, the work of formation became more labor-intensive and now involves more people working in various capacities with human and spiritual, as well as academic and pastoral formation.

In many theologates the role of formation adviser or mentor embraces all matters in the external forum. Usually those who serve in this role work under the direction of the dean or director of formation. Working with the adviser, students are asked to articulate annual goals in the form of personal growth plans that are geared to their individual developmental needs. They identify areas for growth related to all aspects of formation. Beginning students, for example, might concentrate on participating in group tasks in a collaborative spirit, and on learning how ecclesial, liturgical, and spiritual traditions have developed. More advanced students might reflect on how consistent they have become in making judgments with prudence and common sense, and on how they can demonstrate leadership skills in the public arena. These self-assignments then serve as the basis for annual or more frequent evaluations.

Several concerns gained attention when these new programs were implemented.

• First, it was evident that faculty members serving as formation advisers needed education in counseling and psychology to enable them to work more holistically with students. Toward that end, a biannual program for new seminary forma-tors was begun and continues to be sponsored by the NCEA Seminary Department and the American Sulpician Province. Given the diversity of student backgrounds, especially those of students from different cultures, a correct appraisal of students' strengths and weaknesses was becoming more vital than ever before, and yet few faculty had the education necessary to make such assessments.

• Second, advisers wondered how to keep internal and external forum matters separate when serving in multiple roles with weak boundaries, that is, acting as spiritual directors to some and formation advisers to others. Clearer role definitions were needed. Many priests working as spiritual directors believed that the best solution was to refrain from involvement with external matters entirely. For that reason, some seminaries use spiritual directors from outside the school as a way of assuring confidentiality when it is required. A parallel concern of formation advisers was how to balance their function as supporters and advocates of students with that of challengers and evaluators.

• Third, regarding the whole student body the question was asked, How can formation teams inspire and stimulate talented students rather than focusing excessively on students with problems? As the number of entering seminarians who had progressed through a long preparatory program of high school and college seminary dwindled, and as more lay students chose to study for ministry, students altogether were beginning their ministerial education at very different starting points, often with minimal spiritual and theological foundations. Many faculty believed that exceptionally well prepared students were not being adequately challenged because the generally lower level of achievement deflected attention from them. This concern applied equally to all aspects of formation.

2. Human Formation Programs

Rationale for the programs. Since the publication of *PDV* and the fourth edition of the *PPF*, the area of human formation has received new emphasis. In most settings the human and spiritual formation programs are not strictly divided, though each one has a distinct character. Human formation focuses on psychological and emotional development and well-being; it serves as the foundation for spiritual formation, which is directed more toward relationship with God and the Christian community. Certainly the two areas are closely intertwined, as the following quotation from the *PPF* indicates.

> Every seminary must provide a milieu of human and spiritual formation in which seminarians are encouraged to grow continuously and progressively in their personal relationship with Christ and in their commitment to the Church and their vocation. A well-rounded and effective program of spiritual formation presumes and builds upon continuing theological and personal growth and character development consistent with a priestly vocation.[2]

Insisting on the vital importance of developing the human person, *PDV* confirms that human formation has its own unique content and goals.

> The whole work of priestly formation would be deprived of its necessary foundation if it lacked a suitable human formation. . . . Future priests should therefore cultivate a series of human qualities, not only out of proper and due growth and realization of self but also with a view to the ministry. These qualities are needed for them to be balanced people, strong and free, capable of bearing the weight of pastoral responsibilities. They need to be educated to love the truth, to be loyal, to respect every person, to have a sense of justice, to be true to their word, to be genuinely compassionate, to be men of integrity and, especially, to be balanced in judgment and behavior.[3]

The content and structure of human formation programs. Many theologates, especially those with diocesan candidates, have developed programs of human formation that correspond to the requirements stated above. Although formation topics may be treated under any of the four areas of formation, several specific topics are more strongly associated with human formation: (a) vocational discernment and development of commitment to ordained ministry, (b) personal and relational growth in its many forms, and (c) formation for celibacy. The structures include individual guidance and counseling, class formation, and participation in various school activities and special colloquia.

a. Vocational discernment and development of commitment. Helping seminarians discern their vocation is often the first

[2] *PPF,* #264.
[3] *PDV,* #43.

task from both a human and spiritual standpoint. Given their disparate backgrounds, not all students are fully cognizant of the meaning or even reality of their vocation. Human formation is designed in part to present the vocation to priesthood as a mutual call from God and the Church. New seminarians need to receive external endorsement for their vocational decision. The process also leads them to value their vocation and to renew their commitment to the pursuit of ordained ministry. Ideally this commitment will have been made before they enter theology, but given the fact that a considerable number of candidates lack a history of deep involvement with the Church, it cannot be taken for granted.

Vocational commitment requires that the seminarian understand his psychological and emotional strengths and weaknesses, and the directions he must take to ready himself for ministry. According to one former rector:

> More emphasis on human formation is necessary. More intention, effort, energy is needed to help students identify weakness in their lives. They have to have themselves together; one model suggests that prayer and study alone will solve everything. While these are indispensable, human growth must accompany them. It's about the difference between an integration model and an identification model; they need to internalize virtues related to priesthood, not just imitate behaviors they think the faculty may want.

One of the most important goals of human formation, then, is to help seminarians understand their own motivations and desires so that they can consciously make a permanent commitment to priesthood. In discussing this issue, one faculty member reflected:

> We can't take a static approach to commitment these days. The seminarian is being converted to or led to embrace a way of life that requires a dynamic approach, which means continual renewal of commitment. What is being proposed? If the commitment is to remain alive and ever new, it cannot be made once and never changed or revisited. Unless a commitment is dynamic, it will eventually die.

Comparing the commitment to priestly life to that of marriage, a married faculty member noted that "stability in marriage has new meaning these days when people live so much longer. A lifetime commitment means something different now. You have

to keep renewing it, or it won't last. The same is true for priests."
In the past it was part of the culture to make a permanent commitment; now seminarians have to be socialized into the idea.

When asked why there is so much concern about commitment, one rector replied:

> In the past, the seminary prepared men to be pastoral, to de-
> velop those skills. Now the goal of formation seems to focus
> more on preparing the individual for permanent commitment.
> This is driving formation; fear is driving it, fear that priests will
> not be faithful to their commitment to celibacy, to permanence
> in the priesthood. What enables a permanent commitment?
> What else can the program do?

Several formation advisers believe that programs are well designed, but that too much pressure is being put on the seminary
and not enough attention is given to early pastoral assignments. Students do well as long as they are with peers who es-
pouse the same commitment, but it is hard for them once they
get out of seminary. What happens in a diocese? Priests are expected to do the same ministry for a very long time, often in isolated circumstances. They need ongoing support and contact
with each other, opportunities for mutually enriching conversations and encouragement. Especially if they are serving in re-
mote areas and are overburdened with several parishes, they
can become disconnected from the larger Church. Most priest
faculty believe that the quality of priests' lives must be addressed after they are ordained if human formation is to have a
lasting effect. The human formation program can help priests
to cope more effectively, but as their workload increases and
their role becomes more complicated, the diocese must take
more responsibility for their well-being beyond the seminary
years.

In the interest of solidifying commitment that will last into
the future, the most effective seminary programs take into account the developmental nature of human formation. They reflect the need for continual conversion and ongoing growth in
self-knowledge and self-possession. Formation directors work
with students to foster an awareness of how they can tap into
their human potential, their talents, and their intellectual and
pastoral resources. In the area of human development, of utmost importance is an understanding of human sexuality in
relation to a celibate lifestyle. This involves recognizing the ne-

cessity for intimacy as well as the difficulties and obstacles associated with it, especially the professional boundaries that must be respected. The challenges and blessings of relationship are explored with attention to the unique needs of each individual student. The different ages and cultural backgrounds of seminarians make this task both more complex and more crucial than ever before. Because psychological health and spiritual development are so closely connected, the two areas of human and spiritual formation are commonly handled by the same department.

b. Personal and relational growth. Almost every school offers counseling and/or psychological services, and though the use of these services varies considerably from one place to another, overall it is increasing. Typically psychologists assist with testing and consultation during the admissions process, and counselors are available to students throughout their program. The effective use of these services depends on attitudes about developmental counseling on the part of both formation staff and students. Resident psychologists who hold faculty positions are often valuable consultants for other faculty but, depending on their role within the institution, they may or may not counsel students. Some of those who perform both teaching and counseling functions report that classes may provide an entrée into individual counseling, but others identify the teacher relationship as a barrier to counseling. Because of the disparate backgrounds of students, formation advisers are more likely than ever to recommend these services. One difficulty is that of finding appropriate counselors for students from other countries. United States-trained counselors may not have the cultural knowledge to diagnose and handle some of the problems that arise.

Class formation programs are usually arranged by the formation team or director. These programs tend to be thematic and developmental, occurring on a weekly or biweekly basis for an hour or two. From the first to the fourth year, themes progress from personal commitment and discernment, to ecclesial commitment, to pastoral leadership, to transitional issues. In seminaries with around a dozen students or more per class, sessions are usually given for each class level, but in smaller settings classes are more often combined. Conferences, workshops, and courses concerning issues of human formation include sessions on the development of relational skills, self-management, alcohol and substance abuse, family life, celibacy, conflict resolution, and peace and justice, among other topics. Rectors usually offer at least monthly conferences at diocesan seminaries, outside speakers give workshops on specialized subjects, and faculty teach courses on topics related to formation. Attention to the changing nature of the student body is critical so that offerings accord with students' real-life concerns at their stages of development.

Participation in student government is important for the sake of creating community and ensuring that students have a voice in shaping their communal life. Various forms of participation are possible, such as town hall meetings and committee structures, in which students are given the opportunity to learn about group dynamics and to exercise leadership. Since older students with extensive experience along with students from varied ethnic backgrounds are entering seminaries, conflicts about lifestyles and preferences inevitably arise. These are best resolved by the active participation of students rather than administrative fiat. That model also serves as an example for future ministry.

Finally, health and exercise programs receive more or less prominence, depending on the seminary. For the increasing number of students with health-related problems, they are crucial. Self-care is seen as an integral part of human formation, though the ability to balance a sensible regard for oneself with an appropriate work ethic is considered equally important.

c. Formation for celibacy. The phenomenon that bridges human and spiritual formation is celibacy. The main purpose of formation for celibacy is to assist seminarians in attaining a sincere appreciation and personal readiness for commitment to the charism of celibacy. Seminary programs have always provided this formation, but over the past ten years faculty have given it more attention. Two general reasons for the strengthening of celibacy formation are evident: the impact of the sexual abuse by some clergy that has come to light during this period, and the fact that often students' previous religious education has not dealt thoroughly with sexuality from the Church's point of view.

Every area of formation relates in one way or another to celibacy. Human formation concerns psychological and sexual maturity, spiritual formation issues that are linked to prayer and spirituality, intellectual formation an awareness of the theological issues involved in the call to celibacy, and pastoral formation the extent to which intimacy is permitted and professional boundaries must be respected. *PDV* states clearly the importance of explicit training:

> The spiritual formation of one who is called to live celibacy should pay particular attention to preparing the future priest so that he may know, appreciate, love and live celibacy according to its true nature and according to its real purposes, that is for evangelical, spiritual and pastoral motives. The virtue of chastity is a premise for this preparation and is its content. . . . In the seminary, that is in the program of formation, celibacy should be presented clearly, without any ambiguities and in a positive fashion. The seminarian should have a sufficient degree of psychological and sexual maturity as well as an assiduous and authentic life of prayer, and he should put himself under the direction of a spiritual father. The spiritual director should help the seminarian so that he himself reaches a mature and free decision, which is built on esteem for priestly friendship and self-discipline, as well as on the acceptance of solitude and on a physically and psychologically sound personal state.[4]

Theologate faculty have responded to the challenge of providing suitable instruction about celibacy. Depending on their expertise and role, they give seminarians guidance about living a committed life in the celibate state, introduce them to relevant Church documents, and instruct them about relational development, personal intimacy needs, and professional boundaries that must be maintained in ministerial situations. Many faculty members have worked on classes and conferences dealing with celibacy. A director of spiritual formation has developed a comprehensive resource book containing essential documents, commentaries on the tasks and structures of celibacy formation, and other useful articles about how to instruct seminarians on living a life of celibate chastity.[5]

3. Spiritual Formation Programs

Rationale for the programs. With the advent of more developed human formation programs, the essential content of spiritual formation has become more focused. Each group of

---

[4] *PDV,* #50.

[5] Rev. Thomas W. Krenik at The Saint Paul Seminary School of Divinity is the author/editor of *Formation for Celibate Chastity* (1997). The manuscript is being published by the NCEA Seminary Department (1998).

students preparing for ministry—diocesan, religious order, and lay—has its own program orientation associated with the spirituality that is conducive to its ministry. Theologates have designed programs based on the backgrounds, stages of spiritual development, and future plans of students.

The core of diocesan priestly spirituality is prayer and personal faith centered in the sacramental life of the Church. Unlike the situation ten years ago, when extensive literature about the topic was just coming into existence, many pertinent resources in the form of collections of essays, tapes, articles, and books are now available.[6] Each of them helps to define the meaning of diocesan priestly spirituality in the actual contexts in which priests find themselves. The pastor of a large suburban parish, Rev. Robert Schwartz, writes:

> This sacramental spirituality of ordained ministry invites priests to a holiness that authenticates their role as shepherds, prophets, and priests in the Church. To be the sign they were ordained to be, priests must be people of prayer, unifiers, listeners, leaders with courage, conviction, and vision who are able to deal with giftedness, confusion, and conflict, and much more.[7]

Drawing on the experience of seasoned priests, seminarians are asked to develop a spiritual worldview that incorporates the reality of working in parishes. These intense Christian communities expect their priests to be grounded in prayer, able to discern the needs of parishioners, and adept at relating to a variety of groups and individuals. Certain practices and habits help seminarians prepare for a lifetime of parochial ministry in which they are called to service as active contemplatives. Integrating love of God and love of neighbor, their work is essentially Eucharistic in character.

Because of their long traditions, most *religious congregations* have established a significant body of literature about their own charisms and the attendant spirituality that expresses them.

---

[6] For example, Donald B. Cozzens, ed., *The Spirituality of the Diocesan Priest* (Collegeville: The Liturgical Press, 1997) is one of the most comprehensive books on the topic. The twelve contributors include eight diocesan priests and four bishops. Extensive bibliographies are provided.

[7] Robert M. Schwartz, "Servant of the Servants of God: A Pastor's Spirituality," in ibid., 14.

Some congregations focus on preaching or teaching, others on reconciliation or evangelization. Religious practices and virtues emphasized in formation reflect the particular goals and ministries of each congregation, but they also have some components in common with other congregations and with diocesan spiritual formation. Virtually all of them see the Eucharist as central, and most emphasize the importance of Sacred Scripture as the ground of their liturgical prayer and devotional life.

One problem faced by religious formation houses today is the lack of a critical mass of seminarians in communities, which could threaten to abridge the content of the programs offered. With only a few students in some houses, the temptation is to take a minimalist approach to formation. Some formation directors have suggested combining and consolidating small groups so as to lessen the burden on one person doing all the formation in small houses.[8] In theologates where many religious congregations are represented, this practice is already being implemented. The unique charisms of a community are dealt with in separate sessions, but teaching about the vows and prayer life is largely shared by formation directors of several congregations. The understanding of spirituality in religious congregations as a collective reality is expressed in the following excerpt from *PDV:*

> Just as for all the faithful spiritual formation is central and unifies their being and living as Christians, that is, as new creatures in Christ who walk in the Spirit, so too, for every priest, his spiritual formation is the core which unifies and gives life to his being and his acting as a priest.[9]

Lay students enter theological studies with a strong desire for spiritual growth as they contemplate a life of service in the Church. They recognize the increasing responsibilities of the ministries they will assume, and the expectation that they be spiritually mature and able to communicate with others the essence of the spiritual life. Regarding formation for lay ministry, an experienced lay formation director has written:

> From the beginning of their studies, most students perceive the value of engaging in sustained dialogue about where they are in

---

[8] This issue is relevant especially to the Conference of Major Superiors of Men, which deals with formation in religious congregations.

[9] *PDV,* #45.

relation to God, prayer, Church, mission, and ministry with a supportive and skilled director. . . . Spiritual development is perceived as benefiting the individual student and as a needed foundation for future ministry.[10]

Students are encouraged to trace the path of their spiritual growth, to recognize patterns and images in their prayer life, and to integrate the fruits of their spiritual life with their ministry.

The goals of spiritual formation for future priests are outlined in *Optatam totius* and repeated in *PDV:*

> Spiritual formation . . . should be conducted in such a way that the students may learn to live in intimate and unceasing union with God the Father through his Son Jesus Christ, in the Holy Spirit. Those who are to take on the likeness of Christ the priest by sacred ordination should form the habit of drawing close to him as friends in every detail of their lives. They should live his paschal mystery in such a way that they will know how to initiate into it the people committed to their charge. They should be taught to seek Christ in faithful meditation on the word of God and in active participation in the sacred mysteries of the church, especially the eucharist and the Divine Office, to seek him in the bishop by whom they are sent and in the people to whom they are sent, especially the poor, little children, the weak, sinners and unbelievers. With the confidence of sons they should love and reverence the most blessed Virgin Mary, who was given as a mother to the disciples by Jesus Christ as he was dying on the cross.[11]

In essence, the desirable outcome of spiritual formation is that seminarians and lay students will reflect on their experience of God's work within them and will relate their prayer life to the community of believers. Since they will be responsible for nourishing a deeper and stronger faith in parishes and other ministerial settings, they should possess an understanding of their inner life in relation to those they serve. They need a humble, compassionate heart, a deep relationship with and adherence to Jesus Christ, and growing trust in God's love if they are to provide spiritual leadership. In priestly ministry the focus is on liturgical prayer and the many sacramental moments in

---

[10] Virginia Sullivan Finn, "Formation for Non-Ordained Ministry," *The Way* 56 (Summer 1986) 45.

[11] *PDV,* #45.

the life of the parish. In other ministries, God's presence can be discerned and highlighted for the faithful in a multitude of settings—not only parishes but also campus and hospital chaplaincies, diocesan offices, and social service agencies, among others.

The structure and content of spiritual formation programs. A variety of formats, including conferences, workshops, courses, and individual spiritual direction, are employed in spiritual formation programs. The content is also extensive. Fundamental to spiritual formation is celebration of the daily Eucharist, the Liturgy of the Hours, sacramental reconciliation, and prayer services. Diocesan seminarians are required to participate regularly in these exercises during the times set aside for them. Religious-order candidates normally have spiritual exercises in their own communities, but on special occasions they participate with everyone else at the school they attend. In more and more theologates, lay students are also expected to develop spiritual growth plans with a spiritual director or formation adviser; those plans include a pattern of prayer and reflection suited to their calling and state in life.

In diocesan seminaries conferences, workshops, and courses constitute the usual media for ongoing group spiritual formation, and on special occasions students attend days of recollection and retreats. At the class level, weekly formation sessions provide support and encouragement through mutual sharing among peers. On an individual level, students receive spiritual direction and may also be encouraged to keep spiritual diaries or journals, and to discuss with mentors and peers the progress and difficulties of their spiritual quest. A new development in recent years is an intensive spiritual formation program usually a few weeks in duration though in one instance lasting a full academic year. These formational elements and programs supply the groundwork for realization of personal spiritual goals in light of the Church's needs. They are described below in detail.

Conferences and workshops cover many topics relating to the spiritual life. A primary aim is to expose students to dimensions of the Church's prayer tradition, including contemplative prayer, charismatic prayer, *lectio divina* (spiritual reading, especially the Scriptures), the Spiritual Exercises of St. Ignatius, the Rosary, and Eucharistic devotion. All of these experiences familiarize students with ways to enrich their own prayer life and prepare them to be capable and sensitive leaders of prayer.

Many courses are offered in the area of spirituality. Some are more theoretical, for example, the history of Christian spirituality, while others are more practical, for example, the nature and practice of spiritual direction.

Days of prayer and recollection as well as longer retreats give seminarians the opportunity to deepen their relationship with God as they absorb and integrate the many elements of formation. Formats include preached, directed, and guided retreats, conferences, and sharing of faith in small groups. Typically diocesan seminarians take part in preached retreats, but they are encouraged to make at least one directed retreat in their course of studies. Religious-order seminarians are more likely to make directed retreats during the summer rather than the school year. Lay students often participate in days of recollection, but the cost of retreats is prohibitive for many of them. Some theologates arrange and pay for one directed retreat for lay students, who are then expected to cover the cost of additional retreats. With the development of lay formation, program directors voiced concern about how to handle the growing cost of retreats and spiritual direction. Because lay students usually have limited funds, the current solution is for some of those costs to be absorbed by the schools and some by the students.

Prayer forms: communal prayer. Communal prayer has changed little over the past ten years, with the Eucharist and Liturgy of the Hours forming the foundation. The celebration of the Eucharist is the key formative experience and focal point of each day. As one of the seminary catalogs elaborates:

> The Eucharist is the most perfect expression of the community's action of praise and thanksgiving. If the Eucharistic celebration is at the center of Christian formation, it must necessarily occupy the same centrality in any formational program of priestly training. . . . Eucharist forms the center of the daily communal prayer. It reflects the ebb and flow of the liturgical seasons and brings the community together for the prayer of the Church and the celebration of the mystery of Christ.[12]

Seminarians are required to attend Mass daily, and in most seminaries together with other students they are responsible for

---

[12] University of St. Mary of the Lake, Mundelein Seminary, *Catalog,* 1996–1997, 16.

planning the celebrations and for serving in such roles as those of cantor, musician, and minister of the Word. As seminarians progress through their programs, they often do pastoral assignments on weekends and if so are absent from the community Eucharist and from other community activities. Lay students, who frequently study part-time and work in parishes on weekends, are not present either. A weekly celebration of the Eucharist in Spanish is common and, at seminaries where other cultures are strongly represented, some of their liturgical rituals are incorporated when feasible.

Although the Eucharist is spoken of as both the source and the sign of unity, that ideal is not always realized. As in many parish settings, the manner of celebrating the Eucharist can be a source of tension in theologates. The style of celebration, the selection of music, the extent to which other cultural traditions are introduced, the use of inclusive language, and the forms of participation can become points of contention. Disagreements are as evident among seminarians as they are between them and other members of the community. During interviews rectors who felt they had been successful in allaying such problems noted that the best way to handle contentious situations was "to teach, teach, teach." The better the understanding, especially of the historical background of various liturgical practices, the more likely the community is to reach a consensus about their implementation. Many theologate faculty believe that some tension around liturgy is constructive, since the same experience will no doubt be repeated in many parishes.

Prayer life is also sustained by the twice-daily celebration of the Liturgy of the Hours in most diocesan seminaries. The spiritual formation program seeks to foster an understanding and appreciation of this prayer of the Church. To gain experience as leaders of prayer, a primary priestly responsibility, seminarians alternate with faculty members in planning and leading morning and evening prayers. The communal celebration reflects only one dimension, however; opportunities are also offered to gather in small groups or to pray alone, anticipating the varied circumstances that seminarians will encounter in ministry.

The 1993 *PPF* emphasized the sacrament of reconciliation even more insistently than in past editions. At some seminaries priests are available for individual confession before Mass every day, at others on a weekly basis. Sometimes spiritual directors also serve as the seminarian's confessor, and at most seminaries a communal celebration of reconciliation is scheduled seasonally. Such events reflect the desire for ongoing conversion, a hallmark of the Christian life.

These communal prayer experiences represent a variety of prototypes drawn from the wealth of the Church's tradition. Their richness not only enhances the life of the seminary community, but also serves as the matrix for prayer styles to be used in parishes.

Prayer forms: private prayer. Since the 1980s, expressions of private prayer have changed noticeably. While exercises such as spiritual reading and personal meditation continue as before, private devotions have multiplied. Mentioned frequently during interviews, required Eucharistic adoration, Benediction, Marian devotions, Stations of the Cross, novenas, and litanies, among other forms, are spelled out in detail in many formation manuals and catalogs. Remarkably, devotions that are peculiar to Hispanic, Asian, or African American cultures are not commonly found, even though individual seminarians may practice them and ethnic churches may still use them. In part the neglect of specifically ethnic devotions may reflect the complex ethnic composition of the student body at many theologates today. The impossibility of incorporating every group's rituals leads administrators to avoid selective sponsorship because it might cause those not represented to feel slighted. Further, some theologate faculties, particularly liturgists, do not want to emphasize devotions that are not liturgically based.

What constitutes an appropriate devotional life in a seminary? How does effective spiritual formation focus primarily on the public prayer of the Church while recognizing the need for personal devotional prayer? Does the multiplication of devotions and other pious practices signify a more profound spiritual life? Or does it indicate the demise of true religion? These questions asked by interviewees are becoming more urgent as the interest in private devotions grows among seminarians. One spiritual director labeling such devotions as "the new cottage industry of prayer life," faulted some seminarians for spending extensive time reciting devotional prayers though rarely being quiet enough to listen to God's voice within them. Another concerned faculty member put it this way:

> Devotional practices are of a piece with a whole theological picture that, unfortunately, few seminarians have. More and more we have Eucharistic adoration, the Rosary, various Marian devotions, and now before daily liturgy the recitation of the An-

gelus or Regina Coeli. Any attempt to discourage these practices—not in themselves, but because students do not have an
adequate understanding of how they fit with theology and because the practices may be fast becoming a substitute for more
profound spiritual reflection—is perceived by students as just
another attack by liberals on the practices of the Church.

For the reasons just suggested, the relation between devotional practices and the moral content of religion worries some
faculty and formation advisers. One faculty member observed:

> How is it that we have so much clamoring for devotions at a time
> when the personal psycho-social-sexual lives of so many of our
> seminarians are not healthy? Devotional practices put students
> in touch with transcendent symbols—but their lives are not
> transformed by the sprinkling of holy water or being enveloped
> in a cloud of incense. On the contrary, and paradoxically, some
> men who are most inclined to devotionalism are found to be
> lacking with regard to their own basic moral lives. . . . Some-
> times they are willing to cheat on exams, plagiarize papers, and
> present themselves fraudulently as already ordained, being anx-
> ious to benefit from whatever amenities are afforded by the role.

Other administrators and faculty handle the issue of private
devotions at their schools by approaching student interest in
them as an opportunity to teach the history of how these practices developed and how they relate to traditional liturgical practices. The seminary then officially schedules certain devotions
and gives some explanation of how they fit into the overall worship life of the Church. This approach makes it possible to moni-
tor the type of devotions practiced, provide some variety, and
instruct students more generally in the correct use of devotions.

Spiritual direction. In the context of a comprehensive program of human, spiritual, intellectual, and pastoral formation,
individual spiritual direction plays a major integrating role. The
high value placed on spiritual direction arises from its essential
function in inspiring students actively to develop their relationship with God. Because it is so focused on the individual person, however, it may also mirror the cultural inclination toward
individualism and privatization of religion. To the extent that
this is true, spiritual directors are responsible for ensuring that
the experience does not encourage self-indulgence but rather
calls the student to a deeper life in Christ overflowing into effective ministry. In any case students look to spiritual direction

for instruction in the spiritual life, for affirmation and support, and for dialogue to clarify their life choices.

Seminarians must have a priest as spiritual director, whose task is to guide them on their path of personal conversion and growth toward priesthood. Through spiritual direction students develop sound habits of personal prayer, learn to discern the actions of the Spirit, and cultivate their vision of life and ministry. While they are free to discuss anything with their spiritual director, the Church has established specific topics that seminarians must discuss. It is considered especially important for them to deepen their understanding of and commitment to celibate chastity:

> Personal relationships, sexuality, celibate chastity, commitment and interiorization are essential topics for spiritual direction. In this setting, seminarians should be encouraged to speak in detail about their own personal struggles and review their success and failure in living a chaste, celibate life.[13]

Usually seminarians meet on a biweekly basis with their spiritual director. Since a trusting relationship takes time to develop, that between director and student should last for the duration of the seminary program unless it is terminated by mutual agreement. Confidentiality in the spiritual-direction relationship is essential for fostering honesty and self-disclosure.[14] The spiritual director never contributes information about a directee to the evaluation process. Given this requirement, the importance of seminarians also working with an overall formation adviser in the external forum becomes evident. The public nature of the role of priest means that the candidate must be willing to subject his

---

[13] *PPF,* #291.

[14] Seminaries are sensitive to the limits of confidentiality. Typically, three limiting conditions are cited: (1) If directees threaten to harm themselves or another person, the director has the legal obligation to inform appropriate medical and/or civil authorities of the person's intentions, as well as persons targeted for harm. (2) If directees report to the spiritual director that they have physically or sexually abused a minor or vulnerable adult, the director is required to report the abuse to the civil authorities. (3) In cases where spiritual directors are uncertain about how to approach a particular issue, they may consult with another professional (for example, psychologist, another spiritual director). The directee must be informed of the consultation, and the identity of the directee remains anonymous.

attitudes and behaviors to the review of others. In the past it was possible for a student to disregard particular problems by saying, "I'm working on that with my spiritual director." The confidential relationship is still intact, but it is supplemented by the relationship with the formation adviser, in which the subject matter is private but not confidential.

Lay students, though not always required by their program to seek spiritual direction, almost always wish to do so. With the help of the spiritual formation department, they select a qualified director, woman or man, according to their own needs and preferences. Typically, lay students see a spiritual director monthly. Group spiritual direction is sometimes available for those who prefer that mode.

Ideally, spiritual directors should possess wisdom and spiritual depth, with a graduate degree in spirituality or a certificate in spiritual direction if at all possible. If they lack this advanced training, they must have acquired significant experience in the ministry of spiritual direction, demonstrating the ability to listen carefully to people and to respond appropriately. Spiritual formation directors said that, when women were removed from the role of spiritual director for seminarians in the mid-1980s, an adequate number of priests had not been properly trained for this ministry.

Although some priests do have formal training, many others work purely on the basis of their own experience. Therefore it is incumbent on seminaries to provide continuing formation and supervision for all spiritual directors, but not all of them have done so. Spiritual formation directors are aware that priests coming from outside the seminary need to be cognizant of the ethos and formation goals of the school so that they can envision how spiritual direction harmonizes with other aspects of the students' formation. Spiritual directors have the dual obligation of recognizing the aims of the school while also being present as sympathetic listeners.

Intensive spiritual formation programs. As a result of our changing cultural climate and the shallower religious backgrounds and experiences of seminarians, inculturation into seminary life absorbs more time now than ever before. Ranging from a few weeks to a full year, almost every diocesan seminary offers some type of intensive spiritual program in which students are oriented to the community and spiritual life of the seminary. This extended, focused period is dedicated to prayer, reflection, and formation experiences under the supervision of spiritual directors, faculty, and in some cases rectors. It is intended to "teach seminarians to value solitude and personal prayer as a necessary part of priestly spirituality."[15]

The following examples illustrate the variety of available programs. Several schools provide *a type of orientation* for first-year students in which they are introduced to life in the seminary, especially its spiritual dimensions. This two- or three-week orientation may be followed by a retreat that includes individual meetings with a spiritual director. Other schools offer programs of up to six weeks after the first year of theology that concentrate on basic principles of Catholic spirituality and prayer. These programs feature formation experiences such as lectures and readings, prayer, reflection, discussion, and a retreat.

Another format used by several schools is *a three-week intensive course* followed by a retreat during January. Students are immersed in the study of the foundations of the spiritual life through a course like "A History of Christian Spirituality," which highlights key people and ideas in the Catholic tradition. A course like "The Theology and Forms of Prayer" surveys traditional forms of prayer and their practical application. A concluding eight-day directed retreat provides an opportunity to reflect on the subject matter just studied and to experience the presence of God in silence. Often these programs take place away from the seminary in a setting conducive to prayer and reflection.

Some diocesan seminaries structure *a practicum experience* for first-year students that involves interaction with priests who are engaged in parish ministry. It seeks to familiarize seminarians with the spirituality of the diocesan priest, including topics such as prayer, obedience, discernment, simplicity of life, and celibate chastity. A period of concentrated attention to spiritual formation greatly facilitates the process of assimilating academic and pastoral experiences, and arriving at a genuine commitment to priesthood.

While most of these intensive spiritual experiences are scheduled early in the course of theological studies, some schools offer a program each year during January interims or in the summer. Also available are programs sponsored by institutions other than the seminaries themselves.[16] In all cases the purpose is to

---

[15] *PPF,* #321.

[16] One such summer program, "The Institute for Priestly Formation," was founded as a complement to already existing programs conducted

engage students meaningfully with the human, spiritual, and ministerial issues raised during their previous formation. The seminarian is expected to deepen a viable spirituality that will sustain his daily life as a contemporary diocesan priest. Less common is a month-long directed retreat, intended as a unique occasion for the seminarian to face God alone within the context of a silent prayer community apart from ordinary academic and pastoral commitments. The ultimate goal is to enable candidates to reach a fuller awareness of themselves, God, and their calling.

In one setting *a year-long program,* subscribed to by several dioceses, is offered.[17] Here students spend the academic year before first-year theology in intense spiritual formation. The stated purpose of this year is "to help seminarians pattern their lives after the example of Christ, Head, Shepherd, and Spouse of the Church." The program is described as one that emphasizes daily liturgical prayer, times of spiritual reflection, and personal prayer. In addition to daily conferences on the basics of spirituality, liturgy, priesthood, and other topics related to human and spiritual development, students are given an opportunity for spiritual reflection, ongoing spiritual direction, and retreats. The program description states that it is "an investment in the future, providing the seminarian with a unique opportunity to interiorize his configuration to Christ Jesus."

This spirituality year is devoted to an interior development on which the foundation for a life of prayer can be laid. Attitudes necessary in a priest, such as joyful obedience, generosity, self-sacrifice, and interior silence are cultivated. Eucharistic devotion, the sacrament of reconciliation, and Marian devotion are all part of the program. Seminarians are encouraged to reflect openly on the serious obligations and difficulties that pertain to celibate living. The year has intellectual and apostolic components, both of which are marked by prayer and conducted in an atmosphere of prayer. A series of conferences on Catholic spirituality and prayer, human growth and development,

---

by seminaries. Inspired by St. Ignatius Loyola's biblical-evangelical spirituality, it is adapted for diocesan priests and conducted at Creighton University for about ten weeks each summer.

[17] The Spirituality Year is held at Mary Immaculate Seminary in Northampton, Pennsylvania, and welcomes seminarians from several dioceses. Seminarians from the Archdiocese of Philadelphia are required to participate in the program.

conversion and the penitential disciplines, and the theology and spirituality of the diocesan priesthood are among those sponsored. The apostolic component consists of assignments at hospitals, nursing homes, special-education schools, and specialized social programs.

Responses to spiritual formation programs. In the course of interviewing faculty, most expressed approval of the ways in which spiritual formation programs have developed over the past decade. They appreciate programs that encourage an active prayer life leading to effective service and that demonstrate how personal spirituality enriches the way the public prayer of the Church is celebrated. The positive fruits of spiritual formation for future priests and lay ministers become visible when diverse groups within the Church are drawn to worship together in vibrant communities.

Some criticisms of programs were also voiced by faculty and by spiritual formation personnel themselves. They specified three concerns: the apparent lack of attention to Scripture in spiritual formation programs, the relative neglect of social justice, and the separation of spiritual formation practices from the rest of seminary life.

Concerning prayer and Scripture, some faculty believe that the two should be more deliberately connected. They noted that the Eucharist and the Liturgy of the Hours can be powerfully formative if the Word of God is effectively preached and sincerely reflected on by the community. When Scripture is the source and foundation of prayer, it unites the whole community and lessens the tendency toward privatization. A Scripture teacher complained: "Coupled with the evident lack of familiarity with the Word, there is a growing tendency among seminarians to clamor for the introduction of more devotional practices. What about attention to 'the Word' in all its forms?"

Echoing a criticism also prominent ten years ago, another faculty member decried the "lamentable lack of concern that seminarians show for social justice, sensitivity in the areas of racism, sexism, etc. How can this be? True religion is inextricably bound to morality." Incorporating social-justice teachings into the fabric of seminary life, which encompasses prayer, academic studies, and pastoral practice, is no small task. Although spiritual formation programs, including rector's conferences, do address these issues from time to time, many faculty would agree that social justice is not a predominant integrating theme as called for by the bishops in the *PPF:* "In a world that seeks to privatize religious commitment, seminary education should appropriately emphasize the social dimension of the Gospel, its concern for human life, for justice in the marketplace, and for peace in the world."[18]

A third criticism targets how well spiritual formation is integrated with the rest of the seminary program, especially the intensive spiritual formation programs. One problem is the lack of continuity between the intensive programs and later seminary formation. It is difficult for some students to maintain a pattern of prayer when they are faced with the hectic pace of academic studies. Concerns were voiced about students being introduced to styles of life and prayer that might differ radically from what they will find in their subsequent programs. Faculty sometimes concluded that the lifestyle of intensive spiritual programs is too relaxed, "too laid back," so that seminarians have difficulty adjusting to seminary life when pressure and strict deadlines are imposed.

C. Intellectual Formation

Introduction

The overarching consideration in examining formation is to discern how well theologates are preparing lay and ordained ministers for the Church of the twenty-first century. Since every professional minister is called to communicate the faith authentically, intellectual formation is an indispensable part of their preparation. A thorough understanding of the tradition serves as the foundation for teaching and preaching, spiritual leadership, and pastoral care. Students devote a considerable amount of time to academic pursuits for both pastoral and spiritual reasons. As Church documents assert, sound intellectual formation must systematically cover all Christian truths and help students integrate these studies into their faith life:

> Theological formation is both complex and demanding. It should lead the candidate for the priesthood to a complete and unified vision of the truths which God has revealed in Jesus Christ and of the church's experience of faith. Hence the need both to know "all" the Christian truths, without arbitrarily selecting among

---

[18] *PPF,* #20.

them, and to know them in an orderly fashion. This means the candidate needs to be helped to build a synthesis which will be the result of the contributions of the different theological disciplines, the specific nature of which acquires genuine value only in their profound coordination.[19]

Theology courses must be attentive to the relationship between faith and reason and to the requirements of the social and cultural situation of today. Systematic theology should cover the range of Christian doctrine. Fundamental theology, for example, is concerned with Christian revelation and how it is transmitted. Other disciplines, such as moral theology, deal with the Church's social doctrine. The goal of a solid theological foundation is to ground students in the knowledge and wisdom of the Church. The following excerpt summarizes the nature and purposes of intellectual formation:

> A theological education should be comprehensive and extensive. It should witness to the unity of the faith—according to tradition and the magisterium—and its authentic diversity of theological expressions. Such an education should be pastorally oriented, ecumenically sensitive, and personally appropriated by the individual seminarian. It should also be relevant to the world in which the Gospel is preached.[20]

General curricular structure. With guidelines given in Church documents, each theologate has its own way of organizing courses and requirements. Five major fields constitute the curriculum: biblical studies, historical studies, systematic theology, liturgical studies, and pastoral theology. The study of the Bible, sometimes referred to as the "soul of theology," is given the primary place, and course requirements are fairly consistent at all the schools. The arrangement of other theology courses is less uniform: Some schools name systematic theology as a principal field, and include within it dogmatic, sacramental, spiritual, and moral theology courses; larger schools are likely to have separate departments for at least some of the subfields. Liturgical studies is the most distinctive of the curricular areas, with arrangements varying from separate liturgy departments to courses distributed among several departments—pastoral, systematic, and historical. Pastoral theology

---

[19] *PDV*, #54.
[20] *PPF*, #339.

usually consists of courses in pastoral ministry, canon law, pastoral care and counseling, homiletics, and religious education. Pastoral field education is almost always a separate department, with the director serving on the administrative team of the school. The various degree programs are delineated next, followed by descriptions of each curricular area with reference to goals, structure, and faculty assessment.

Degree programs. Most theologates offer at least two or three degree programs, and many of them now have a pre-theology undergraduate-level course of studies.

The master of divinity (M.DIV.) is designed to prepare students for professional ministry, so every theologate in the United States offers this degree. Since the mid-1980s most theologate faculties have reviewed the M.DIV. degree requirements, reconceived its underlying principles, and adjusted the content of the curriculum to respond to a new generation of students and new ministerial circumstances. Nevertheless, the overall number of credits and their distribution among disciplines have changed only slightly (see chart A below).

Chart A: Credit Distribution for the Master of Divinity Degree

	1987	1997
Scripture	17.6	17.1
Systematic Theology	26.6	30.5
Moral Theology	11.2	10.5
Historical Studies	8.6	8.9
Pastoral Studies*	23.9	22.5
Field Education	11.8	10.8
General Electives/Other	8.0	11.9
Total	107.7	112.2

*Includes the following credits: Pastoral Theology/Skills 8.2; Homiletics 5.6; Canon Law 4.8; and Sacramental and Liturgical Practica 3.8.

As the chart indicates, about five additional credits, the equivalent of two courses, are required: On average one more course in systematic theology is required and one more general elective or other course outside the five traditional areas of study is allowed. The increase in systematic theology credits is in large part a response to the generally less adequate theological background of incoming students. The other additional credits are usually in electives or courses that cover the exercise of ministry from a multicultural perspective. Most theologates still maintain a heavily prescribed and crowded curriculum.

Pastoral studies and field education together have lost the equivalent of about one course. This relatively small reduction can be explained by one of several factors. In some cases the same amount of work is required as before, but fewer credits are awarded; in other cases a pastoral year without credit substitutes for part of the concurrent field education. In a few cases faculty have determined that students need formal academic courses more than practica or field experience, thus keeping alive the long-term debate at some schools between those favoring an academic and those favoring a pastoral orientation of the curriculum. Most schools have applied their efforts to integrating these two dimensions of the formation program, but at a few schools the issue remains controversial. Perhaps more critical than the number and distribution of credits are the teaching methods used by faculty. As is evident below where each discipline is described, faculty have made extraordinary efforts to teach students from disparate backgrounds and who will enter ministry in a Church with a changing Catholic population and ministerial structures.

Pre-theology programs for seminarians were introduced for the first time during the past decade in at least fifteen theologates, and ten other schools revised their programs to conform to the requirements of the fourth edition of the *PPF*.[21] Significantly the number of credits in philosophy was increased from eighteen to twenty-four, and in theology twelve credits were required for the first time.[22] In conjunction with intellectual formation, human, spiritual, and pastoral formation were also prescribed. In theory the program takes two years, but in practice requirements are sometimes waived and substitutions made based on previous experience or studies.

According to informal reports by directors of pre-theology programs, the result is that less than half of the seminarians actually take two full years. A total of 287 pre-theology students

---

[21] *PPF*, #209–48.

[22] Typically six specific philosophy courses are required: ancient, medieval, and modern philosophy, philosophy of human nature, logic, and metaphysics. Two other philosophy courses, usually electives, complete the twenty-four credits. In theology the usual requirements are a biblical course, Church history, spirituality, and ethics.

were enrolled in the twenty-five theologate programs operating in 1997–98.[23] The average enrollment numbered about twelve. Extensive resources have gone into providing these programs, and many rectors lament the duplication of programs, but none is willing to give up their program since, once enrolled, students usually stay at the same school for theological studies.

Other graduate degree programs. Together the 42 theologates offer 26 different degrees for a total of over 150 degree programs, about 4 per school. After the M.DIV., the *master of arts in theology* (M.A.T.) is offered most frequently, at thirty-eight schools. Five theologates in the United States have the right to offer pontifical degrees (S.T.B., S.T.L., and S.T.D.) on their own along with the American College in Louvain, three confer the S.T.B. in conjunction with a Roman university, as does the North American College in Rome. Relatively new degrees are the *master of arts in pastoral studies* or in *pastoral ministry* (M.A.P.S. or M.A.P.M.), conferred by fourteen theologates. Usually two years in duration, these degrees are intended for lay students who are pursuing professional ministry but not earning the three- or four-year M.DIV. Three different doctoral degrees are offered, including the *doctor of philosophy* (PH.D.) at three schools, the *doctor of sacred theology* (S.T.D.) at five, and the *doctor of ministry* (D.MIN.) at seven. Most of the other degrees are at the master's level in one or another area of specialization, and seven schools also offer a bachelor's degree. Considering the size of faculties, the number of degrees offered is extremely large and no doubt contributes to faculty perceptions of being overworked.

1. Sacred Scripture

Sacred Scripture is fundamental to intellectual formation and holds a primary place among the disciplines. Since Vatican II, Roman Catholics have become more attentive to the Bible. Consequently those preparing for ministry are expected to master a method of interpreting the Bible, study a range of books from both Testaments, and acquire the skill of applying the Scriptures. Especially in preaching and teaching they are expected to draw heavily on Scripture as the basis of their discourse, and more frequently they are asked to lead Bible study

---

[23] A total of 531 pre-theology students were enrolled in 1997–1998, of whom 244 attended one of 25 college seminary programs. In 1987–1988 the total number enrolled in pre-theology was 192.

groups. In other situations they will use Scripture, for example, when spontaneous prayers are called for at special religious occasions or in the course of pastoral counseling in or out of the confessional. In effect all of ministry requires a broad knowledge and clear understanding of the Bible.

The *PPF* and *PDV* both address how Scripture study is to be approached. They insist that students be introduced to the approved approaches to Scripture and become acquainted with the appropriate statements of the magisterium. The study of the Word of God is fundamental and should serve as background for all other theology—the Fathers of the Church, the liturgy, the history of the Church, and the teachings of the magisterium. In particular, homiletics should be taught so that students can communicate the Gospel in an effective and appropriate manner.[24]

Over the past hundred years the teaching office of the Catholic Church has issued three major documents on the study of the Bible: *Providentissimus Deus* (1893), *Divino afflante Spiritu* (1943), and from Vatican II *Dei Verbum* (1965). More recently the Pontifical Biblical Commission has authored *The Interpretation of the Bible in the Church* (1996). Each in its own age, these documents speak to ways of understanding the Sacred Scriptures and together give a history of interpretation. Faculty value these works notably because they help students accept the authoritative legitimacy of the historical-critical method and other newer approaches to the Bible. Influenced by the current resurgence of fundamentalism, in particular as it pertains to biblical interpretation, seminarians with limited theological backgrounds tend to be suspicious of what they are taught about the Bible; thus these documents strengthen the position taken by faculty.

Goals. Faculty who teach Scripture articulate several goals for the study of their discipline. After developing a deep acquaintance with the content of the Bible, students should learn how to use the methods of biblical interpretation and the skills of exegesis. Depending on the particular course, different contents are emphasized. Some provide understanding of the historical setting and religious institutions of the period they represent. Others focus on hermeneutics, including traditional methods

[24] See especially *PPF,* #356; *PDV,* #54; and *PPF,* #377.

like source and form criticism, along with new approaches like literary criticism, feminist hermeneutics, and canonical criticism. Still other courses examine basic doctrinal, paraenetic, and theological themes and their implications for the life of the Christian community. Investigation of ethical perspectives and homiletic potential can also be the main consideration. The common goal is to imbue students with such a deep knowledge and love of the Scriptures that all of their life and ministry will be informed by its power.

Structure. A background in Scripture is considered indispensable to other academic courses and equally important to good pastoral practice. Hence almost every theologate requires students to take two Scripture courses during the first year of theology and four others during the remaining years.[25] The *PPF* states that "in Scripture, the core should include Introduction to Old and New Testaments, Johannine Literature and the Synoptic Gospels, Pauline Epistles, Pentateuch, Psalms, Prophets, and Wisdom Literature."[26] A typical curriculum covers these eight areas in six required courses, three each in the Old and New Testaments.

Generally, the first course is one of three: introduction to biblical studies, methods and Pentateuch, or Old Testament interpretation. This course gives attention to exegetical method and practice, helps students acquire a historical perspective, and teaches them about the cultural background of the Bible. Usually the course includes at least the Pentateuch. In a separate course the Psalms are studied for language, form, and theology, using representative types from praise to lament. Except at a few schools, the third Old Testament course combines the Prophets and Wisdom Literature, examining the origins, character, and role of prophecy, and exploring the themes and

[25] The number of credit hours required in Scripture in M.Div. programs is as follows:

				1997	1987
12 hours	=	4 schools			
13–15 hours	=	10 schools	Mean	17.1	17.6
16–18 hours	=	17 schools	Median	18	18
18.7–21 hours	=	8 schools	Mode	18	19–21
26 hours	=	1 school	Range	12–26	12–28

[26] *PPF,* #369.

methods of the Wisdom tradition. Occasionally schools require two separate courses.

A few schools require an introduction to New Testament, but more often methods of interpretation and the history of early Christianity are incorporated into the Synoptic Gospels course. A study of Johannine and Pauline literature completes the mandated curriculum. Biblical languages are required only at the American College, Louvain; but most schools offer at least introductory Greek and Hebrew, courses subscribed to by a minority of students. Those specializing in biblical studies are, of course, required to study these languages. Were it not for the already crowded curriculum, faculty and most students agree that more courses in Bible would be desirable. Other courses hinge on knowing the Scriptures, and much of pastoral ministry is concerned with the Bible, including preaching, religious education, and adult Bible study.

Faculty perceptions. Faculty members who teach Scripture are universally enthusiastic about their subject matter and often use highly creative teaching methods. They understand the preeminence of their discipline in the curriculum and see the importance of integrating Scripture with other courses, though most acknowledge how difficult it is to achieve that integration. The enthusiasm of faculty stems largely from their own love of the Word of God.

Several Scripture faculty speak to the relevance of the Bible in their lives and teaching. Daniel Harrington, S.J., writes: "I find God largely in and through the Bible. Most of my academic, spiritual, and pastoral life revolves around the Bible. It is for me the most important way to come to know, love, and serve God."[27] Donald Senior, C.P., addresses the relationship of Scripture to preaching: "The preacher is the *servant* of the Word, a scribe *for* the kingdom, mediating a message that dips into the very reality of God. . . . Preaching with a biblical character should be expansive, evocative and visionary rather than didactic, moralistic, or trivial."[28]

---

[27] Daniel Harrington, "How Can I Find God? Another Look," *America* 177 (30 August 1997) 11.

[28] Donald Senior, "Scripture and Homiletics: What the Bible Can Teach the Preacher," *Worship* 65 (1991) 394. See also Donald B. Cozzens, "Tender of the Word," *The Spirituality of the Diocesan Priest*, ed. Donald B. Cozzens (Collegeville: The Liturgical Press, 1997) 42–58.

Based on his teaching experience, Ronald Witherup, S.S., describes several ways in which the proper study of the Bible can contribute to both intellectual and spiritual formation: By teaching students how to read critically and increase their power of observation and attention to detail in the reading process, by promoting good biblical preaching and more cooperation between other areas of theological study and the biblical field, by fostering a desire for ongoing education, and by serving as a model of intellectual integrity in ecumenism and in the faith dimension; it represents an area where the intellectual and the spiritual can truly be wedded.[29]

Special teaching methods also enhance the study of the Bible. Team teaching is commonly used. Scripture and homiletics faculty are the most likely groups to work together, striving in their courses to ensure effective proclamation of scriptural texts. Moral theologians join with both Old and New Testament faculty to investigate ethical perspectives in the Bible. In courses on creation, suffering, prayer, and other theological themes, systematic theologians combine their perspectives with those of Scripture faculty. At one school, faculty have developed a concept paper showing how the biblical prophets can provide the foundation for contemporary pastoral ministry.[30] Many schools sponsor field study in the Holy Land or in other settings where study of the Bible is the focus. In one model course entitled "Prophets: Foundational Ministry in a Global Context," students are expected to learn how to understand culture through the example of the Prophets. They read about the cultural engagement in the prophets and then live in a Mayan village, where they begin to explore how Israel's questions are questions for today. "They pair the practical with dense theological inquiry."[31]

Despite their intense enthusiasm, Scripture faculty are also frustrated in their teaching. A major concern stems from the prevalence of fundamentalist interpretations of the Bible, which many students have absorbed. Inclined toward a literal interpretation of the Bible, they are troubled by the historical-critical

[29] Ronald D. Witherup, "The 'Intellectual' Formation of Priests," *The Priest* (August 1993) 49–51.

[30] Jesuit School of Theology at Berkeley, unpublished paper by fourteen faculty members and students, "Pastoring Prophetically in a Global Church: An Approach to Congregational Analysis."

[31] Dr. Gina Hens-Piazza teaches this course at the Jesuit School of Theology at Berkeley.

method. Another major concern, even more alarming to faculty, is the negative attitude toward the study of Scripture that some students embrace. These students diminish the importance of Scripture altogether, preferring instead to focus almost entirely on the writings of the Fathers of the Church. A third disappointment for faculty is the absence of required language studies either before or during theological studies. This lacuna limits the ability of students to do textual criticism and exegetical analysis.

Two other concerns are widespread: One is the deficiency students show in historical and literary background, and the other is their failure to connect biblical studies with spirituality. One faculty member expressed strongly what many others also mentioned:

> I find that students have a lamentable lack of knowledge with regard to the content of the Bible. . . . The emphasis in *Dei Verbum* on the spiritual nourishment that comes from not only the Table of the Eucharist but also the Word, seems to be lost on the majority of students, and few show a great interest in developing biblically based spirituality. I am always amazed, and somewhat appalled, at the negligible interest seminarians show in using the Scriptures as a place of encounter with God.

In spite of the weak backgrounds of some students, the reluctance of others to accept newer methods of study, and the resistance of a few to studying Scripture at all, most come to appreciate the crucial role of Scripture in their future ministry. In a survey of priests who have been ordained for five to nine years, Scripture was named as the course of study that was most helpful in priestly ministry, and 93 percent of respondents stated that the theologate prepared them well or very well in Scripture.[32] These encouraging outcomes are a tribute to the effectiveness of Scripture faculty and an indication of the importance of the field.

2. Historical Studies

Because it illuminates the impact of the past on the present and so fosters the ability to make wise judgments for the future,

---

[32] Eugene F. Hemrick and Dean R. Hoge, *A Survey of Priests Ordained Five to Nine Years* (Washington, D.C.: National Catholic Educational Association Seminary Department, 1991) 13–14.

Church history is an ideal foundation for the study of Scripture and theology. Consequently most theologate programs require students to take courses in historical studies, sometimes called church history, during the first year of theology. Knowing how the Church has lived for two thousand years enables students to develop skill in reading the signs of the times and to see that history has a bearing on the twenty-first century. To that end, the *PPF* recommends that the core curriculum "should include Patristics; Early, Medieval, Modern, and Contemporary Church History; and American Church History. American Church History should be taught in a way that reflects the multicultural origins of the Church in the United States. Among historical studies, the study of Patristics is of special importance."[33]

Goals. Students of Church history first need to acquire a knowledge of historical method and an ability to use historical documents critically. Second they should become broadly acquainted with the major phases in the social, cultural, and institutional development of Christianity, thereby gaining an awareness of the life of the Catholic Church as it has been experienced over twenty centuries. A third goal is that students learn to appreciate the historical character of the Church, the development of doctrine and practice, and the value of the apostolic tradition. Such study reveals how the interaction of human freedom with the providential guidance of the Holy Spirit has shaped the Church. This understanding leads to a fourth goal: that the direction for the new millennium be based on a thorough knowledge of history. In pursuing these goals, some schools emphasize the internal history of the Church, its thought and structure, its missionary expansion, and the impact of external conditions on its functioning. Others focus on the Church's relations with secular society and civil government, as well as the influence of its members in the secular, intellectual, cultural, social, and political spheres. Most balance the two perspectives.

Structure. At almost every theologate, the faculty who teach Church history are organized in a separate department that is identified in one of several ways, most commonly as historical studies (16) and church history (10); two or three church history

---

[33] *PPF,* #372.

departments, respectively, are designated as ecclesiastical history, historical theology, history, and history of Christianity; and several others form part of systematic theology, biblical studies, or cultural studies departments. The requirements also vary in name and number, but are relatively uniform in content.[34]

Depending on the number of courses required, the chronological span of the survey courses varies. Typically the first course covers early Church and medieval history, and the second covers the Reformation and modern church history. In a few cases patristics is listed as a separate course on the writings of the early Church Fathers through Augustine. The third required course is often in American church history, but this may also be an elective. A few schools offer interdisciplinary courses, especially in conjunction with sacramental and liturgical theology.

Faculty perceptions. Approaches to teaching historical studies depend significantly on the backgrounds of faculty. Many are educated in theology as well as history, and some have specialized in social and cultural studies; thus the perspective of some may be more related to internal church matters, and that of others to the external context. In either case, faculty value the study of history because it looks at the decisions others have made and the consequences these decisions have had for the Church. As one faculty member noted: "It is important to learn from the mistakes of others; for example, it is beneficial to know that overreaction to some problems has hurt the Church. The Church is always in need of reformation, but the way changes are implemented will determine how well they are accepted."

Faculty who have special training in social or cultural studies tend to emphasize how the Church is affected by the larger society. Science, art, music, and politics all have repercussions on the internal life of the Church. By paying attention to the impact

---

[34] The number of credit hours required in historical studies in M.Div. programs is as follows:

				1997	*1987*
< 6 hours	=	1 school			
6 hours	=	10 schools	Mean	8.9	8.6
7–9 hours	=	14 schools	Median	9	7–9
10–12 hours	=	13 schools	Mode	6	6
> 12 hours	=	2 schools	Range	3–14	3–15

of the external context on the Church in earlier times, students are taught the importance of the present-day context as well.

Almost all faculty in historical studies teach students the historical-critical method and encourage them to use primary sources in their research. Most faculty prefer the traditional lecture-discussion format for classroom teaching, but recently some have added media resources and the use of technological aids to present their course material.

The most frequent complaint of church history faculty concerns the educational backgrounds of students. In the judgment of someone who has taught for more than thirty years:

> These days students have no real depth in the humanities, in literature, or in history. Knowledge of the classics, for example, can open their eyes and enlighten them about life, but they have not been exposed to these studies. They often have a business, legal, or scientific background and a mindset that makes the study of history difficult for them. They don't know how to work with ambiguity, and they don't know how to understand images or symbols.

Faculty noted that students often have an idealized, uninformed view of the Church. This representative comment was made by one faculty member: "They can't accept any readings—even of the Fathers—that critique the Church. I believe they have to examine the shadow side, the messiness that is part of our history. Without solid grounding in the tradition, they have fixed ideas about the past without having studied any of it." Faculty try to assess the effect of prior educational lacunae on how students think and to teach them new ways of looking at the past. They invite students to consider how historical events affect us now and to ask questions about the future in light of the past. Faculty "want students to see that all of experience is not wrapped up in the present," and to think about issues from fresh perspectives.

In spite of these concerns, the overall satisfaction faculty find in their teaching is exemplified by this remark:

> It is wonderful to see students come alive and to see them make connections, get into their tradition, be critical, but also be appreciative of the tradition as it gives focus to their lives. In other words, I feel that being here I'm not just peddling academic truths. What we teach, the way we teach, and the scope of history we cover is meant to—it does—impact on their lives and on the future of the Church.

3. Systematic Theology

Recognizing that the study of systematic theology provides essential knowledge about the beliefs of the Catholic Church, faculty give particular attention to the approaches, content, and methods employed in teaching it. Following the emphasis articulated in *PDV*,[35] faculty urge students to be aware of the relationship between faith and reason. Faith is the point of departure and, in the context of Catholic theological studies, those who reflect on the truths of the faith are believers and members of the Church. During theological formation for ministry, both the statements issued by the magisterium and discussions by theologians are applicable. In the words of *PDV:*

> The living magisterium of the church and theology, while having different gifts and functions, ultimately have the same goal: preserving the people of God in the truth which sets free and thereby making them "a light to the nations." This service to the ecclesial community brings the theologian and the magisterium into a mutual relationship.[36]

The *PPF* stresses the role of the magisterium: "The normative function of the magisterium should be presented as a vital, integral, and essential component of the theological enterprise."[37] Further, the pastoral nature of theology should be incorporated so that the Gospel message is proclaimed through the cultural modes of the age and penetrates the very life of cultures. *PDV* makes a similar point: "A further problem strongly felt these days is the demand for the inculturation of the message of faith."[38] Therefore the study of systematic theology should include magisterial teaching, theological discussion, and recognition of the cultural context.

Systematic theology constitutes a substantial portion of the curriculum. Various theologates organize and designate the courses that are central to the field in different ways. Some theologates refer to dogmatic and moral theology on the one hand, and sacramental and liturgical studies on the other, but many separate the relevant courses into three subdivisions: dogmatic, moral, and sacramental. Likewise distinguishing between dog-

---

[35] *PDV,* #353–55.
[36] *PDV,* #55.
[37] *PPF,* #383.
[38] *PDV,* #55.

matic and moral theology, the *PPF* specifies that the core dogmatic courses should include "Fundamental Theology, Theology of God, One and Three, Christology, Creation, the Fall and the Nature of Sin, Redemption, Grace and the Human Person, Ecclesiology, Sacraments, Eschatology, Mariology, Missiology, and the Theology of Priesthood."[39] Following the *PPF*'s divisions, theologate requirements in moral theology and liturgical studies are considered in the fourth and fifth parts of this chapter.

Goals. Systematics faculty expect students to become generally familiar with the history and development of the Church and its doctrines. To this end the principal theological questions are treated in a systematic fashion, and the Church's official teaching is clearly delineated. The second goal is that students examine the Christian message of salvation in Christ in its entirety and so gain an appreciation for the core mysteries of the Christian faith and revelation: the Trinity, christology, Christian anthropology, eschatology, and the Church. The third goal is that they become acquainted with a variety of topics, doctrines, and beliefs expressive of their faith. Finally students must develop an understanding of the diversity of theologies and methods of theological reflection within the Catholic tradition.

The *PPF* devotes several paragraphs to the question of method, mentioning in particular the significance of St. Thomas Aquinas as model and guide for study and research in theology. In general, students learn to evaluate the strengths and limitations of various theological viewpoints, and to comprehend "the distinction and relation between truths revealed by God and contained in the deposit of faith, and their theological mode of expression."[40] Besides the primary areas of study within dogmatic theology, the *PPF* prescribes that students also study both spirituality and ecumenism.

Structure. The list of courses included in the area of systematic theology depends on the overall structure of the curriculum.[41] The standard required dogmatics courses are (1) fundamental or foundational theology, (2) ecclesiology, and (3) christology. Three other courses are almost always required but

---

[39] *PPF,* #370.

[40] *PPF,* #380–82.

[41] In order to compare the requirements of 1997 with those of 1987, systematic theology is defined as encompassing dogmatic and

may be named and combined differently: (1) Trinity, doctrine of God, or mystery of God; (2) Christian anthropology or theology of grace; and (3) creation, sin, and eschatology. When offered, ecumenism and Mariology also fall under dogmatic theology;[42] but they are rarely required as separate courses. Mariology is studied in ecclesiology courses, while ecumenism, with few exceptions, is offered as an elective. A course on priesthood and orders may be listed under dogmatic theology or as part of liturgy and sacraments. Missiology is rarely mentioned, even though the *PPF* specifically requires it. Also according to the *PPF,* the core should include an introduction to spirituality and spiritual direction. In fact, most theologates require only one course in the history of Christian spirituality, and a course in spiritual direction is seldom prescribed.

Together, dogmatic theology courses provide a comprehensive overview of the major doctrines of the Catholic faith pre-

---

spirituality courses in addition to sacramental and liturgical courses. Practica and skills courses are not included. The number of credit hours in systematic theology required in M.DIV. programs is as follows:

				1997	*1987*
6 hours	=	6 schools			
7–9 hours	=	13 schools	Mean	10.5	11.2
10–12 hours	=	12 schools	Median	10–11	11
13–15 hours	=	8 schools	Mode	12	12
< 15 hours	=	1 school	Range	6–18	6–24

[42] The *PPF* pays considerable attention to ecumenism and to the study of the Eastern Churches:

> During their study of ecumenism, seminarians should become well acquainted with the ecumenical teachings of the Church, especially *Lumen gentium, Unitatis redintegratio, Nostra aetate,* as well as *The Ecumenical Directory* and its guidelines. They should also be aware of the ecumenical and interfaith dialogues in which the Church participates, worldwide and in the United States (#378).

Further:

> In the various theological disciplines, attention should be given to the ecumenical and interfaith dimension of each area of study. A knowledge of the history and theology of other churches and religious bodies prominent in the region where the seminarians will serve as priests is particularly helpful (#384).

Finally: "Courses in all areas of study, especially in theology, history, and liturgy, should highlight the role and contribution of the Eastern churches" (#385).

sented synthetically and integrally. Grounded in Scripture and tradition, the subject matter of these courses is elaborated through the teachings of the magisterium, contributions of theologians, and contemporary experience. Analysis of and reflection on the truths of faith lead students toward a deeper understanding of these truths, their relation to one another, and their relevance for Christian life and ministry.

Faculty perceptions. More than faculty in other fields, systematic theologians centered their comments on student readiness to study theology. They also discussed teaching methods and the content of their courses. Again and again faculty repeated the point that students who have a philosophical background acquired through an extended program designed to prepare them for the study of theology are best equipped to undertake systematics courses. With such a background, students prove more able to explain and express the truths of the Christian faith. Without it, they lack the vocabulary and methods needed to examine theological concepts, are less able to deal with abstractions, and find creative and imaginative study burdensome.

Another concern noted by faculty is that students yearn for certainty about matters of faith and consider the new *Catechism of the Catholic Church* to be "the book with all the answers." Many faculty attribute this longing to the erosion of a Catholic culture. As one faculty member put it:

> In their laudable desire to be orthodox teachers of the faith, they fear discussion of any theological concept, any controversial issue that might disrupt their preconceived notions. To study theology, they think they need only personal conviction and factual knowledge of the Church. Any critique of ideas is considered dissent. They resist learning anything that doesn't fit their grid.

Another faculty member noted that

> Students have a deep-felt need for security, and so they tend to be reactionary and anti-intellectual fundamentalists. They grab a few icons from the 1950s and devote themselves to them. Their concept of God and religion is very narrow, culture-bound. They resist the Church as it is and are extremely selective about the teachings of the magisterium.

Despite the prevalence of such sentiments, other faculty reported an openness and readiness to learn on the part of many students. Questions brought from pastoral field placements enlivened classroom discussions and lent a realistic quality to the subject matter, they said.

Approaches to teaching also concerned many faculty. One of them lamented: "Students are not prepared to learn what we teach, and we are not prepared to teach them what they need to learn. What do they know, and when did they learn it?" To find a common starting point, a way of situating them in the tradition, is a difficult task. One helpful approach was to relate theory and practice, for example, asking students to connect faith and science, creation and Scripture, or to reflect on men and women in society, on ecology, or on the Trinity at work in the world. These assignments helped students realize how their own experiences correlate with seemingly abstract theological ideas.

Some teachers talked about providing heuristic images, a conceptual or cognitive map of their courses, or an overview that would show students the direction being followed. As much as content affects their teaching, so does interaction with students. One teacher explained how he helps students understand a controversial point: "If I raise an objection to what a student says, it doesn't do much good. It is more effective if I ask them to justify what they are saying, to explain themselves. I want them to realize their presuppositions, to understand the basis of their beliefs and why they hold them."

Faculty also expressed the hope that students would grasp the connection between the substance of an idea and the pragmatics of ministry. Those teaching christology and ecclesiology, for instance, wanted students to be able to relate Christ, Church, and culture. As one faculty member said:

> We teach christology because of soteriology, what Jesus has done in saving us. His passion connects us with our own and the world's passions, its crosses. This vision of Jesus—the kenotic Christ—makes the most sense. Reading the signs of the times in light of the tradition opens our eyes to the suffering of the world.

In the same vein, another teacher commented:

> The Church is not a cultural entity that stands apart from the world; it is shaped by the language, values, and symbols of each culture. Because of this, there is pluriformity in the Church. Yet the Church has a tradition, a pearl to share with the world that provides cohesion and continuity.

Systematics faculty were eager to see students develop the capacity to relate the subject matter of their courses to the faith of all believers. Many faculty referred to the role of the Church on behalf of the poor, insisting, for example, that "the Church has to be on the side of the poor, aware of racism, conflicts, crime, drugs, poverty, hunger, and injustice. It has to be the wounded healer, recognizing its own poverty and brokenness, while representing God's grace and salvation." Students "need to have their theology smell of life, to shift from propositions to seeing God's revelation in life, to be aware of how God overwhelms us." As these observations suggest, systematic theology is about God's presence in the world, especially through the Church's representation. Intimately related to the experience of every human person, it deals with sin and grace, creation and redemption, and thus is essential to the formation of future priests and lay ministers.

4. Moral Theology

Catholic moral principles and the moral teachings of the Church offer an increasingly secularized society the basis for making right judgments about human actions. Pastoral ministers therefore need both knowledge of the content of the Catholic moral tradition and the ability to communicate the rationale for it. *PDV* notes that the cultural situation "strongly demands a high level of intellectual formation, such as will enable priests to proclaim, in a context like this, the changeless Gospel of Christ and to make it credible to the legitimate demands of human reason."[43] The assumption is that, in a secular society, moral guidelines based solely on religious claims will not be persuasive.

The *PPF* highlights the social teaching of the Church, which "should be presented in its entirety with appropriate principles of reflection, criteria for judgment, and norms for action. The systematic study of the social encyclicals of the popes is especially recommended."[44] Prescribed core courses include fundamental

---

[43] *PDV,* #51. *Gaudium et spes,* #10, reflects the same sentiment: "(The Church) also maintains that beneath all those changes there is much that is unchanging, much that has its ultimate foundation in Christ, who is the same yesterday, today, and forever," in *Vatican Council II: The Conciliar and Post-Conciliar Documents,* ed. Austin Flannery, O.P. (Northport, N.Y.: Costello, 1996) 172. Earlier the document speaks of the many changes in the world. The issue, of course, is what to define as "unchanging."

[44] *PPF,* #371.

moral theology, medical-moral ethics, sexuality, and social ethics. The *PPF* also emphasizes that knowledge of moral theology is critical for administering the sacrament of penance.

Goals. Faculty who are teaching moral theology articulate several important goals for their discipline: that students approach moral dilemmas in the light of revelation and the teachings of the Church; learn to deal systematically with ethical issues in a Catholic theological context; and model their lives on the life of Jesus Christ, whose words and deeds are normative for a truly human and Christian moral life. Each of these tasks has numerous ramifications for the pedagogical process, and for human and spiritual formation programs.

Students must first grasp the underlying principles[45] and norms of morality so that they can begin to answer the question, How are moral decisions to be made? The response to that question needs to be situated within church teaching on major issues, including an examination of both historical and contemporary examples. Additionally students are asked to discern the method that will best help them apply moral insights and convictions to particular situations. Most important, the study of moral theology shows how the Christian life should be lived because morality flows from the words, deeds, and person of Jesus Christ. For this reason morality is not simply about law, but about deepening one's life of faith.

Structure. Moral theology is positioned in the curriculum in various ways: as a separate department, within a department of systematic theology, or combined with spirituality in a department named "Christian Life," or given a similar title. Typically

---

[45] My colleague Rev. William C. McDonough notes that the word "principle" can be misleading. In Latin "principia" means "starting points, where to begin from." In English it has come to have an almost mathematical meaning, namely, first truths from which everything else gets deduced. According to Father McDonough, Walter Kasper (*Theology and Church*, 174) has a balanced way of putting the dilemma:

> General principles are necessary, but not enough. . . . Practical directives cannot simply be deduced in the abstract from general principles. They presuppose an evolution of the particular situation into which general principles have to be translated. . . . Here the Church is dependent on human experience, human judgment, and the relevant human sciences.

theologates require three or four courses in moral theology.[46] The initial course deals with moral principles and norms, the use of Scripture, the role of the magisterium, natural law theory, proportionalism, a vision of the common good, freedom and conscience, sin, intrinsic evil, and virtues, as well as other Thomistic themes such as truth, lying, honor, and fidelity. Variously named fundamental moral theology, christian moral principles, introduction to moral theology, or foundational moral theology, this course is highly valued by faculty because it guides students in discovering the importance of discerning a method for dealing with moral dilemmas across a broad spectrum.

The other two commonly required courses concern personal morality and social ethics. The first of the two, a study of pastoral and moral perspectives on human sexuality, is most often called Catholic sexual morality. Topics covered include sex and marriage, premarital sex, contraception, natural family planning, abortion, sterilization, technological reproduction, masturbation, the psychology of human sexuality, homosexuality, chastity, and celibacy. Because of its sensitive subject matter and its personal significance, faculty find this course very demanding to teach. The content of social ethics, the third required course, relates to the social teachings of the Church. The titles usually assigned to it are social doctrine and social ethics, faith and justice, or Catholic social teachings. Using encyclicals and pastoral letters as a point of departure, the course addresses such issues as peace, world hunger, racism, sexism, rights and duties, and the common good. In this area of moral theology, the biblical understanding of justice is foundational.

Some theologates require a fourth course or offer other electives in moral theology. The most common additional requirement is biomedical ethics, which identifies and assesses the moral dimensions of health care issues: the physician-patient relationship, allocation of resources, genetic medicine, reproductive

---

[46] The number of credit hours required in moral theology in M.DIV. programs is as follows:

					1997	1987
6 hours	=	6 schools				
7–9 hours	=	13 schools	Mean		10.5	11.2
10–12 hours	=	12 schools	Median		10–11	11
13–15 hours	=	8 schools	Mode		12	12
> 15 hours	=	1 school	Range		6–18	6–24

technologies, organ donation, abortion, and euthanasia—issues that traverse the human life span.

A revitalized field gaining much popularity now is virtue ethics.[47] The course under that name retrieves the tradition of virtue as a basis for moral theological reflection. Sometimes organized around the traditional categories of cardinal virtues and theological virtues, it may instead focus on themes such as intentions, practical reason, faith, and the cultivation of virtues. Examples of other available electives on contemporary issues are business ethics, truth telling, church-state relations, clergy ethics, and rural and urban problems.

Faculty perceptions. Of all the curricular areas, perhaps none is more difficult to teach than moral theology, according to many faculty who were interviewed. The following comment represents the thinking of numerous faculty:

> Students are looking for black and white answers to every conceivable moral dilemma. We need to create a safe environment in our classes so that they feel free to look at different sides of issues, to wrestle with complex problems.

In the words of another: "Students rely on an appeal to authority rather than reasoned and persuasive argument. This stance is very difficult in our country because it is part of our culture to believe that the force of the better argument will prevail." Some faculty feel that many students have an adolescent way of viewing authority and are themselves unable or unwilling to judge the weight of various pronouncements. These faculty would seek to educate students so that they can think through a moral issue, cognizant of the teachings of the Church. As one faculty member remarked:

> In all my classes I try to get students to appreciate why the Church teaches what it does. Morality is about more than developing a legal code; it is not just rules, but rather it is a paradigm that gives life. I want them to be able to apply moral principles in a pastoral setting, not to depend on a book of rules that couldn't possibly cover every eventuality.

---

[47] See William C. McDonough, *"The Church in the Modern World: Rereading Gaudium et Spes after Thirty Years,"* ed. Anthony J. Cernera (Fairfield, Conn.: Sacred Heart University Press, 1997); and Jean Porter, *The Recovery of Virtue* (Louisville: Westminster/John Knox, 1990).

However, some faculty members believe that their main responsibility is to impart the content of Church teaching rather than a method for reaching moral decisions. They feel that time does not permit going into depth or probing the rationale for the teaching(s) to any extent. Their main text is the *Catechism of the Catholic Church.*

Numerous faculty stressed the importance of character formation, of teaching people to live a life of virtue. They explore with students how a community of faith lives a moral life, how the dignity of the human person is respected, how friendship plays a role in developing moral character, and how one's relationship with Christ serves as the foundation for living. In this context faculty spoke of conversion as a necessary component of the moral life. Several also expressed a strong commitment to the poor. One said:

> As scholars we need to be accountable to the poor; for example, I am responsible to the poor in what I publish. Really radical questions of justice may not be of interest to the academy, but I need to address them. John Paul II's speaking out for human rights is very helpful in this quest.

Many faculty expressed their concern that despite the clear, unquestioned role of justice in Catholic moral theology, students often seem inattentive to both academic and pragmatic dimensions of social justice.

Faculty in moral theology are extraordinarily conscientious about the teaching methods they use. They encourage students to think carefully and speak openly, to raise questions and express doubts in an accepting environment, and to make sound, prudent judgments. The nature of the subject matter lends itself to case studies involving moral dilemmas. Some students also appreciate the use of novels and videos that pose moral questions and present stories of ordinary people living lives of heroic virtue.

The process of formulating and interpreting moral principles more precisely is enhanced by featuring panels of married couples in courses on human sexuality, and of physicians and nurses in courses on biomedical ethics. In social ethics courses, some faculty take their students to shelters for the homeless and to other settings that bring alive the consequences of systemic injustice. Attuned to the realities of the present cultural situation, most faculty members encourage students to anticipate realistically the issues they will face in their ministry. All of these methods and tools are recommended for teaching the complex field of moral theology.

Most faculty want students to realize that their desire to be faithful to the teachings of the Church requires them to discern a method for moral decision making. Without a framework for thinking through issues, their ministry will suffer as new moral questions arise. Good judgment is necessary, especially in counseling situations and at the sacrament of reconciliation. Students are more concerned about this area of study than any other. They worry that they will not be faithful to the teachings of the Church, or that they will not have answers for all the moral questions they will face. For some students, the anxiety may be related to their yearning for black and white answers in contexts that lend themselves more to careful reflection and nuance. Faculty believe they have reached their goal if they are able to develop thoughtful pastors who are prepared to think through the myriad questions they will encounter in ministry.

5. *Liturgical Studies*

Each theologate has its own way of organizing and teaching liturgical studies, but in all cases courses offered in this area form a bridge to other disciplines in the curriculum. In order to present a comprehensive view of the field, it is discussed here as a whole, regardless of how it may be segmented at various schools. In some cases liturgical studies is included under systematic, moral, and pastoral theology; in others sacramental and liturgical theology comprise a separate department, along with all the practica associated with these courses.

Approaches to the subject may be primarily historical, systematic, spiritual, pastoral, juridical, or some combination of those. Theologates with strong liturgical studies programs require many courses and employ several faculty, whereas other schools require few courses and employ faculty who either are not specifically trained in liturgy or are serving as part-time, adjunct members.

However a given school approaches liturgical studies, it occupies a pivotal place in the life of the Church. The *PPF* mentions liturgy in several contexts, with special attention to the form it should take in the spiritual life of the seminary. Only a few statements are made about its academic content: The core should offer an introduction to liturgy and courses in the historical, spiritual, and juridical aspects of liturgy. The *PPF* further recommends that liturgical practica include the celebration of the Eucharist and the sacraments, with emphasis on the sacrament of penance. Students should also be introduced to music and its role in liturgical celebration.[48] Under the heading of Spiritual Formation, *PDV* refers to the Liturgy of the Hours and the sacraments, especially the Eucharist and the sacrament of penance, as essential elements of the spiritual life, but it does not mention specific courses in its section on Intellectual Formation.[49]

Goals. The goals articulated for liturgical studies at theologates depend on the importance attached to the field. They begin with the aim of teaching students about the centrality of Christ's action in the sacraments and providing a guide to their proper celebration. Students are expected to recognize the communal-sacramental nature of Roman Catholicism as they learn to appreciate and pray the texts of the liturgy. More advanced goals presuppose a deep commitment to the sacramental and liturgical life of the Church, since they have an unparalleled impact on the typical Catholic.

Understanding the sacramental liturgy from scriptural, doctrinal, canonical, and pastoral perspectives requires students to integrate several fields. Ultimately they must be prepared to preside prayerfully at worship services in a manner that reflects their knowledge of the rites and the roles of other ministers. As one faculty member summarized the liturgical studies agenda, "The main goal is to get students to think as sacramental theologians do."

Structure. Departmental organization and course offerings are both important considerations when examining the structure of liturgical studies. Thirteen theologates have separate departments in which all the liturgical and sacramental courses and practica are taught, two do not specify departments, and most of the remaining twenty-five allocate liturgical studies courses among the departments of systematic, sacramental, and pastoral theology. A few offer practica in sacred music, and a few others have integrating or interdisciplinary studies courses that include liturgical subjects.

There are thirty-three different titles for the departments that teach liturgical studies at the forty schools, giving an indication

---

[48] *PPF*, #375 and #376.
[49] *PDV*, #48.

of the many ways in which this discipline is structured within the curriculum. A definite independence of approach to their discipline characterizes the faculty. Although numerous categories could be used to indicate the way courses are classified, three are typical: sacramental theology, liturgical theology, and sacramental and liturgical practica.

The topics covered by the normally required sacramental courses are the sacraments of initiation, the Eucharist, reconciliation and anointing, orders, and marriage. These topics are combined in various ways, with on average nine credits of the entire curriculum assigned to sacramental theology. One three-credit course in liturgical theology is usually taught from a historical perspective, and practica averaging a total of four credits deal with celebration of the sacraments, especially the Eucharist and reconciliation.[50]

In reviewing the requirements associated with liturgical studies, my general impression is that the courses cover similar material but the approaches—for example, historical or pastoral or juridical—and the importance assigned to the discipline vary among theologates more than they do for any other area of the curriculum. Differences in the depth and breadth of liturgical studies from school to school produce graduates with strikingly different levels of competence and understanding. Since the liturgical life of a parish is so central to its vitality, these studies deserve considerable attention.

Faculty perceptions. Faculty who teach liturgy, students, and other members of theologate communities who commented on liturgical studies spoke more often about how liturgies are celebrated than about course content. The quality of liturgical celebrations has particular relevance for future ministry, especially for priesthood candidates. In the words of one respondent:

> The liturgies, especially Eucharistic celebrations, are significant here. It is our central act of worship, and one that can unite or divide us as a community. Everyone has an opinion about how worship is conducted. Students who prefer private devotions sometimes find it difficult to enter into a public celebration, and

---

[50] As in my study of ten years ago, sacramental theology and liturgical theology were counted with systematic theology and sacramental and liturgical practica with pastoral studies. The total number of credits required in each is approximately the same.

they complain to the rector about the amount of participation required.

Because the Eucharist is the cornerstone of the Catholic faith, students have an immense investment in learning about its historical sources and present forms. Liturgical studies are regarded by many students as critical to their future ministry. According to faculty, the more experience students have had before and during theological studies with diverse congregations and the diverse forms of celebration allowed in the Roman rite, the more likely they will be to embrace liturgical studies.

However, since many students have limited experience with the Church's traditions, they need to develop a sense of symbol and discern the meaning of grace, the assembly, and the Church's teaching about the reality of the Eucharist. Faculty acknowledged the necessity of attending to the "mental maps" of students, which derive from their past experiences of liturgy and the sacraments. Several faculty remarked that students are "imprisoned by lack of religious imagination," "limited by knowing only one way to celebrate a liturgy," and "unaware of cultural adaptations." This narrowness may lead students to become "liturgical and sacramental censors" even before they have studied the history of liturgy and the Church documents pertaining to it. Some students have been influenced by observing nontraditional celebrations of the Eucharist on television, and to the dismay of faculty they begin to adopt some of these idiosyncratic practices.

Keeping the limitations of student backgrounds in mind, faculty have adopted many creative ways of teaching liturgical courses. One person described the progression of methods in his courses as follows:

> I begin with lectures, especially when we are dealing with historical material, but as soon as possible I get students actively involved, participating in the presentation of material and in demonstrating how the rites should be celebrated. We also talk about collaboration, whether it is with other ministers in setting up programs, with those who will be receiving the sacraments, or with parents who are preparing their children. When possible I bring parents into the class to talk about everything from marriage preparation to helping their children get ready for the sacrament of reconciliation.

Faculty use professionally made videos to illustrate various liturgical practices and to create a case study based on common experience. Students also videotape each other in practica courses to see if their gestures express what they want to communicate as they preside. Often faculty arrange for students to move beyond the classroom; for example, they may attend baptisms in several types of parishes, or visit a cemetery and pray for the dead, or teach a sample class for parents of first communicants—and then analyze the experience. "The point of enlarging their horizons," according to one faculty member, "is to put them in touch with the hopes and fears and longings of people. Before they can preside and pray with people, they need to know about the people and the circumstances that surround the event. Only then can they be welcoming." One rector affirmed that emphasizing the ministry of hospitality in the school's liturgies is the best way to teach students to be hospitable.

A pressing predicament is how to prepare students for liturgical ministry in cultures other than those in which they have previously experienced the Church. The problem has several dimensions. Anglo students are ill prepared to enter multicultural parishes, and students from other cultural backgrounds have generally had few occasions to become familiar with religious practices in the United States. For faculty, the difficulty of teaching students with dissimilar cultural backgrounds and educational needs is compounded by lack of training to teach liturgy and sacraments from a multicultural perspective. A few schools in the South and West have more experience with diversity than those in other parts of the country, so that they are able to incorporate the practices of specific ethnic communities; but overall much progress in this area is needed.

6. Pastoral Studies

When considering the question of how effective theologates are in preparing future priests and lay ministers to serve the Church, an area that has particular practical relevance is pastoral formation.[51] Catholics are directly affected by the teaching, preaching, and pastoral care afforded them in parishes and institutions. The quality of their later ministry demonstrates the quality of students' pastoral formation. The development of a

---

[51] Pastoral studies courses are one of two major components of pastoral formation required by theologates; the other, pastoral field education, is described in the section that follows the description of courses.

pastoral outlook, as realized through the integration of pastoral courses and experience with human, spiritual, and intellectual formation, has a major impact on the way ministry is exercised.

Through human formation, students develop the attributes required of those who work in public ministry in the Church. Through spiritual formation, they grow in prayer and virtue so that as ministers they will be able to recognize God's action in their own lives and in the lives of others. Through intellectual formation, they gain understanding of the history and theology of ministry, the necessary foundation of faith. Pastoral formation, which in its broader sense includes field education, is the culminating and integrating force that bridges the practical and the academic as well as the spiritual and the organizational dimensions of church ministry.

Goals. Church documents testify to the determinative role of pastoral formation: "Formation in its different aspects must have a fundamentally pastoral character. . . . The whole training of the students should have as its object to make them true shepherds of souls after the example of Jesus Christ, teacher, priest, and shepherd."[52] Both *PDV* and the *PPF* dedicate significant space to the subject of pastoral formation, each document with its own emphasis. *PDV* addresses both the theological and the practical sides of pastoral formation, stating that it needs to be studied as the true and genuine theological discipline that it is. The document specifies some of the ways in which pastoral formation should be implemented.

Students should learn "the interior habit of evaluating problems and establishing priorities and looking for solutions"; they should exercise "evangelical discernment of the socio-cultural and ecclesial situation in which the particular pastoral action is to be carried out"; and they should develop awareness of the church as 'communion' so that they can carry out "pastoral work with a community spirit, in heartfelt cooperation with the different members of the church." In particular, they must be prepared for "cooperation with the laity."[53]

Thus in addition to its function as an organizing principle for all aspects of ministerial preparation, pastoral formation is also

---

[52] *PDV,* #57, quoting *Optatum totius,* #4; the *PPF* also stresses the centrality of pastoral formation.

[53] *PDV,* #57–59.

part of intellectual formation, consisting of academic courses and pastoral field education. The *PPF* describes the academic courses as components of the core curriculum and devotes a separate chapter to field education, the pattern followed also in this research. Usually organized under departments of pastoral studies or pastoral theology, the courses cover the areas of (a) pastoral ministry, (b) homiletics, (c) canon law, (d) pastoral care and counseling, and (e) religious education. Pastoral field education is conducted through apprenticeships, internships, and immersion experiences. The rationale for each of those arrangements, along with specific field education requirements, follows the description of pastoral courses below.

a) Pastoral theology and pastoral ministry. Within the broad discipline that constitutes pastoral studies, most theologates offer courses in pastoral theology and ministerial skills.[54] These courses may concern the theological principles underlying the various ministries and institutions of the Church, or the dioceses or congregations where ministry takes place, or the pastoral skills needed for administration. Some theologates also include their liturgical and sacramental practica under this department.[55]

The goals of pastoral theology and ministry courses vary more than those of most other disciplines because of the variability among pastoral courses. Pastoral theology presents a theoretical framework for pastoral activity. Beginning with the pastoral situation, it draws on Scripture and tradition as they relate to concrete pastoral questions. According to one catalog,

---

[54] The average requirement in pastoral ministry is four semester credits. Nine schools require no courses specifically in pastoral ministry, but all make courses available.

[55] The liturgical and sacramental practica are described under liturgical studies, section 5. Those academic credits are added below to the other pastoral studies credits for the sake of comparison with the 1987 data, and because most schools include their practica under this section. Thus the combined number of credit hours required in pastoral studies in M.DIV. programs is as follows:

				1997	1987
< 13 hours	=	2 schools			
13–18 hours	=	10 schools	Mean	22.4	23.9
19–24 hours	=	15 schools	Median	22.5	24
25–30 hours	=	8 schools	Mode	23	24
> 30 hours	=	5 schools	Range	12–37	9–38

The task of pastoral theology is to elucidate the theoretical framework which will inform pastoral practice. Pastoral theology strives to understand contemporary human experience in the Church as well as in the world, so that pastoral ministers may empower people in the community to realize a fuller appropriation of the gospel in their lives.[56]

Ministerial skills, as well as skills associated with liturgical and sacramental practica, are used for the analysis of ministerial situations, for the exercise of suitable parish administration, and for the realization of proper pastoral practice. Through their knowledge about and practice of these skills, students become more aware of the connections between culture, Church, and ministry. They develop the ability (1) to identify beliefs, attitudes, and values in a multicultural society and their impact on ministry; (2) to examine the nature of the Church and the parish in American society; and (3) to reflect on the relations among various ministries. Some courses deal with administrative skills such as facilitating groups, creating a collaborative spirit, resolving conflict, and using human and financial resources effectively. In general, these courses and experiences are designed to prepare students to serve competently as pastoral practitioners and leaders.

b) Homiletics. Like several other fields of study, homiletics correlates with many areas of the curriculum. Effective preachers must be well versed in the Scriptures, have a solid grounding in all branches of systematic theology, exercise keen moral discernment within the Catholic tradition, and be cognizant of the pastoral situation in which they are preaching. Homiletics courses teach the principles and skills that are essential for apprehending and communicating the Word of God. Along with academic preparation, students must be spiritually mature in order to preach well, since their homilies reflect the depth of their relationship to Christ. Prayer, knowledge, skills, and practice are all required to reach a high level of competence in preaching. Most theologates have followed the *PPF*'s prescription that homiletics should occupy a prominent place in the curriculum and be integrated into the entire course of studies.[57]

---

[56] Seton Hall School of Theology, *Immaculate Conception Seminary Academic Bulletin,* 1991–1993, 54.

[57] *PPF,* #377. The document does not specify the number or type of courses needed. In practice, theologates require 5.6 semester credits in

Faculty from many disciplines contribute to the formation of good preachers, and those teaching homiletics have specific responsibilities. Some students need remedial work in basic communications skills, after which they progress to preaching courses. Schools usually require a beginning and advanced course in homiletics, or less frequently several courses of one or two credits each. The first-level course generally covers the organization, composition, and delivery of the homily, while the second helps students develop a practical hermeneutic for preaching from the texts of the lectionary, with emphasis on pastoral exegesis and theological reflection. Some schools regard the preparation of a homily as a collaborative effort involving a parish liturgy committee, other laity, and priests; faculty encourage students to include representatives from parishes as they prepare to preach. Obviously the task of training effective preachers extends far beyond the faculty.

Homiletics faculty have been especially conscientious about upgrading their skills, and most of them are now full-time faculty members who hold credentials appropriate to their field. Their professional organization, the Catholic Association of Teachers of Homiletics (CATH), sponsors workshops and conferences that deal with improved teaching methods such as videotaping homilies for critique, requiring more supervised delivery of homilies, and involving other faculty in assessment of student preaching. One faculty member commented on how much can be gained from careful evaluation of student homilies: "Hearing seminarians preach gives an excellent insight into their personality and ideology—and their relational skills. It is an indispensable part of their formation."

Because preaching touches every believer directly, it is not surprising that faculty regularly hear criticism of homilies from parishioners. Excellent courses in homiletics do not necessarily translate into well-crafted homilies, especially by beginning preachers. Since the art of preaching incorporates so many areas of learning and experience, it may take years in some cases to become a distinguished or even adequate preacher. One of the most difficult aspects of teaching is providing a judicious critique without being so discouraging as to dishearten students. Faculty recommend that everyone who preaches, even those with

_____

homiletics. All but seven schools require at least two courses in homiletics, and those seven require one course.

years of experience, seek evaluation so that the standard of Catholic preaching will be raised.

c) Canon law. The purpose of studying canon law is to understand how the spirit of the Gospel is concretized in the life of the Church. Canon law is concerned with juridical principles and laws, and with how the entire system of ecclesiastical government and discipline functions. As specified in the *PPF,* two courses in canon law are typically required: a general introduction, and the canon law of individual sacraments (especially marriage).[58] Many faculty who teach in this field serve simultaneously in diocesan tribunal offices, thus bringing depth and realism from their field experience to the classroom. Although attention to legal texts themselves and pastoral considerations are both essential components of canon law courses, faculty members are inclined to emphasize one or the other, the latter more often than the former. Those representing the latter position argue, for example, that the goal of canon law studies is "to interpret faithfully and compassionately the pastoral law of the Church," whereas the former position is reflected in phrases like "a presentation of canonical legislation" or "a focus on church order." Teaching usually involves the use of case studies, and most faculty report that initial resistance of students to this area of study gives way to interest and enthusiasm as they perceive the pastoral importance of understanding church law.

d) Pastoral care and counseling. Faculty who teach pastoral care and counseling make a distinction between becoming a professional pastoral counselor, and attaining foundational knowledge and skills in pastoral counseling sufficient for engaging in ministry. In the one or two courses usually required by theologates,[59] students "develop the counseling skills suitable to the opportunities and demands of general ministry, with a focus on the brief encounter," and they "learn standards of professional ethics for pastoral care and counseling."[60] Most programs teach mainly the procedures for evaluation and referral. At only a few

---

[58] *PPF,* #373. Theologates require 4.8 semester credits in canon law. Twelve schools require one course, and the rest two or more courses.

[59] Theologates require 3.1 semester credits in pastoral care and counseling. Five schools require none, eight require two courses, and the other twenty-seven require one course.

[60] Weston Jesuit School of Theology, *Catalog,* 1997–1998, 56.

schools, usually those that require two courses, do students have the opportunity for supervised practice of counseling techniques. Faculty express apprehension about future ministers inclined to play the role of professional counselor when they should be referring individuals with serious psychological problems. Helping students determine the limits of their competence is a critical goal.

e) Religious education. Perhaps one of the most neglected areas of study in theologates is religious education. Less than half the schools require a course in it,[61] though almost all future pastors will have oversight responsibility for religious education programs. Partly because of extensive curricular requirements, the *PPF* states only that pastoral studies should "provide an introduction to initiation rites for adults and children."[62] Several theologates stipulate that students are expected to gain an understanding of the Rite of Christian Initiation of Adults (RCIA), but few offer a separate course devoted to that program. As is the case with other pastoral subjects, few full-time faculty are employed to teach religious education. Diocesan and parish religious education directors express concern about the minimal education of seminarians in this area given their future supervisory role. However, with the focus of formation directed elsewhere, it is unlikely that this pattern will change.

----

[61] Theologates require an average of only 1.1 semester credits in religious education, which means that seventeen schools require one course or a field practicum of two or three credits. Twelve schools have courses available but do not require any, and the remaining thirteen schools offer no religious education courses. Four theologates have extensive offerings: Sacred Heart Major Seminary, Michigan; SS. Cyril and Methodius, Michigan; Mount St. Mary's of the West, Ohio; and St. Vincent Seminary, Pennsylvania. Other theologates, especially those affiliated with universities or those with separate programs for lay students, offer full programs in religious education, but the courses are not necessarily required of or available to M.DIV. students.

Among the thirty-one diocesan seminaries, those in the Midwest are nearly twice as likely (about 70 percent) to require a religious education course as those on the coasts (about 40 percent). Among the schools for religious-order candidates, only one requires a course (11.1 percent). In some cases students will have taken education courses before they begin theological studies, but very little is available to them as theology students.

[62] *PPF,* #379.

Structure. Unlike the other major divisions of the curriculum, pastoral studies is subdivided into distinct areas of study and in many cases employs part-time faculty engaged in the ministry associated with their particular discipline. Perhaps for that reason, pastoral studies is emphasized less than Scripture, systematic, moral, or sacramental theology. The areas of canon law and homiletics have uniformly moderate requirements, pastoral care and counseling has uniformly minimal requirements, and religious education has the least requirements. Pastoral ministry shows the most varied requirements, ranging from no credits to as many as fourteen, and including courses as disparate as the practice of collaborative ministry, social analysis, ministry to families, leadership in parish settings, and ministry to the multicultural community.

Disagreement among faculty continues about whether students should dedicate their years of study to courses that are considered more academic or to more practical courses. Those favoring academic courses believe that the often deficient educational backgrounds of students indicate that they should spend as much time as possible on Scripture and systematic theology. Those favoring practical courses believe that, in the absence of a pastoral dimension, academic studies will produce graduates who are unable to meet the ordinary ministerial needs of people. Although not new, the controversy has become more pointed in recent years, since most priests now have only a short apprenticeship before becoming pastors, whereas twenty-five years ago they would not have become pastors for ten or more years. Thus in almost all theologates, pastoral field education, described in the next section, carries the burden of providing the knowledge and skills necessary for ministerial service.

Summary analysis. Do the curriculum and the way courses are taught adequately prepare the teachers, preachers, and spiritual leaders needed by the Church in the decades ahead? As the foregoing reports on curriculum indicate, both positive and negative claims can be made. Positive features such as improved teaching, competent coverage of basic subject matter, and appreciation for the social and cultural context of ministry are immediately evident. On the negative side, meager student backgrounds, numerous curricular requirements, and a lack of support for continuing education diminish the possibility of providing a truly superior ministerial education.

The positive features deserve some elaboration:

a) Creative teaching methods. Of great interest to faculty are developments in teaching methods and techniques that correspond to the way students best learn. As indicated in their previous comments, faculty have updated and improved their teaching by attending programs sponsored by professional organizations and peer groups. For example, since 1996 and continuing until 2001, faculty from a total of twenty theologates will participate in a summer conference at Keystone, Colorado, inaugurating a six-year project on "Theological Teaching for the Church's Ministries."[63]

Devoted to the personal and collegial formation of theological school faculties, this program looks at various educational issues, in particular those raised by the diversity of contemporary student bodies. Each school selects a topic such as teaching students from other cultures, relating to students with an affinity for diverse religious ideologies, and reorganizing the curriculum in light of new ministerial requirements.

Faculty are urged to discuss various teaching methods and the content of their own courses as compared to courses taught by other faculty members. On that basis methods and content are both enriched and expanded. Amplifying the typical lecture/discussion format, they introduce case studies, role playing, field experience, and new technologies. Some faculty, for example, ask students to e-mail questions relating to the next-day's readings or the previous day's lecture, or to respond to exam questions. Use of multimedia is a growing practice, and computers are beginning to appear in the classroom. As students enter theological studies from settings where these educational tools are widely available, including electronically based libraries, faculty are seeing the need to expand their own knowledge. With the help of funding and professional organizations, faculty have responded well to such opportunities.

b) Coverage of extensive content. Besides creative teaching, faculty at most schools have constructed a curriculum that covers a range of content corresponding to the backgrounds of stu-

---

[63] Another, broader program with similar goals of helping to build enabling environments for good teaching and learning is sponsored by The Wabash Center for Teaching and Learning in Theology and Religion. Among other projects, the Center hosts programs that help faculty deepen their vocational commitment to teaching and keeps them abreast of advancements in their disciplines.

dents. Aware of the enormous demands placed on those who serve in ministerial roles, the typical curriculum is designed for students who need to learn basic theological and pastoral concepts, as well as gain a more mature understanding of their faith that will foster their development as leaders and teachers. Considering the magnitude of the task, faculty have succeeded in sending out graduates who for the most part are well regarded by their supervisors, coworkers, and those who receive their ministry.

c) Consideration of the religious, social, and cultural context. Many faculty begin their teaching careers in theologates with considerable experience in a variety of ministries. Priests have often served in parishes or, in the case of religious priests, in the ministries of their congregations. Often laypeople and women religious faculty members have ministered in parishes, schools, and other Catholic institutions, thus bringing variety of experience and breadth to their teaching. These experiences alert them to the context in which their students will be ministering in the future; accordingly they design the curriculum, teach their classes, and serve as mentors with full cognizance of the religious, social, and cultural realities that make service in the Church so complex today. Many priest faculty continue to work in parishes on weekends, and other faculty remain in touch with life outside the theologate through their families, communities, and their own participation. Interviews revealed the involvement of faculty in many aspects of religious and civic life, which they bring to bear on their teaching.

Although the positive aspects of intellectual formation are significant, several distressing problems remain:

a) The meager backgrounds most students bring to theological studies. The chapter on students describes their backgrounds in general; relevant here is their academic preparation, which is often deficient in both learning skills and content. In an age dominated by fast-paced media, proficiency in reading and writing is often minimal, and less than half the students who begin theological studies have been well schooled in their faith. The curriculum must address these many deficiencies and accommodate the expected level of study to the students' backgrounds.

In contrast to their counterparts ten years ago, fewer and fewer seminarians have been enrolled in college seminary programs. Most lay students, even those coming with a Catholic college education, have done limited course work in philosophy and theology, and the liberal arts all together. One institutional response has been to increase the prerequisites for admission, fulfilled either in a college or a pre-theology program.

Because of the added requirements set out in the *PPF,* many seminarians now enroll in two-year pre-theology programs, which were virtually unheard of ten years ago. Lay students, too, are required to take courses that will address deficiencies in their education, but they usually enroll in one or two classes each semester while continuing to work. They seldom participate in a pre-theology program that includes human and spiritual formation. However, the older lay students often make up for this lacuna with their previous ministerial experience and consistent, long-term practice of their faith.

b) The numerous curricular requirements of most programs. A second response to the inadequate backgrounds of students has actually contributed to another concern of faculty, that is, an overcrowded curriculum. Many students, especially those who are under thirty, enter theological studies having only a minimal acquaintance with the Church, so that faculty cannot depend on understanding that comes from either lived experience or academic study. Hence initial theological courses often cover basic knowledge of the faith that would have been assumed in earlier years. Further, more areas of study are required by the *PPF,* and pastoral demands create other grounds for adding courses. The proliferation of course requirements and pastoral experiences has led to a reduction in elective courses and, in some seminaries, programs that are almost entirely prescribed. At the same time, students complain that the crush of work leaves no time for them to integrate their learning experiences. An ethos of overwork pervades many theologates and is felt by both students and faculty.

Even with all that is required, some topics are addressed insufficiently or not at all. First among these is teaching students to minister to a changing Catholic population, especially in multicultural settings. Few faculty—despite their willingness to learn—are prepared to teach about such ministry. Courses dealing with evangelization, religious education, ecumenism, and collaboration are seldom required ostensibly because of already full programs, even though the last two are two of the four major themes proposed for seminary curricula by the *PPF.*

Other topics, for example, pertaining to new parish structures or ministry to multiple parishes, are not usually available even as electives. Although faculties try to take advantage of the time during which students are enrolled, some topics are not treated at all or tangentially within another course. Some theologate faculty and administrators question the template for curriculum design, and perhaps they will find more productive ways of conveying the corpus of knowledge required.

c) The need for continuing education. A third problem, which carries elements of both hope and discouragement, is the need for required continuing education without the structures or financial support to provide it. Both priests and lay ministers would benefit from access to courses that could not be accommodated during theological studies, in part because of lack of time and in part because some topics are not conducive to classroom study without practical experience, for example, parish administration. Moreover, with new developments in theology and pastoral practice, professional ministers should be updating their knowledge and skills. Faculty are concerned, however, that few priests and professional lay ministers are able or willing to engage in a systematic program of continuing education.

This attitude has had serious repercussions on the structure of the curriculum. One academic dean described the situation thus:

> While arguments can be made why continuing education should be given greater emphasis, the more fundamental problem that its underemphasis points to is the lack of a developmental model for ministry. Priests are expected to "get it all" within four (or six) years; they can't depend on having time to study in any significant way once ordained. Therefore we feel compelled to develop curricula that are so jammed that even bright students groan under the burdens imposed. The *PPF* has moved away from course prescriptions to topic prescriptions; that actually is progressive if schools began to reconsider how topics can be interwoven as students gain their bearings as theological thinkers. Imagining new models will not occur unless ministry is seen as developmental in every aspect over an entire lifetime. We can indeed get better at what we do; it will not substitute for a developmental perspective.[64]

---

[64] The statement was made by Dr. Victor Klimoski, academic dean at The Saint Paul Seminary School of Divinity at the University of St. Thomas, whose background is in adult education.

The issue is of importance because so many priests become pastors only a few years after graduating; laypeople also become directors of programs within a relatively short time, though not as quickly as priests become pastors in most dioceses. Usually neither group has received the particular training appropriate to the positions they assume. If further education were required, agreements could be reached between theologates and continuing education offices to assure that all critical subjects were available for study when the individual most needed them.

In conclusion, the answer to the question of whether the curriculum adequately prepares teachers, preachers, and spiritual leaders for the Church is both yes and no. Yes, teaching methods are usually creative, innovative, and appropriately geared to the level of the students. At a basic level the content is comprehensive, and the presentation reflects the reality of the Church at the turn of the millennium. Yet some shortcomings are inevitable, particularly in light of weak student backgrounds, an overcrowded curriculum that leaves no time for some topics, and inconsistency in continuing education policies that would ensure availability of advanced courses on specialized subjects.

Given all the data, I believe that most curricula as currently constructed serve resourceful students very well. After they graduate and encounter lacunae in their expertise or education, they will delve into areas that require their special attention on their own, with mentors, or through continuing studies. Less talented students are served by the present curricula as well as possible, but extending the time of their enrollment might be beneficial to them. In addition careful mentoring after they leave theological studies is imperative. Unfortunately those who need additional knowledge and assistance are often least likely to seek it, so that requiring supervised apprenticeships may be the best way to supplement the years of formal theological education.

D. Pastoral Field Education

Introduction

The development of more useful and effective pastoral field education programs is one of the major accomplishments of theologates over the past ten years. The content of interviews with directors of field education ten years ago was often in the mode of lament. Then they reported that in many instances supervisors were not adequately prepared for their role, the involvement of parishioners was limited, faculty were unsupportive and uncooperative in helping with theological reflection, and student experiences were disjointed. Some of the earlier programs were of course already well developed, but many others have benefited from the reorganization undertaken by field education directors; now only a few directors complain about the former shortcomings. Moreover directors' credentials are more suited to the tasks required of them, and their competence has resulted in better programs.

Purpose and goals. The purpose of pastoral field education has always been to help students become effective practitioners. Through supervised field placements and theological reflection, they begin to acquire the skills and attitudes appropriate for ministry. For the most part the learning experiences take place in the context of student ministry.[65] The length of time, the placement settings, the involvement of those inside and outside the school, and the quality of supervision vary, but the overall aims are remarkably similar. As stated succinctly in one seminary catalog, the pastoral program is designed to enable students "to use their academic training in a pastoral situation, thereby giving pastoral insights to academic studies and enhancing ministry with a solid theological foundation."[66] The concept of integration is essential to the process of students' coming to understand the ongoing relationship between theory and practice. With the guidance of supervisors, they work toward personal integration of theology and ministerial experience, perceiving in the process how ministry informs theological study and how theology informs and deepens the meaning of service.

Several more specific goals are also common to pastoral field education programs. Some goals are related to the students' personal growth, while others are linked directly to ministry. Vocational choice, personal qualities and attitudes, and pastoral

[65] Twenty-eight of the forty-two theologates call the program field education, while eleven call it pastoral formation or pastoral ministry. Supervised ministry, professional ministry, and community service and development is the nomenclature used by the remaining three schools.

[66] Pope John XXIII National Seminary, *Catalog,* 1995–1997, 16.

skills are dimensions of personal growth that can be tested and developed in field placements. The opportunity to learn more about future colleagues and future parishioners—the various cultural, ideological, and chronological groups in their future congregations—in addition to the breadth and depth of the services they will be expected to offer all pertain to ministry.

On a personal level, one major goal is to promote students' emotional and vocational maturity. Especially those with little experience in parish settings or other church-related institutions need to test their disposition toward and aptitude for ministry to see if these correlate with their own sense of identity. A field education director commented on how a pastoral placement can meet this goal: "It is essential for vocational discernment. The vocation is not just an intellectual affair. The call is tested in reality. In the context of ministry, the vocation grows stronger or is called into question."

A complementary goal, once vocational choice is confirmed, is to deepen ministerial self-understanding and self-confidence. While learning to recognize the value of their unique gifts and prior experiences, students also become aware of their liabilities and limitations. With the assistance of supervisors, they reflect on how they tend to act and react in pastoral situations. They begin to identify areas for personal and professional growth, gradually coming to appreciate the importance of cultivating new attitudes and new pastoral skills. Thus they learn to be more secure in themselves and less fearful of encountering new situations. In the words of one seminarian:

> My pastoral experience helped me to develop a sense of "I-can-ness." I used to wonder if I had what it took for ministry, but now I know I have some gifts. I also recognize my shortcomings, and I want to develop the skills I need to overcome them.

Further, relationships with a wide range of people help students learn about the ethical requirements for the practice of ministry and the delineation of appropriate boundaries. In light of recent clergy abuse cases, theologates are determined to reinforce guidelines for ethical professional conduct. At the same time, students need to enter into dynamic relationships and to understand the place of intimacy in the exercise of ministry. Building community, working collaboratively, extending compassion, and offering hospitality are all part of effective ministry and require interpersonal transactions. Concerning this indispensable personal presence, one ministry supervisor remarked: "As leaders and listeners in the Church, we all need to be bridge builders. That means being comfortable with the people we serve, looking them in the eye, being a 'people person.'" From the point of view of the schools, assessing how students behave in ministerial settings enables them to identify problems and intervene early by advising students to change the way they exercise ministry; if students prove incapable of adapting, they are often asked to leave the program.

An additional goal is to situate theological study within the life of the Christian community. Students experience first-hand the tensions involved in exercising personal pastoral abilities under the pressure of public ministry. Indispensable to good practice is an acquaintance with the context of ministry and a realistic understanding of its possibilities and limits. As students work within the structure of the Church, they face what it means both to exercise authority and to submit to authority. In some situations, field placements give students opportunities to work with personnel in archdiocesan offices. Being introduced there to the people and services provided by the diocese, they realize the many resources available to them. Connections with the Church at large, for example, hospitals, nursing homes, and other institutions, also broaden their perspectives.

Other goals are met through parish ministry. According to one seminary's catalog, experiencing the ambiguities of life in a parish community will

> prepare students for the emerging reality of collaborative ministry, e.g., other churches and religions, male/female, ordained/lay," and "expose students to issues of social justice and to the importance of social analysis leading to the development of appropriate ministerial responses, e.g., empowerment, advocacy, and networking.[67]

In almost every diocese, parishes—especially the larger ones— have a sizable lay staff, facilitating the goal of learning how to work collaboratively with other professional ministers and volunteers. In one interview a field education director stated emphatically: "One of our main objectives is to be sure our seminarians are willing to work with lay people. This is not debatable; they *must* learn how to do this or they won't be able to

---

[67] *Ibid.*

function as leaders in this diocese or any other." Similarly another director spoke about the necessity of supporting the role of women in the Church: "Students need to be able to work with courageous and talented and strong women. Today so many parish ministers are women, both lay and religious. Collaborating with them is absolutely indispensable."

Pastoral experience heightens students' awareness of the parish, the diocese, and other ministerial settings in which the Church addresses a variety of human needs. The heterogeneity of American Catholics requires ministers who can be flexible in the midst of complexity and sensitive to the needs and aspirations of people in many circumstances. Introducing students to parishioners with diverse linguistic and cultural backgrounds, a range of ideological positions, and varying educational backgrounds, gives them a sense of how expansive the Church is in this country. When disagreements occur, pastoral leaders are called to work through difficulties and misunderstandings so that everyone—young and old, women and men—will feel included. A faculty member who participates in theological reflection with students commented:

> We try to introduce them to the wide range of people they will have to serve. The backgrounds of people, their religious education and views of church, their spiritual needs and expectations of parishes—all these things give ministry a face, make it real. I think our obligation is to help students find the middle road, to reach out from the center to serve as many people as they can. If they can learn to communicate, negotiate, and manage conflict, the program has accomplished what it set out to do.

An indirect benefit, if not a specific goal, of pastoral placements is that numerous persons engage in the formation and evaluation of future priests and lay ministers. Especially when students remain in the same parish or other ministerial placement for a long period of time, supervisors can offer sustained, meaningful feedback. Often several individuals become part of a group officially assigned to accompany students during the field placement, serving additionally as a theological reflection group. At their best these groups provide insightful formative and summative evaluations of the student. Critical to the usefulness of such parish committees is their preparation for the role, lest their function be reduced simply to affirmation of the student. A realistic critique of students' readiness for ministry should both reinforce positive qualities and identify, with a view to correcting, negative ones. As a supervisor in one parish said: "The value of this (pastoral internship) is that the whole church gets involved in preparing future leaders and has a chance to say to the seminary staff, and ultimately to the bishop, 'This is the kind of leader we need.'"

Pastoral field education likewise benefits students by acquainting them with the rewards and the tensions that are inherent in ministerial service. Seminarians profit by observing the lifestyle of the parish priest as they prepare "for ministry as celibates and (to) reflect upon the implication of such a life call as these indications emerge from their ministerial practice."[68] At every stage of development, pastoral formation equips all students to reflect on their pastoral identity and to grow in appreciation of their ministerial role.

Personnel. Many people assist with pastoral formation, including field-education directors who administer the entire program, and faculty who teach pastoral courses and moderate theological reflection sessions. In the field, trained supervisors, parish committees and staffs, and others who work with students in placements outside of parishes comprise the personnel. Many program directors noted that the most significant improvement in pastoral field education over the past ten years has been in the preparation of field supervisors. Almost every school now provides an extended orientation for new supervisors as well as annual in-service sessions for experienced ones. Consequently the retention rate of supervisors has increased, as has their ability to advise and evaluate students.

The key figure in pastoral field education is the administrator of the program, who is usually accorded the title Director of Field Education. Some schools substitute "pastoral" for "field" in the title, as in Director of Pastoral Formation or Pastoral Life. The director's position title almost always corresponds to the program title. Who are these directors? With respect to their *vocational status,* fourteen of them are women religious, another fourteen are diocesan priests, six are laywomen, five are men religious, two are Protestant ministers, and one is a layman. The proportions are similar to those of ten years ago, except that there are fewer men religious and more laywomen. The following table gives the *credentials* of the forty-two directors:

---

[68] Kenrick-Glennon Seminary, *Catalog,* 1996–1997, 24.

Degree	Number	
Ph.D.	7 (incl. 2 candidates)	⎫
S.T.D., Th.D., Ed.D.	4	⎬ 33.3 percent
D. Min.	3 (plus 1 with Ph.D.)	⎭
M.Div. only	9	⎫
Master's (two degrees)	11 (incl. 1 with D.D.S.)	⎬ 66.7 percent
Master's (one degree)	7	⎬
B.S.	1	⎭

Ten years ago a larger proportion of directors held doctoral degrees (41.9 percent). Faculty status was accorded to all but two directors then, whereas in 1997 four are not listed as faculty members. Altogether, however, a higher proportion (47.6 percent) now hold academic rank than in 1985–1987 (37.5 percent). The credentials of current directors, especially those with doctorates or two master's degrees, are more often directed specifically to the competencies needed for this work, and the diocesan priests who hold only an M.DIV. degree often have extensive pastoral experience. The programs of professional organizations, both the Catholic Association of Theological Field Educators (CATFE) and the association for both Catholic and Protestant field educators, the Association of Theological Field Educators (ATFE), have strengthened the competence of directors. In all cases, their experience and education give them more confidence in leading pastoral field education programs than was true ten years ago.

Structures. Theologates provide pastoral field education at several venues, implementing many arrangements and formats.[69] The two most common models are concurrent and intensive, each having several variations. Some form of the concurrent model is used by virtually every school, requiring students to take courses and be involved in a pastoral placement during the same semester. The intensive model usually requires students to spend a period of time from several weeks to a year working full-time in a particular ministerial setting. Each model has advantages for certain students and disadvantages for others, so that field education directors will adapt program requirements to fit the needs of the individual student.

---

[69] The average requirement in pastoral field education in 1997 was 10.8 semester hours, compared to 11.8 semester hours in 1987.

Typical of concurrent programs is a developmental approach, with students progressing from observation to participation to leadership. First-year theology students prepare for field placements over one or two semesters by studying the foundations of ministry. They also learn the basics of theological reflection, an exercise that involves the selection and analysis of a ministerial experience based on Scripture and Tradition. In dialogue with supervisors and peers, theological reflection helps these students gain new insights and discover new approaches to the ministerial experience. Sometime during their second semester or at the beginning of second-year theology, students begin actual pastoral work. At first this ordinarily means either working with a small group or teaching a catechetical class.

During the second and third years, students participate in more intensive and time-consuming placements, often in a parish setting. If a full-time placement is not required, the ministerial service expected during these years is more extensive. The level of responsibility increases with each semester, until a student may be responsible for planning and teaching the RCIA program (Rite of Christian Initiation for Adults), organizing a parish census, or executing a similarly complex assignment. On average, students spend six to eight hours per week for two or three semesters in this type of placement, in addition to one hour of supervision and two hours of theological reflection. If the program also requires a full-time placement, the time for the concurrent work is usually limited to less than five hours per week, and its duration to a semester or two. A few programs prescribe that students stay in the same parish for all of their ministerial experiences, but most programs move students around to various settings and not always to a parish.[70] Nonparish placements may be on campuses, in prisons, with social service agencies, or in an AIDS ministry. Hospital ministry presents a special case and receives more consideration than many of the other nonparish placements. Of the forty-two theologates, twenty-four

---

[70] Among the advantages of being in one place are getting to know people well enough to render meaningful service, experiencing consistent supervision where issues have time to surface, and more nearly replicating the actual ministerial settings where most students, especially seminarians, will spend their lives. The disadvantages are that students encounter less variety in the people they serve and in the types of ministry practiced.

require either CPE (Clinical Pastoral Education) or an extended hospital internship. Many of the remaining eighteen offer a hospital experience as one alternative among several.

The full-time placements are of several types, ranging from a few weeks to a year. Summer placements are most common, with eleven schools requiring one or two summer experiences, and two others recommending them. Each of the following intensive experiences is required by one or two schools: (1) a five-week period after the end of the semester for three summers; (2) a ten-week period, a semester or quarter with a consecutive summer, or a full-time diaconal internship; or (3) a pastoral internship year, which requires a break in the academic program. Six seminaries require this internship and four others recommend it. Many dioceses require a year in a parish, regardless of the school's policy; often the school's field-education director will assist with supervision, and the school may or may not give credit for the placement. Both diocesan seminarians and those belonging to religious orders may elect to participate in an intensive placement, whereas lay students usually prefer concurrent programs because of time and financial constraints.

The aims and advantages of extended field placements for seminarians were spelled out at length during interviews and appear in the schools' documents. One catalog describes such placements as "an intentional educational process structured to achieve the human and faith maturation of the person as a minister while seeking to develop competence in pastoral skills through theological reflection in the actual practice of ministry."[71] Another catalog articulates why a seminarian might spend a year in an internship:

> It not only enables the student to test and develop his pastoral skills, but also provides an opportunity for him to better achieve the level of personal growth and spiritual maturity that are essential for a priest in the Church today. A pastoral year internship permits the seminarian and his diocese or religious community to discern his calling to the priesthood in a more authentic setting, in that the internship takes place within the context of the local church or religious community ministering with the local presbyterate.[72]

---

[71] Oblate School of Theology, *Catalog*, 1997–1999, 35.

[72] Pontifical College Josephinum, School of Theology, *Catalog*, 1996–1998, 34.

The settings for intensive placements are often in ordinary parishes in the United States, though many schools are developing alternate sites. Opportunities for students to live in another culture or another country are increasingly valued because of the multicultural membership of the American Church; most sociological studies indicate that the proportion of Catholics in the United States who are Latino, African American, or Asian is approaching 50 percent. Often the programs that take students into another culture are called immersion experiences. At least thirty such opportunities are provided by the theologates, most of them in the Hispanic community (fifteen); the remainder are in the Holy Land, Rome, Appalachia, and other rural and urban settings with different ethnic communities. Apart from field experiences, thirteen schools offer extensive Hispanic programs, and sixteen others Spanish language courses. Additional academic courses deal with the exercise of ministry in a culture that is not one's own by birth.

All of these programs have advanced tremendously over the past ten years, though most attention by far is given to Hispanic culture. A few schools have exemplary language programs and courses in ministry that refer to a multicultural setting.[73] Attention to Asian communities is growing as the number of Asian students increases, for example, at Notre Dame Seminary in New Orleans special programs are in place, some to assist Asian students with inculturation and others to familiarize other students with Asian culture. At the Catholic Theological Union several programs on ministry in the African American community have been introduced, among them the Augustus Tolton Pastoral Ministry Program cosponsored with the Archdiocese of Chicago.

While multicultural programs, courses, and field experiences are more prevalent now than they were ten years ago, few faculty members teaching in Catholic theologates derive from Hispanic, African American, or Asian cultural traditions themselves. The predominant group of Anglo faculty members expresses uncertainty about how to teach and form students from

---

[73] Several theologates are quite well known for their Hispanic programs: St. John's Seminary, Camarillo, California; St. Vincent's Regional Seminary, Boynton Beach, Florida; Catholic Theological Union, Chicago; Mount Angel Seminary, Mount Angel, Oregon; and Oblate School of Theology, San Antonio, Texas.

different racial and ethnic backgrounds. The task is further complicated by the substantial number of seminarians who have recently immigrated from Eastern Europe. The growing ethnic and racial diversity among theologate students, and the increasing number of Catholics in the United States who have recently come from other countries, makes it imperative that theologates provide field education placements that will help students prepare for ministry in multicultural settings.

   Outcomes. In light of the goals, the personnel, and the structures that support pastoral field education, what are the desired outcomes of this considerable effort? Besides assisting students with individual and ministerial growth, pastoral placements give faculty more occasions to observe the readiness of students for ministry. As they observe, faculty ask such questions as, Can students integrate theological study and apply it to ministry in a contemporary setting? Within a local parish community or some other ministerial placement, do students exhibit qualities needed for the practice of ministry? Are they capable of further developing their abilities? The desired outcomes[74] relate to the witness of faith, the methods of ministry, the style of ministry, and the context of ministry. If programs fulfill their goals, students will be able to

- sustain a daily prayer life and continue spiritual direction;
- witness to a life of faith and communicate it to others;
- maintain a positive attitude toward the Church and pass that on to others;
- relate the Gospel to everyday life by word and example, share the Gospel with the alienated and the unchurched, and communicate a sense of God's love and forgiveness;
- apply pastoral theory and theological knowledge to ministerial situations;
- incorporate the practice of theological reflection on pastoral experience as part of the ministerial lifestyle;
- identify the theological and pastoral issues implicit in the experience of ministry;
- advance the mission of the Church through effective leadership, communication, collaboration, and celebration;

[74] Collated from information in interviews and current theologate catalogs.

- perform competent pastoral care and engage in effective group work;
- take initiative, assume responsibility, and be accountable;
- realize their own unique ministerial leadership role in the community, and develop good interpersonal relationships with parishioners and parish staff;
- reach a clear understanding of the diversity of ministries in the community and the connections between them;
- recognize the tensions inherent in ministry and utilize appropriate resources to help resolve them;
- make an informed pastoral response to contemporary issues in the context of the global mission of the Church;
- cultivate sensitivity to matters of social justice, including sexism and racism, and to the role of the Church in the world.

Summary analysis. When we compare the state of pastoral field education ten years ago with the situation now, we see that many improvements have been made though some areas remain undeveloped. Recalling the issues that were uppermost in the minds of directors of field education at that time,[75] it is possible to gauge the distance that has been traveled since then. So, what advances can be discerned over the past ten years? How effectively do current programs prepare future priests and lay ministers? What more should be done?

Of the ten objectives mentioned by field education directors a decade ago, considerable progress has been made on six of them. The first was to bring about full acceptance of pastoral training and field education by faculties in theologates. At only a few theologates is the significance of pastoral field education now queried or the program not accorded academic credit. Faculty have a greater appreciation of how ministerial experience enlivens classroom discussion and focuses questions. For example, students express awareness of the concerns of young people about sexual issues and of parents about faith formation for their children.

A second positive change has been in clarifying the meaning of theological reflection and the role that faculty play in this process. At many theologates faculty willingly engage in dialogue with students about pastoral incidents drawn from fieldwork.

[75] See Schuth, *Reason for the Hope*, 193, 196, 199–200.

The third and fourth objectives were to train supervisors in field settings to perform their evaluative function with greater skill, and to broaden participation by parishioners in the field education process. Both of these objectives have been addressed by providing orientation for new supervisors and in-service programs for those with experience. The programs focus on training in the art of supervision. A few field education directors sponsor summer workshops at their schools to teach their peers and to exchange ideas about successful practices. Directors notice the difference this preparation makes for themselves and for on-site supervisors when it comes to evaluating students. On-site evaluation is universal, and some supervisors are invited by the schools to take part in the annual comprehensive evaluation of students.

A fifth objective of many directors ten years ago was to implement a more coherent and progressive program that would reflect more systematically the range of student backgrounds. Achievement of this objective has been aided by that of the sixth, namely, to upgrade the credentials held by most directors. Now both their degrees and their own pastoral experience are better suited to the task of establishing pastoral programs and assessing the capabilities of students.

Although many advancements have thus been reported, not all schools have completed the work of improvement, and four areas remain problematic. Ten years ago, pointing to the diminishing number of clergy and increasing involvement of professional lay ministers, field education directors sought to incorporate appropriate changes in field placements. Ten years later, with parishes still working on new structures and procedures, students cannot yet benefit from fully developed patterns of practice that would anticipate their own future ministries more accurately than do some of the present arrangements.

A second problem, less appreciated ten years ago, is the restricted time students have available for pastoral placements. This problem has two dimensions: On a week-to-week basis, other formation claims more time, and students feel rushed when they are also expected to do concurrent pastoral work; over the longer term, bishops and vocation directors sometimes ask students to accelerate their programs so that they can be ready for ordination sooner. Several faculties have recommended a pastoral year as a program requirement, but this proposal has been rejected by boards and bishops in the interest of reducing the time required for formation before ordination. Many field education directors believe that a full-year internship would be advisable for almost every student because pastoral competency and the habit of theological reflection cannot be developed in a short time.

The other two unresolved problems remain less in the hands of theologates than in those of the wider Church, but both are perplexing for new priests and lay ministers. Facilitating the transition from theologate to parish ministry is the first issue. Some schools do see this as their responsibility, but few have the personnel or resources to carry it out. The final issue is closely related, and even more difficult for theologates to manage, that is, arranging for supervision through the early years of ministry as a means of ensuring continuity and growth.

Why is this so important for the Church? When priests and lay ministers begin working in parishes and other ministerial settings, they often encounter unexpected obstacles—sometimes because of problems with coworkers or supervisors, sometimes because they are not adequately prepared to do particular tasks that they are expected to do. If these obstacles are not addressed early, discouragement sets in and sometimes results in the person's leaving the priesthood or ministry. Even though everyone recognizes the need for ongoing personal and professional development, the amount of time available for apprenticeship once the candidate is ordained or certified for ministry is limited or nonexistent, so that all the more is help with transition needed.

An additional issue not mentioned ten years ago is the need for students to be prepared for ministry in multicultural settings. As described earlier, field education directors have developed many placements in various racial and ethnic communities, but not all students are in a position to do fieldwork in these settings; yet in fact most students will minister in multicultural parishes. More attention should be focused on opening up more placements that include people from various cultural backgrounds.

Credit for the many program refinements and improvements goes primarily to the field education directors themselves, but the support of parish personnel, faculty, and administrators has been significant as well. Movement toward more adequate pastoral formation is also evident in the formation documents already cited. The improvements still needed are especially urgent because so many expectations are placed on pastoral programs. Students must assume the responsibilities of ministry as soon as they finish their degrees, and for most of them the main locus of experience is in their field placements.

Field education models that foresee the seminarian as a pastor in just a few years are most beneficial. Not only have a number of positive changes occurred over the past ten years, but also the present situation contrasts dramatically with that of twenty-five years ago, when a brief diaconal internship of teaching and limited pastoral work was considered sufficient for pastoral formation.

Part IV. The Future

■ ■ ■ ■ ■ ■ ■ ■ ■

Introduction

During interviews for this research, we explored ideas about Church, ministry, and priesthood through questions such as the following: What is your vision for the future of the Church? What are some of the ways in which ministry in the Church will need to be exercised, and how should this affect preparation for priesthood and lay ministry? What is the image you have of priesthood? What is involved in being a priest today, and what will be involved in the future? These and other questions elicited responses from faculty, administrators, and students that coalesced around several broad themes, or topics, concerning Church and culture, ethnic and ideological diversity, and ministerial personnel and structures. The themes are listed below, followed by reflections on various images of priesthood and the role of priests in the future.

A. Perceptions about Church and Ministry

The five topics regarding the Church and the future of ministry mentioned most often by interviewees were

1. the nature, identity, and role of the Church in a pluralistic and multicultural society;
2. the heterogeneity of the Catholic population, including cultural, racial, and ethnic differences, as well as economic, educational, and age differences;

3. extreme ideological diversity and an attitude of intolerance among many church members;
4. acute ministerial needs, especially for evangelization, adult formation, religious education, enhancement of family life, care for the poor, and spiritual development; and
5. evolving church structures, collaboration, and the changing roles of priests and lay ministers.

Even if these five topics cover a wide spectrum of issues, the list is not intended to be exhaustive. Rather, as an attempt to summarize the discussions held with all categories of interviewees, it represents the major concerns of those who prepare others, and those who are themselves preparing, for ministry. Ultimately it will be instructive to examine how closely these themes correspond with concerns of parishioners, lay ministers, and pastors.

1. The Nature, Identity, and Role of the Church in a Pluralistic and Multicultural Society

Respondents expressed much enthusiasm as they imagined prospects for Catholicism in the future. Their comments highlighted the role of the Church in contemporary society, the stance it should take toward culture, and the identity of the Church with reference to Vatican II. Divergent views on these topics, especially between students and faculty, surfaced repeatedly.

Many respondents commented on the Church's vision in response to the pluralistic culture that characterizes the present American context. Since the 1960s, attitudes and values have shifted dramatically. Now in the postmodern era absolutes are not readily accepted, and beliefs and behaviors are far less uniform. The expectation is that each person will believe and act in his or her own way. The heightening of individual differences can be attributed in part to the changing ethnic and religious makeup of our society, to the improved economic and educational status of many citizens, and in the Church to ecumenical and interfaith connections along with an influx of Catholics from Latin America and Asia. Western European Christianity is less dominant, and the assumption that a single perspective should determine the practice of Catholicism is vanishing.

The Church is confronted with two converging realities: (a) American cultural attitudes are less uniform, individualism prevails in all facets of life, authority is no longer automatically accepted, and Christianity has lost its dominance as a cultural force; and (b) large numbers of new immigrants with diverse views on how Catholicism should be practiced are arriving daily, longer-term residents from non-Western European countries are claiming leadership roles and confronting Church structures, and other denominations and faiths are influencing Catholic religious practice. Faculty and students alike realize that new responses to the many faces of pluralism will be called for as ministry is exercised in the future.

A related issue raised by many interviewees pertains to what stance the Church should take in relation to the culture. Should the Church engage with and participate in the culture, or should it repudiate and separate from the culture? What will it mean to be Catholic in this culture in the twenty-first century? Respondents cited models ranging from "Christ against culture" to the "Christ of culture," corresponding to the classic paradigms of the relationship between Christ and culture proposed by H. Richard Niebuhr.[1] Students more than faculty viewed the culture as negative and saw themselves in conflict with it. The definition of culture is important in this discussion. Broadly understood it includes all that surrounds us: values, ideas, rules, rituals, language, and artifacts. In a narrower sense it may refer only to "popular culture," music, movies, television, and other media. Many students subscribe to the latter definition, further legitimating criticisms of those members of the religious press and other media who lament the harmful effects of this narrower view of culture. If seen as blatantly in conflict with the whole of culture, faculty fear that the Church will become irrelevant.

Faculty struggle to convey a broader understanding of culture, insisting on engagement with it in the exercise of ministry, a view that more closely represents the Church's teaching. Echoing the thought of Paul VI, several respondents asserted that the Church cannot speak to the modern world if it is not engaged in dialogue with it. They stressed the importance of being interconnected with society, finding out how systems work, and bridging gaps with business, technology, medicine, and science. They affirmed that the Church should be active in the wider culture as witness and prophet, announcing a new world while weaving together the strands of Church and world. One faculty member asserted:

---

[1] H. Richard Niebuhr, *Christ and Culture* (New York: Harper & Row, 1951) 39–44.

The Church needs to really struggle with how our tradition lives in this age; we often are seen as if we are selling out by paying attention to the culture; rather we *should* pay attention, for example, to biomedical and sexual issues, marriage and family, who is being ordained in other traditions. Some things are changing in this world; we must have a conversation about them, *admit* to the struggle. This does not necessarily mean to change, but to *engage*, not retreat from the world.

Likewise a student remarked: "Having had the experience of God, we need to be concerned about how people are living. How do we understand ourselves as bearers of the gospel to the culture?"

Several deans wondered how well their curricula foster deliberate comprehension of the impact made on the Church by our modern secular and pluralistic culture. One of them mused:

Secularization is a problem that the Church must understand. This is a Church immersed in the cultural milieu, a milieu that is far from God. Reintegration of the Catholic vision of life is required if the Church is to be a sign and witness to new life. We need a coherent picture of what is good. Catholics can make a difference by living out their faith; we can't be anonymous or isolated.

Regarding the watershed of Vatican II, some respondents believe that the Church is still undergoing an identity crisis brought on by discrepant degrees of adherence to the teachings of the Council. According to one rector:

The image of the Church is in disarray because the Church is confused; the 1950s image is gone beyond repair; at the same time a reactionary stage against Vatican II has set in. Personally I believe that opposition to Vatican II in the name of orthodoxy is actually unorthodox and is responsible for much of the confusion.

Another added:

The sense of development since Vatican II is absent; a quilt of progressive and traditional elements is in place, but we have lost direction. This blend of ideas is part of what it means to live in a postmodern era. We live and let live when we should instead be in dialogue about our differences.

Reactions to this confusion tended toward opposite poles. On the one hand, some people long for the exercise of a magisterial control under which Church teachings would be set out with no expectation of discussion or disagreement. Those who prefer more order and discipline are typically disturbed by attention to the insights of Vatican II. For example, a student remarked that "faculty are too concerned about the Vatican II Church and the early Church, but not about what happened in between; Vatican II is emphasized too much." On the other hand, some would prefer a more collaborative, less hierarchical Church. This second group appeals to the priesthood of the faithful, and holds a less clerical view of the Church. Deriving priesthood more from baptism and confirmation than from ordination, it believes that laity need to claim and live their rightful roles in the Church more fully. In the words of one seminarian of this persuasion, "All people in the Church are important; I think of the Church as the people of God, so becoming one with them and gaining a *sensus fidelium* is something I will strive to do."

Both students and faculty have considered how to minister in the midst of such polarity. Most want to serve the entire Church, to respond to diverse theologies with solid Church teaching. The Church, they feel, must be in conversation with all its members, talking and listening to different sectors of the community. Recognizing the conflict between groups representing pro-Vatican II and anti-Vatican II positions, the goal of faculty is to teach students to be sensitive to all sides. As one moral theologian commented:

> I want students to consider what it means to minister in a Church which is varied, which has a whole spectrum of people from right to left, a multicultural Church. I ask them to think about what is unique about the Church. How do they identify God's action in Christ? Do they have any use for Jesus? These broader questions help them move beyond ideology to understand what Christians hold in common.

Although divergent views can detract from church unity, the overall appraisal of the Church by respondents is at once hopeful and realistic. Many voiced their conviction that the mystery of God is working, that the Spirit is alive and well. One theologate president declared:

> I am hopeful because it is not our Church; the present difficulties are in God's hands. We need to know history and its similarities to the present to keep from despairing. We need to have pride in the future, to project a positive view of the Church. People need to believe that the Church cares about them, works for the welfare of people. When we minister we need self-consciously to

let them know that we care, to project a sense of family not of a cold institution.

2. The Heterogeneity of the Catholic Population— Cultural and Social Diversity

When respondents reflected on the future, almost all expressed their awareness of the tremendous heterogeneity in the Catholic population. As they explored the meaning of that reality, it became clear that notions of diversity are themselves diverse. More than two-thirds spoke of multiculturalism within the Church—the ethnic, cultural, and racial variations among Catholics; others mentioned differences in family structure, age, education, and income level; and still others referred to dissimilar ideological perspectives. Faculty especially are conscious of the effects that such heterogeneity has on the ways in which dogma is understood, prayer is experienced, and evangelization is to be adapted to meet the needs of the particular group being addressed—in sum, how ministry is practiced.

Most obvious and immediate are concerns about ethnic, cultural, and racial diversity, awareness of which is especially strong in the South and West. One faculty member at a western seminary noted that "diversity is not new, to be sure, but the way it is manifested is different. It is represented by new faces and more variety. The global dimension of the Church is a visible reality; we have moved beyond parishes that are primarily Hispanic or Anglo or Vietnamese, to being truly multicultural. The end of the ethnic model of parishes is in sight." Faculty want students to become more aware of the Church as a worldwide reality, to think of themselves as members of a Church that is neither culturally nor politically bound. Conveying a universal vision of the Church is crucial as heterogeneity increases.

Mission outreach, evangelization, and religious education are becoming critically important as huge groups of new immigrants—Latino, Korean, Vietnamese and others—populate parishes. One faculty member lamented:

> We are behind in reaching out to new immigrants. There are too many, too diverse, coming too quickly for us to prepare ministers to work with them. Language problems are a factor; so much work has to be done in their native language, but they have no priests of their own to do it.

Faculty question whether missionaries from Spain, for example, can serve Americans of Latino origin. Experience has shown that such a substitution may or may not be effective or acceptable depending on the minister's knowledge not only of the native culture, but also of American culture which many immigrants are eager to adopt. What is the goal in this instance? Not a separate Church and language, yet respect for Latino culture, which may be realized through traditional approaches to the sacraments, more devotional practices that reflect Latino culture, and more focus on family and the domestic church. Sometimes ministers lack the desire to enter into these communities and learn their traditions; both faculty and students report that members of immigrant communities have occasionally felt discriminated against by representatives of the Church. Dealing with racial and cultural bias—conscious or not—is on the agenda of a number of theologates. Indeed unless the Church responds more effectively to the spiritual needs of new immigrants, more of them will be lost to the Church, continuing a trend already set in some dioceses. Thorough cultural and social analysis, including age, family patterns, education, and religious practices, is required if these new communities are to be approached with integrity.

Respondents also emphasized the economic, educational, and age differences among ethnic groups in the Church. Economic and educational differences often run parallel, with those who immigrated decades ago likely to be at the higher end of both scales. Compounding the problem is the fact that many people who are highly trained in a secular profession lack a corresponding level of religious education. Further, descendants of immigrants from largely western European countries are more likely to be older than recent immigrants. These disparities create inordinate strain for parishes attempting to respond to rich and poor, educated and uninformed, settled and newly arrived in this country.

The reality of cultural and social diversity is acutely felt among members of different age groups and those living in different family structures. Research shows that some groups of young people find that most church services are geared to an older population with little awareness of how to engage young adults, especially those without families. Then too, families themselves are more diverse, including many single-parent families, divorced and remarried couples, and multigenerational families, among others. In planning parish activities, Church leaders should study each situation carefully so that the spiritual needs of all those present can be met. Finding common humanity and faith in the midst of diversity will help to heal the rifts that are so prevalent in today's Church.

3. Extreme Ideological Diversity and an Attitude of Intolerance among Church Members

In light of the many social and cultural variations among Catholics, it is not surprising to find religious variations as well. In reflecting on the future of the Church, respondents mentioned ideological differences and polarization within the Church more than any other topic. More profoundly than some of the tangible manifestations of diversity, these differences affect how the Church functions in peoples' lives and how ministry is exercised in parishes. Although the degree of acrimony produced by divergent theological views and perceptions of how the Church should function is much debated, future ministers agree on its negative impact.

Many respondents spoke about a divided Church, about their awareness of conflictual situations, and about their hope of finding ways of living with both poles in a polarized Church. With great sadness, more than a few respondents mentioned "schism talk" and their longing to bridge the gap between groups of Church members, including on occasion their own peers. Strongly present in the discussion are issues involving gender. According to one rector: "Many women have felt the sting of exclusion because of reversals in liturgical language and because few gains in membership in decision-making groups have been realized, to say nothing of the discussion of women's ordination."

These issues, for example, lay ministry and gender equity, create difficulties in parishes and other Catholic institutions. Seminarians are often apprehensive about working with women in parishes, and laywomen preparing for ministry are worried about being accepted in the positions that they have been trained to fill. One faculty member summed up the attitude of several others when he said:

> Until Church leaders in this country address the role of lay-people in professional ministerial positions and acknowledge the growing need for their services, our school is limited in what it can do to reinforce the importance of collaboration between men and women, and between ordained and lay professionals.

Anxiety is acute for those who wonder how they will work effectively in parishes where positions on religious education, liturgy, inclusive language, and moral questions, among others, differ so markedly. Seminarians favored two possible approaches: About two-thirds would choose to tread carefully when confronted with controversial questions, seeking to understand conflicting viewpoints, empathizing with people's experiences, and helping them to become reconciled. One commented, "We have to be honest and firm in sharing the teaching of the Church, but we can't expect to impose our understanding without discussion." The other third would take a more controlling approach, presuming to tell people what they must believe and how they must act. Some of these students have an overriding desire for uniformity, as suggested by this remark: "I wish Latin were imposed again; it would bring unity in the way we celebrate Mass, and unity in belief would follow." One faculty member worried aloud about how such students would fit into parish life:

> Some say the Church has to change to accommodate the students who are being ordained. Should not the newly ordained be willing to participate in the changing Church, and themselves make accommodations to respond to the reality of the Church today?

At stake in this discussion is the understanding seminarians have of what it means to be "pastoral" in conflictual contexts, how to work with groups holding dissimilar views on vital issues. Being pastoral, according to the first group identified above, would mean inviting parishioners to strive for a deeper understanding of each other's views, and of the Church's teaching rather than attempting to impose a narrowly defined position without discussion. The aim would be to present fully and nuance accurately the teaching of the Church without alienating people. The second group, however, would regard the mode of the first group as compromising the truth. Defining their own mode as one of "being loyal to the pope" (although their loyalty is quite selective, especially regarding some of the social teachings of John Paul II, which they deemphasize), they would not encourage open exchange.

Lay students also expressed anxiety about working in parishes riven by factions and conflict. Many lay students are already doing pastoral ministry, in most cases in sizable parishes with people whose expectations about liturgy, religious education, and many other topics cover a broad spectrum. Lay students with this practical background voiced fears about the "resistance to change and conservative retrenchment" that they have experienced from some of their seminarian classmates. "It is my goal in my ministry to bring together left and right hard-liners," said one. "If we can't even get along in the parish, how can we ever teach the gospel?" The Catholic Common Ground Initiative inaugurated by Joseph Cardinal Bernardin is one hopeful response designed to promote dialogue among Church members. It originated from the perception that division among Church leaders and members hinders efforts to strengthen and carry out the mission of the Church.

Even though differences between those preparing for ministry, especially some seminarians, and those already serving in ministerial positions seem to be sharpening, research shows that most Catholics stand nonideologically in the middle. They care about how to raise their children in the faith, their own spiritual growth, meaningful liturgies, active service to those in need, and how to live out their lives as faithful Catholics in the world. They want church authority to be exercised with compassion and fairness; they want priests and lay ministers to reach out, calling people to be better than they are. They envision the Church as a source of healing and reconciliation that will bring people back to God. The desire for unity in the midst of plurality is strong in this painful and difficult time.

4. Acute Ministerial Needs: Evangelization, Education, Care for the Poor, and Spiritual Development

The most urgent ministerial tasks, according to most respondents, are to evangelize, educate, care for those in need, and help people deepen their spiritual lives. Ideally these areas of ministry intersect, since people who are truly evangelized, knowledgeable about their faith, and spiritually alive act for the sake of others, especially for those who most need assistance. In practice each of these ministries has multiple layers that may not always seem interconnected. They involve reaching out and teaching members of various ethnic and racial groups of varying ages; generating support for the poor, the lonely, and the afflicted; and providing liturgical and devotional services for individuals with widely disparate preferences and desires. Teachers of ministry and the future ministers who learn from them have different perspectives on ministry. Faculty are discouraged that so few students seem interested in working with the poor or even motivating others to do so. Students worry that they will not be able to satisfy heterogeneous groups of parishioners drawn to diverse forms of worship, education, and interaction.

Evangelization. Faculty expressed their awareness of the need for evangelization at several levels: self-conversion, spreading the gospel message to people who have not yet heard the Word, reevangelizing those whose commitment has wavered, and strengthening those who desire a deeper commitment.

Evangelization requires being present to people—calling them together and determining where their faith is leading them. It is a time-consuming process that is complicated by the many ways in which people are hurting. Confronted with dysfunction, abuse, and oppression in society, people are searching their faith for ways to transcend suffering and find meaning. Alienated Catholics—both those who are on the verge of leaving the Church and those possibly returning—may hope for everything from celebration of the sacraments to social action. For the Church to enter deeply into the life of the community with appropriate models of evangelization, the consensus of faculty was that future ministers will have to engage in careful discernment and critical social analysis to discover where to focus their time and energy.

Education. Virtually everyone in our post-Vatican II era acknowledges the lacunae in the comprehension that most Catholics have of their faith. Religious education encompassing a substantial range of topics is needed across the individual lifespan. Some Catholics wish to augment their knowledge of the faith, perhaps after years of graduate-level secular education, leaving a gap between their professional and spiritual development. Others turn to the Church to help them with pressing problems involving family life: how to strengthen their marriages, how to raise their children in the faith, or how to care for their aging parents.

Two problems concerning adult religious education were mentioned during interviews, especially by those with direct experience in parishes. First, they noted that too often only a few parishioners participate in parish education programs. As one student, a laywoman who also works full-time in a parish, explained the situation: "People have so much to do, they don't attend functions or take the time to form community. We need to discover more effective ways of engaging our parishioners, perhaps using technological resources like video, internet, e-mail, and the like."

The second problem mentioned by pastoral theology faculty is the difficulty of finding people who have the training required for specialized ministries such as pastoral counseling, youth activities, or music ministry. Some faculty worry that the Church is being irresponsible by allowing untrained people to perform some of these ministries. Perhaps the two problems are related: Parishioners may not be attending educational programs because those who offer them are not sufficiently trained or attuned to the desires of their audience.

Education of young people was also identified as a crucial issue for the future of the Church. The task of translating into religious language what young people can grasp on the basis of their experience takes ingenuity. Too often youth ministers are ill prepared to teach the faith to young people, and many youth ministers stay in a parish for only a short time, so that programs lack planning and continuity. Thus Catholic youth are not intensively involved in Church activities and may lose interest in the Church.

According to one seminarian: "The graying of the Catholic Church needs to be examined. No one under thirty-five seems to be in church these days. How can we meet young people where they are? Realistically, can we speak the truth in a way that will be relevant to them?" Catechetical training for young children poses yet another dilemma. Differing views on the how, who, and what of religious education create tensions: methods of teaching—from strict memorization to open discussion; who should teach the classes—religious education teachers or parents; and what should be the content of the classes. At every level of religious education, such questions wait to be answered.

Care for the poor. Moral theologians more than any other group of interviewees stressed the importance of spreading the good news to the poor, and of attending to their material as well as spiritual needs. Against a background of growing socioeconomic inequality in our society, the Church is compelled to speak for the disenfranchised, the unemployed, and those without the means to raise their families. More than giving them voice, several faculty members advocated meeting the needs of the poor by providing direct social services. Like their counterparts ten years ago, most students are not immediately attracted to this form of ministry; however, as the number of new immigrants increases and the gap between rich and poor widens, the Church has an unarguable obligation to assist those who lack basic human necessities.

The failure of the Church to respond to some situations has already led many immigrant and poor Catholics to other denominations that are more willing to attend to their material needs. A few students are committed to ministering in poor neighborhoods and in parishes structured to meet the needs of the poor, perhaps in conjunction with social service agencies. Yet the ethos of most students preparing for ministry is not sympathetic to the poor, and their stance is of grave concern.

Spiritual development. People of all ages are seeking a deep relationship with God; both seminarians and lay students understand this spiritual ministry to be one of their major responsibilities, and they prefer it to any other one. What is necessary for people to grow in an awareness of the Spirit in their own lives? What do they seek from the Church community? Sacramental life, Eucharistic liturgies, and communal and individual prayer are some aspects of religious experience that are being sought. Of immense interest in the larger society, spirituality transcends religious boundaries. In the words of a pastoral theologian:

> The Church is made up of people who are on a spiritual journey, who go beyond the boundaries of the Roman Catholic Church to other religions and movements, for example, Buddhist thought, New Age religion; we can't be blown away by that, but rather we must discern how to keep in touch with people who have become involved with these movements.

What makes Catholic spirituality distinctive? One Scripture teacher commented:

> Traditionally the Church has emphasized its liturgical and sacramental basis, and more recently it has renewed its biblical and service-oriented dimensions. People want to gather in light of the Word; small faith communities encourage discussion of the Word. I wonder if we do enough to help our students learn about the power of breaking open the Word in faith-sharing groups. If these groups are led well, people who participate in them will be moved to engage in tremendous social action.

Noting that the Catholic Church is more and more comprised of people who are members by choice rather than merely by birth, a liturgy professor observed: "The quality of presiding and preaching has to be excellent; laypeople don't 'fear hell,' and so they won't show up unless the services respond to their spiritual needs. The homily is critical; people need something to lift them up, to be life-giving." In the same vein, the few full-time music faculty who are teaching in seminaries worried about the quality of music at worship services. Most parishes are still contending with the long-standing problem of choosing inspiring music that will raise the congregation's hearts and minds to God. One music teacher said:

> If one of the critical concerns of the Church in America is poor church attendance, reflecting a waning faith, the problem is that people have lost their sense of mystery connected with the liturgy. The profane has found its way into the temple. Our work is to restore the sacred in a way that touches people in this age.

Seminarians and lay students alike appreciate the significance of fostering the spiritual development of the faithful. A spirituality that is truly Catholic will lead people to live out the commands of the Gospel: love of God, neighbor, and self in the manner of Jesus. This area of ministry is high on the list for most future ministers of the Church.

5. Evolving Church Structures, Collaboration, and the Changing Roles of Priests and Lay Ministers

According to many interviewees, increased parish size and modified parish structures are significantly influencing the way ministry is and will be exercised. Parish size is being altered by the rapidly growing number of Catholics in the United States and by demographic movement from rural and urban to suburban areas. Structural changes are due largely to the decline in the number of priests coupled with a growing number of laypeople serving in ministerial roles. Affected are both large parishes, where roles are differentiated and staff members numerous, and small parishes, where a single priest or layperson may be in charge of virtually every aspect of parish life, sometimes for two or three parishes.

Seminarians from rural dioceses expressed anxiety about working in multiple parishes as the only ordained minister, and future lay ministers were concerned about conducting liturgical services in the absence of a priest. In suburban settings, where parishes are becoming larger rather than more numerous, other aspects of the issue surfaced. Suburban pastors often function as leaders of a professional lay staff of thirty or more persons who work as youth ministers, directors of religious education for youth and for adults, family life ministers, liturgists, music directors, and business managers. The focus of priestly ministry in these complex settings varies from person to person. The priest may function primarily as a manager, or he may devote extensive time to sacramental ministry and hire someone else to do the administrative work.

Whether the context is large or small, rural or urban, most priests and lay ministers realize that collaboration is now an inalienable aspect of ministry. The future, almost all believe, will include further structural changes such as parish consortia—several locations with a centralized administration—or very large parishes divided into subgroups served from one location. These models resemble some of the nondenominational megachurches already found in and around large urban areas.

That collaboration between lay personnel and clergy is necessary for the proper exercise of ministry is one of the main findings of this research. The very nature of ministry implies the presence of a community where interaction unfolds and relationships are formed. The *PPF* presents collaboration as one of its four integrating themes:

> Future priests should be trained to work effectively in the collaborative situations that are characteristic of ministry in today's Church. The theme of collaboration should be integrated into all phases of seminary education.[2]

Although the theme of collaboration was mentioned with more urgency in some parts of the country than others, almost every faculty member interviewed advocated educating ministerial leaders, both lay and ordained, so that productive collaboration is enhanced. A Church historian concurred:

> Where there is resistance, students need to be reminded that ministry exercised by a variety of people is not "untraditional" when considering twenty centuries of Church history. From the very beginning the disciples depended on the service of many different followers, and that pattern has been incontrovertible ever since.

Both faculty and administrators affirmed the positive effects of working together. In the words of one rector, "Pastoral leadership with a collaborative spirit bespeaks the peace and love of Christ; it is not about turf wars and ideology, but about being in service to the people of God." A field education director amplified the point:

[2] *PPF*, #22.

As Church we are not simply a collection of private individuals, but rather we have the grace of community. The communal spirit is essential to the Catholic parish and should be modeled by those who lead it. Important in building that community is the capacity to respect relationships and systems that are in place and, together, to support others who will extend the mission of the Church.

Similarly a faculty member who teaches only seminarians remarked that one of his goals is to "get students to believe in the power of other ministries, to think of them as a precious gift for the Church." While some seminarians still do not appreciate the role of lay ministers, compared with the situation ten years ago current attitudes are generally more accepting. Nevertheless the latent opposition of some seminarians to working collaboratively with laypeople, especially laywomen, in ministry concerns faculty and parish field education supervisors. Trying to understand the mentality of individuals who oppose collaboration is a challenge that must be faced. An academic dean shared this insight:

Priests *must* be able to work with women. One of the primary factors shaping the new Church is the participation of women; what women are able to do in the Church makes the difference between reaching a wide range of people and touching only a few. Can men and women really work collaboratively? Not until both men and women are holy as God is holy. But shouldn't that be the goal of all of us who work in the Church?

One of the fundamental responsibilities of theologate faculty is to teach students how to collaborate as they implement educational programs, liturgies, parish celebrations, fund-raising, and other aspects of parish life. Structures that will facilitate a collaborative style of ministry are gradually emerging, but this pioneering work is demanding. Students must learn how to enable, empower, and cooperate with a variety of people. Teaching the skills needed for collaboration in the absence of immersion in full-time parish ministry requires vision. Pastoral field education bears much of the burden for combining the reality of the parish with theories about collaboration. These days more and more theologates, especially those where lay students are enrolled in significant numbers, are developing courses and programs designed to prepare students specifically for ministry in collaborative settings. The task is difficult enough because of the many types of ministry, the personalities involved, and the

complex definition of ministry altogether. It is further complicated by the option of many bishops for schools that enroll only
seminarians, with the result that in the educational setting opportunities for collaboration are limited.

Part of the uneasiness over collaboration between priests and
lay ministers seems to derive from the notion that the role of the
priest will be reduced if lay ministry is overemphasized. However, most faculty realize that the development of the latter does
not diminish the former. A lay male professor of ecclesiology
remarked:

> I appreciate the Church of the laity, yes, but I also want to qual-
> ify that by saying that the most influential people in my life have
> been professed religious. We need to recognize the value of min-
> istry by those who are ordained, professed, and lay. The Church
> as the people of God is not so clearly delineated according to
> one's state in life. All have a role.

Uncovering the hopes and fears connected with the changing
structures outlined above will lessen anxiety. Highlighting examples of the positive effects of enlightened practice will likewise
be beneficial. One pastor who also teaches homiletics observed:

> Priests have to be enormously skilled managers and enablers
> who can organize and build the community, hire and coordinate
> paid staff and volunteers, and validate the ministry of others;
> professional ministers will go to the parishes where pastors
> know how to manage and are not hostile and insecure. Burdens
> are lifted for pastors when a wide range of people take respon-
> sibility for the Church and become involved on parish staffs and
> committees.

Priests must be animators who educate, teach, preach, celebrate, and pray together with large staffs; and staffs must have
the flexibility to tend a Catholic population in flux. Enlivened by
the presence of the Spirit, members are finding many opportunities for service to the Church as new structures replace out-
moded ones in this time of change.

B. Perceptions about Priesthood

Priestly identity, the meaning of priesthood, and images of
the priest are topics that permeate documents and conversations about seminaries. In *PDV* all of chapter 2 ("The Nature and

Mission of the Ministerial Priesthood") is devoted to the theology of priesthood, as is chapter 1, article 1, of the *PPF* ("Doctrinal Understanding of the Ministerial Priesthood"). The latter summarizes the teaching presented in several other documents:

> Configured to Christ, head of the Church, and intimately united as co-workers of the bishops, priests are commissioned in a unique way to continue Christ's mission as prophet, priest, and king. Their primary duty is to proclaim the Gospel to the whole world by word and deed. . . . The preaching of the Gospel finds its source and culmination in the Eucharist. Priests exercise the office of sanctifying the Christian people in the celebration of the sacraments of the Church. . . . Finally, priests exercise the office of shepherd, because of the "specific ontological bond which unites the priesthood to Christ the high priest and good shepherd." . . . In these and similar ways, priests are servants of Christ present in the Church as mystery, actuating Christ's presence in the sacraments; as communion, building up the body of Christ; and as mission, heralding the Gospel.[3]

The theology of priesthood as spelled out in the *PPF* and other documents was often reflected in the relevant responses of interviewees—faculty, administrators, and students. The questions concerning priesthood asked of each interviewee were, What is the image you have of priesthood? What is involved in being a priest today? and, What will be involved in the future? Depending on the group and the particular seminary, points of emphasis varied considerably; and as might be expected, seminarians answered the questions more fully than did lay students. The opposite situation prevailed in answer to questions about ministry in general.

In their responses faculty, administrators, and students identified (1) their preferred images of priesthood, as well as (2) the qualities needed for effective ministry, (3) the main role and functions of priests, (4) dispositions required for ministering as priests today and tomorrow, and (5) concerns and cautions. The views about priesthood held by faculty and administrators are crucial, since what they envisage influences the formation offered to seminarians. Also determining the future of ministry will be which priestly identities seminarians choose to embrace from the myriad possibilities, both internally and in relation to other ministers.

---

[3] *PDV,* #33.

1. Faculty and administrators presented the predominant images of priests as those of public witness, servant-leader, shepherd, and spiritual leader; secondary images were those of prophet, disciple, bridge builder, and priest as sacrificial victim. Others presented the priest as witness to the faith, bearer of tradition and of mystery, and exemplary Christian. The communal and active nature of priesthood was also noted.

Seminarians shared some perceived images with faculty and administrators but diverged from others. Paralleling their mentors, seminarians named most frequently the image of shepherd, followed by servant, pastor, and spiritual leader. Missing from their most-frequent list was the concept of priest as public witness. Secondarily seminarians referred to the priest as representative of Christ crucified, a wounded healer, and one who would be self-sacrificing and willing to die for the mission of the Church. A few also mentioned foot washer, friend, and bridge builder. A more spiritual pastoring role was the prevailing image. Most seminarians apparently assume that being a priest will not be easy and will require spiritual strength.

2. The qualities that faculty and administrators identified as necessary for priests today were numerous. Above all they mentioned integrity—consistency between the priest's public and private life—as most critical to the credibility of his ministry. Likewise interviewees named inner strength born of a sound spiritual life as a high priority. A priest who is to lead others to God must be an integrated, balanced spiritual person who has depth, knows how to pray with and for the community, and loves those he serves. Wisdom and prudence are also expected of those claiming to be pastors. Other respondents believe that flexibility and openness to an uncertain future are indispensable qualities in these times.

Seminarians listed similar qualities but in a different order of priority. Most frequently they spoke of being personally holy, being a person of prayer, loving the Eucharist, being in love with Christ, knowing Christ and knowing *about* Christ, and having confidence in God. Like their mentors but much less frequently, seminarians mentioned the importance of being real and authentic if one is to have credibility. Because of the inevitability of change, several referred to faith, trust, and hope as essential, in addition to patience and endurance. From another perspective the need to be compassionate, approachable, and humble was variously expressed. In contrast to their mentors, seminarians seemed less aware of qualities relating to the community, though when they spoke of the roles and functions of priests they were clearly aware of the relational dimension.

3. Corresponding in many ways to the images and qualities identified above, interviewees spelled out the *roles and functions of priests* as they understood them. Most faculty and administrators acknowledged that priests will play multiple roles, both in a specific parish at a given time and over a lifetime in several ministerial settings. Common conceptions of the priestly role included being open to whatever service the Church requests, being a "jack-of-all-trades," and being a general practitioner. However, others cautioned that priests should avoid "being a mile wide and an inch deep," responding to every need, and failing to delimit their role. Especially priests serving large parishes or several small ones can be "worn to a frazzle" by countless responsibilities.

Almost every faculty member stressed the centrality of Word and sacrament, but specific conceptions of the priest's role varied somewhat according to the respondent's discipline. Scripture and homiletics faculty often emphasized preaching and properly interpreting the Bible; systematic theology faculty were more likely to note the importance of understanding doctrines thoroughly so as to be authentic teachers of the faith; liturgists and musicians upheld the importance of liturgy and the sacraments; moral theologians frequently highlighted social justice and care for the poor; and those in pastoral theology called for particular competence in ministries ranging from hospital visitor to presider to youth minister. Across disciplines faculty described the ideal priest as a visionary, a planner, and a skilled manager.

Considering the topic of role and function from another perspective, a faculty member commented about the "narrowing of the definition of priesthood" as an unintended result of the intense demand for priests in parish ministry. Not only are diocesan priests essentially restricted to direct pastoral or diocesan service, but religious-order priests are being asked more frequently than ever before to provide ministry for parishes. In effect, an immense shift has taken place causing the whole sector of nonparish ministry to suffer great diminishment both in absolute numbers and proportionately.

Seminarians' ideas about the role and functions of priests were shaped not only by faculty but also by their local parishes. The ideas of seminarians from areas of the country where priests are proportionally more numerous contrasted with those of their counterparts from dioceses where the small number of priests has already deeply affected the character of priestly ministry. Common to both groups was an insistence on the centrality of sacramental ministry, especially celebration of the Eucharist. Some preferred this emphasis on a cultic role and called themselves "sanctuary priests," despite their awareness that many faculty disapprove of this narrow definition.

More often seminarians spoke of wanting to go beyond being "dispensers of the sacraments" and "traveling presiders at Eucharist." They recognized the need for a broad ministry taking plural forms. Beyond the sacramental role, they aspired to spiritual leadership involving among other expressions, "helping people see God in their lives," "communicating the love of Christ," and "walking with people on a spiritual journey." Seminarians also expected to be teachers of the faith through the Rite of Christian Initiation of Adults (RCIA), evangelizing, and answering questions. Some felt that their teaching should be geared to "protecting the orthodoxy of the Church," whereas others (while certainly wanting to teach the faith authentically) considered a defensive or apologetic stance ineffective in today's society. The latter group would focus on sharing faith, communicating Christ, and being present and listening to people.

4. Addressing dispositions required for the exercise of priestly ministry, faculty and administrators spoke of the need for passion and zeal, for caring deeply enough about the Church to spend one's life in its service. Many faculty mentioned the necessity of being skilled in human relations—"an expert in humanity," one person said—not afraid of the intimacy appropriate to a celibate person, confident enough to enter into people's lives at emotional and sometimes difficult moments, and comfortable with silence. Almost all interviewees regarded a team approach to ministry as essential; at different stages and for different projects, this could involve networking, orchestrating, collaborating, or leading the pastoral team. Most agreed that priests must accept the uncertainty and ambiguity of the future.

Seminarians reflected on their own dispositions as they considered doing ministry in the future. A strong sentiment among many is that they are facing an evolving ministerial situation potentially filled with difficulties and demands of all kinds. Afraid of burnout, they talked frequently about being balanced and taking time for themselves, especially for prayer. Many expressed the desire to find friendship and fraternity among priests, though they are fearful in some cases that this will not be easy. Several said that they realize they "can't be on a power trip," and "won't be put on a pedestal." The majority seemed quite realistic about the life that awaits them, approaching it with enthusiasm on the one hand and trepidation on the other. Without the benefit of ministerial experience, seminarians appeared less aware of the support they will receive from those with whom and to whom they will minister.

5. Respondents also identified several *concerns and cautions.* First and foremost was the apprehension that priests are more and more perceived as "sacramental machines," "circuit riders," or "Mass presiders." Particularly in smaller dioceses and in areas of the country where the declining number of priests is more noticeable, priestly ministry is becoming narrowly focused on a few essential functions so that the fuller meaning of priest-hood is obscured. Especially neglected in this scenario is the role of evangelization, proclaiming "the Gospel to the whole world by word and deed."[4]

A second concern, reported by several faculty members con-centrated at a few schools, was that some current seminarians and recently ordained graduates have set themselves up to be judges of the actions of other priests. Our interviews with semi-narians confirmed that these men, operating out a form of neo-conservatism, believe that priests who continue to promote the renewal brought on by Vatican II should be restrained. Faculty recognized the potential for a rupture of fraternity and for polari-zation within presbyterates should these self-appointed judges prevail. More often than not, the advocates of this critical posi-tion are not native to the diocese where they seek to rectify abuses but rather arrive from elsewhere to "help" the local bishop put things in order.

A third concern of many interviewees referred to clericalism. Given the reduced number of seminarians and consequently of new priests, those who are in the system easily feel entitled to special privileges by virtue of vocation. This way of thinking is manifested, for example, in their seeking out the most expensive material goods, such as cars, clothes, and restaurants, and their limiting the amount and range of work they will accept—in effect "taking care of themselves first," as one interviewee put it.

---

[4] *PPF,* #33.

Although all students—lay, religious order, and diocesan—shared common perceptions about priesthood, some differences became evident. Those preparing for lay ministry were most concerned about how priests will share ministerial responsibilities with them in parishes and other settings. They worry specifically about collaboration, authority, role differentiation, structures, and salaries. Diocesan seminarians are more likely than religious-order candidates to be preparing for ministry in parishes, so that their focus is on parish management, especially providing basic liturgical and pastoral services.

Although religious-order seminarians are sometimes preparing to serve in parishes, many will be working instead in educational institutions, chaplaincies, retreat centers, and missions.[5] The importance of evangelizing, engaging in missionary activity, and serving the universal Church received greater attention from members of religious orders, both faculty and students. The pressing demands of parochial ministry make these activities less accessible to diocesan clergy.

In conclusion, three points deserve special mention. The first concerns the image of priests: Faculty and administrators stressed the importance of priests as public witnesses and servant-leaders, whereas students emphasized interiority, spirituality, one's relationship with God, and the desire to accompany people on a spiritual journey. Both dimensions of a priest's life are indispensable for the Church's ministry. Formation must be attentive to helping seminarians integrate the two dimensions so that as future priests they are not torn between being active and being reflective.

The second point concerns the role and functions of priests: As the number of priests decreases, the shape of their day-to-day ministry is changing; more and more time is needed for the sacramental and liturgical life of the parish, but at the same time priestly responsibilities for administration and staff leadership are also increasing. The threat of burnout is growing as priests try to maintain their traditional roles in much larger parishes or in several small ones. Priests will serve more effectively for a longer time if they have places where they can gain strength and personal support, as well as connect with other priests. Formation must lead seminarians to collaborate effectively with

---

[5] See *A Concert of Charisms: Ordained Ministry in Religious Life*, ed. Paul K. Hennessy, C.F.C. (New York: Paulist Press, 1997).

lay ministers and other parish members so that they can sustain a reasonable workload and benefit from the talents of others who are also educated to serve the Church in a variety of positions.

The third point concerns virtues and attitudes that will enhance priestly ministry. Many were mentioned by those interviewed, but several seem particularly crucial at this time. Integrity is important for everyone serving in a public role, and for priests it is imperative. Prayer is the basis for a life of integrity, and if a priest fails to pray his ministry will be hollow and his effectiveness limited. The fruit of prayer will be a life that corresponds to the life of Jesus—one of simplicity, love for every person, and zeal toward bringing about the reign of God. Formation must be attentive to helping seminarians continue to be receptive, after they are ordained, to guidance and evaluation from a spiritual director, superiors, peers, and coworkers. A priest who is open and honest, not secretive and isolated, will be respected for the integrity he exhibits.

Conclusion

. . . .

"Do you still have hope?" "How—and how well—are men and women being prepared for the Church's ministries?" These questions have served as guideposts throughout this study. As the reader may infer, many reasons for hope pervade reports from students and faculty, administrators and parish leaders. Yet even as these positive signs come to light, critical concerns can also be detected. This study describes in detail *how* formation for ministry—human and spiritual, academic and pastoral—is constructed, but judgments about *how well* it is constructed are more difficult to make. Certain components of formation programs are well conceived, conforming to the ministerial needs of the roughly sixty million United States Catholics today. The strongest of these positive components are highlighted in the next section under "accomplishments." At the same time, because of the multitude of changes in the Church, among them the composition of the Catholic population and the configuration of ministerial teams, as well as in the schools themselves, other less positive components lag behind current demand and are discussed in the subsequent section under "critical concerns." In neither case are the lists exhaustive, but they do illustrate the major trends present in theologates at this time.

1. Accomplishments

While each theologate legitimately claims a unique set of accomplishments over the past ten years, some accomplishments have been shared by almost all schools and so they can be regarded as "positive trends" for the whole community. These accomplishments fall into one of three categories: Some pertain to management, including the presence of more effective board members, more stable and qualified administrators, and more knowledgeable partners in theological associations; others pertain to programmatic developments, including human formation for seminarians, multicultural programs, and pastoral field education, as well as new programs, in particular pre-theology; and the third group consists of numerous improvements in campus facilities and technological resources. Other accomplishments at some schools were not persistent enough to be considered a trend.

a. Management. Since the mid-1980s the governance and administration of theologates have shown signs of new life, benefiting from the accrued experience of board members and administrators who have now served their institutions for an extended period of time. Considering first the governing boards of theologates, most have been in existence for thirty years or less. During their first two decades they sought to find an appropriate role in the life of the institution, which entailed asking questions about how much authority they would be allowed to exercise, who would constitute the membership, and what were suitable ways to interact with faculty and administrators.

Since the time when governing boards were first created, ordinaries (bishops and religious superiors) who sponsored theologates have discussed the issue of authority with their board members and school representatives. Together the parties have reached a clear understanding of the degree of authority—always ultimately in the hands of the ordinaries—delegated to the boards. Most board members have been satisfied that their suggestions and recommendations were taken seriously and, except in rare circumstances, accepted. The clarification of their role has invigorated many board members—now more numerous and more diversified than they were ten years ago—to devote greater time and energy to board activities. A side effect of considerable benefit has been an overall improvement in fiscal policies, fund-raising, and related financial matters.

A second accomplishment in the area of management involves administrators. Those now serving in major administrative positions have spent a longer time in office and are better prepared than were their counterparts ten years ago. Consequently, along with experienced faculty members, these administrators have become more knowledgeable partners in theological education.

As noted earlier, the terms of rectors/presidents who are currently in office average 5.8 years, an increase of one year since 1988, when it was 4.8 years. For academic deans, the terms of those in office now average 5.3 years, an increase of more than one year since 1988, when that figure was 3.9 years. With longer terms, theologate leaders can elaborate a vision and realize its key aspects more completely, especially in connection with fiscal matters (including fund-raising) for rectors/presidents and with curricular planning for deans.

Among other administrators who have made significant strides in the past decade are pastoral field educators. They have organized and enhanced their area of expertise with beneficial results—improving relations with parish leaders, training on-site supervisors, and helping students discern effective ways to minister. Moreover, many administrators and faculty have engaged in collaboration with colleagues from other seminaries—Protestant and Catholic—principally through the Association of Theological Schools (ATS) and the NCEA Seminary Division. Most Catholic theologates have been members of the ATS for about thirty years. In recent years they have become senior partners, offering substantial insight and service to this professional organization. These advancements stand as a tribute to theologate leaders.

b. Programmatic developments during the past decade have been substantial. Human formation for seminarians, multicultural studies, and pastoral field education have all experienced growth and development, and at many schools whole programs have been added, most notably in pre-theology. The section on human formation in Part III described how schools have responded to changing student bodies by establishing programs appropriate to their developmental needs. Given the range of students, assessment of their spiritual, psychological, and emotional development leads to the creation of programs intended to prepare students to be mature Church ministers. Influenced by *PDV,* recently revised formation programs require seminarians to give more attention to personal growth, celibacy formation, and commitment to the Church and their vocation. Lay students are equally called to personal maturity, commitment, and spiritual life commensurate with their own vocations. As recommended by *PDV,* programs are designed to prepare "balanced people, strong and free, capable of bearing the weight of pastoral responsibilities."

Recognition of the changing ethnic, racial, and cultural composition of the Catholic population is of utmost importance, since almost every parish and other ministerial setting is touched by the new faces of Catholics. Theologates have expended extensive time and resources amplifying and refining existing multicultural programs. Especially at schools located in the South and West, where the Hispanic population is already substantial and still expanding, theologate faculties have initiated language and cultural studies, courses and pastoral internships, to acquaint students with the heritage of this growing segment of the Church. However, as indicated under "critical concerns," much more remains to be done in the Hispanic community, as well as in African American, Asian, and Native American communities, which represent distinctive and vital constituencies within the Church.

Pastoral field education is a relatively new phenomenon in Catholic theologates. Only during the past two decades have programs been established at most schools. In an earlier era seminarians may have served as deacons in a parish where they taught religion classes and assisted with liturgical ministries. Little connection was made with the theologate and supervision was not part of the program. Now all students who are earning a Master of Divinity degree are required to participate in well-organized and supervised field placements. Field education directors have worked with parish leaders and lay committees to ensure close collaboration with those on site, and with faculty who mentor students in theological reflection. Although some bishops and vocation directors express reservation about the time required, these programs have become a crucial part of ministerial preparation, especially because newly ordained priests in many dioceses begin functioning as pastors after only a brief interval and without the benefit of any other apprenticeship.

Many new degree programs are now being offered by theologates in response to changes in numbers and composition of Catholics, and growing diversity of students. Several schools have instituted multicultural programs, sometimes in the form of an independent degree program and sometimes by adding courses or specializations to already existing programs. The most significant innovation, however, has been to inaugurate pre-theology programs. The fourth edition of the *PPF* calls for a two-year program that will bring candidates up to an appropriate level of readiness for theological studies. More than twenty such programs have been established and several others reorganized to meet the standards stipulated in the *PPF*. Theologate faculty acknowledge the positive impact that two full years of formation has had on students before entering theology, not only academically but also personally and spiritually. Because these programs have been so beneficial, the sponsoring schools hope to persuade more bishops and vocation directors to subscribe to a full two-year pre-theology program.

   c. Numerous improvements in campus facilities and technological resources were reported in the survey of rectors/presidents. Partly to maintain a competitive edge in the recruitment of seminarians, more than a dozen theologates have made major renovations to their facilities, especially to residential buildings, and one entirely new administrative and residential facility has been built. These improvements have been anticipated for some time, since many theologates have just passed or are approaching a century of service with many of their original buildings still in use. On the whole, depreciation has not been funded, so the renovations represent a major capital outlay symbolizing confidence in the future.

   The other major capital investment has been in technological resources: A decade ago computers were appearing at a few schools, but electronic mail, internet, web sites, and home pages were not yet on the scene. Now almost every theologate is allotting substantial human and financial resources to technological hardware and the personnel needed to operate it. The rate of investment is likely to increase as the society becomes more attuned to these instruments. Major expenditures on facilities and technology call for continual reassessment but are likely to remain an essential item on the agenda for the future.

2. Critical Concerns

   Several critical concerns must be addressed more adequately over the next decade. Some are so comprehensive that, even though much has been done already so that they overlap with areas of accomplishment, much still remains to be done. First among these concerns are curricular issues, especially those relating to multicultural studies, ecumenism, and collaboration. A second set of concerns relates to students: recruitment of more students with an aptitude for ministry, scholarships to attract lay students, and human and spiritual formation programs for lay students. A third area, linked to both curriculum and students, is faculty development, designed to help faculty improve their teaching methods and course content on the one hand and to build and maintain faculty unity on the other. Finally, planning and evaluation across all aspects of institutional life are critical, especially as these processes relate to personnel and students, and to technology and finances.

 a. Among curricular concerns, the need to further multicultural studies, ecumenism, and collaboration takes precedence. The development of multicultural programs is listed as an accomplishment, and indeed some schools have made substantial progress in preparing students for the reality of serving a multicultural Catholic population, but the task has by no means been completed. In regions of the country where the Catholic population continues to be mainly European in origin, schools have been slower to create programs that take into account the overall shift to a multicultural Church; even in other regions of the country where greater diversity is already present, more attention needs to be given to multicultural studies.

 Curricula do not adequately reflect the new multicultural reality, and few faculty or administrators, especially those of Hispanic, African American, Asian, and Native American backgrounds, are prepared or available to develop these programs. Major efforts will have to be made to overcome the shortfall, which is evident when one compares the schools that have made little investment of resources with those that have instituted full programs consisting of language studies, liturgical services, academic courses, and pastoral experiences. The environment of these few latter schools is permeated by a "feel for diversity," faculty are knowledgeable about preparing students from varied backgrounds, and students are eager to serve in ministries for a multicultural Church. When a program is fully implemented, every element of the school from liturgy to courses, from personal and spiritual formation to field education reflect the diverse racial and ethnic heritages represented in the Church.

 In recent years ecumenism and interfaith relations have come to occupy a more prominent place in Church teaching, and Roman congregations have issued related documents, chief among them *Ut unum sint*[1] in 1995, and "The Ecumenical Di-

---

[1] John Paul II, *Origins* 25 (June 8, 1995).

mension in the Formation of Pastoral Workers" in 1998.[2] In the *PPF* "Ecumenism and Interfaith Relations" is named as one of four integrating themes for priestly formation, and at least twenty-three separate references are made to that theme. The topic also has practical implications for ministry; for example, approximately one-third of all marriages in Catholic churches are interfaith, and in some dioceses the proportion is well over half.

However, with few exceptions, theologates have given little consideration to ecumenism in their curricula, and relevant courses are offered only as electives at most schools. Given the growing commitment to ecumenical and interfaith dialogue, theologates will be compelled to forge ahead with it in the near future. During interviews faculty acknowledged the importance of promoting ecumenical dialogue, but students often expressed resistance to learning about other traditions and how to relate to those of different denominations and faiths. More than a few indicated that they felt their own faith would be threatened by doing so. Thus considerable energy must be devoted to this endeavor before the standards proposed in various documents are met.

Collaboration, a third curricular concern, is also represented among the four areas for thematic integration put forward in the *PPF*. According to the document, "Future priests should be trained to work effectively in the collaborative situations that are characteristic of ministry in today's Church. The theme of collaboration should be integrated into all phases of seminary education."[3] This admonition applies equally to lay students preparing for ministry. Some individual faculty members have made efforts in this regard, but as noted earlier the concept of collaboration is neither clearly understood nor widely practiced in theologates or in the Church more broadly. Collaboration is sometimes viewed by seminarians as a practice that will diminish their authority and control when they come to serve as pastors. In isolation from real ministerial settings, theologate programs can teach about collaboration, but effective collaborative practice must be based on good examples provided by parish and institutional staffs. Promoting a collaborative style of ministry

---

[2] *Origins* 27 (March 19, 1998) by the Pontifical Council for Christian Unity.

[3] *PPF*, #22.

requires cooperation at many levels and is perhaps the most critical of the "critical concerns."

Each of the concerns mentioned here—multiculturalism, ecumenism, and collaboration—demonstrates the importance of faculty maintaining contact with dioceses, parishes, and other institutions to ensure that preparation for ministry is correlated with real ministerial situations and settings. Only if students have opportunities to encounter diverse ethnic and racial groups, people of other denominations and religions, and multiple parish staff situations, will they be well prepared to serve in similar circumstances. Therefore theologates will have to plan their curricular and pastoral experiences, as well as their human and spiritual formation programs, deliberately.

b. A second set of concerns relates to students: recruitment of more students who have an aptitude for ministry; scholarships to attract lay students; and human and spiritual formation programs for lay students. Rectors/presidents listed the recruitment of both seminarians and lay students as a more critical and more problematic responsibility than any other that they face. Each year fewer seminarians are entering theologates, and when the present enrollees are compared with those of ten or more years ago, the data take on even greater significance. Until the mid-1980s most seminarians studying at theologates were beyond the pre-theology stage, that is, enrolled in first- through fourth-year theology. Now with a year or two of pre-theology added, and sometimes a pastoral year, students are often enrolled for six or seven years.

Despite longer programs the total enrollment is down about one thousand seminarians since the mid-1980s. The few schools that can pride themselves on increasing their enrollment of seminarians recognize that, unfortunately, their additional students are merely choosing to enroll in their schools rather than another and thus the overall enrollment is not increased. Further, a large proportion of seminarians (about one-fourth) are recruited from outside the United States, and many of them will return to their own countries, making the low numbers even more striking. Encouraging vocations to the priesthood is generally not a role assumed by theologates; they depend on vocation directors and other external personnel for enrollment.

With the decrease in seminarians and the compensatory commitment to lay ministry, theologates are enrolling lay students in record numbers. Many of these students are able to attend only part-time because of lack of scholarship money, so that recruitment of lay students is also competitive. In dioceses where ministries are available for the nonordained, are satisfying to those working in them, and pay adequately, these students are more likely to enroll; but present trends worry theologate leaders, who believe that in the future lay students will be as scarce as seminarians. For admissions committees an uneasy balance exists between the pressure to enroll enough students and the imperative of maintaining a qualitatively respectable student body. With a few exceptions, theologates have adhered to reasonably high standards for admission, but the few that have not are known to accept students who have been rejected by other theologates. Whether these eventual graduates perform satisfactorily as ministers has not been researched, but the fact of their enrollment troubles many in leadership positions.

Related to enrollment is the problem of providing scholarships for lay students, who are not supported by religious congregations or dioceses. Lay students seldom have the resources to support full-time study and the prospect of low ministerial salaries limits their ability to assume debt. Without sufficient scholarship funds forthcoming from theologates, lay students sometimes choose to pursue a degree at Catholic colleges and universities that offer academic courses though generally not pastoral training; or at Protestant seminaries where they are unlikely to receive much instruction in Catholic theology; or in nondegree programs sponsored by dioceses at low cost. The suitability of the alternative forms of preparation raises questions about the quality of Catholic ministry that may result. Therefore, adequate scholarship funds are absolutely vital for the ongoing viability of the schools and the competence of their graduates.

Human and spiritual formation programs for lay students are found in various stages of development in two-thirds of the theologates that have been enrolling a sizable number of lay students for more than a decade. Lay students regularly articulate their desire for more structured and more focused human and spiritual formation. The early programs tended to replicate formation for priests and religious, but, as the phenomenon of lay ministry has evolved and matured, practitioners recognize that a distinct program is essential. A few schools have invested significant resources in personnel and so have been able to provide suitable programs for their lay students, but most are still unsure of how to proceed. Lay ministers presently working in ministerial positions, current lay students, and staff teaching at schools with developed lay formation programs all should be consulted if progress is to be made.

c. Faculty development has several important purposes, among them to help faculty update their teaching methods and revise course content, but also to maintain faculty unity. During the past three or four years, foundations and professional organizations have offered programs to assist faculty with the first two of these objectives.[4] Especially since the advent of technology for education, experienced faculty are seeking ways to update their methods and adapt the content of their courses to new media. Several schools are also adding "distance learning" to their curricula; here technology is a prerequisite for communicating with students at locations away from the main campus. Moreover as student bodies become more diverse, faculty are looking for better ways to reach students with special learning needs or those accustomed from their undergraduate years to reliance on visual aids, as well as to students from other cultures. Both for new faculty and for experienced faculty trying to adapt to new circumstances, faculty development will remain high on the agenda.

The other reason for faculty development—to promote greater unity of purpose—is a relatively unfamiliar theme. Until recently faculty came from the generations that matured before the close of Vatican II, but newer faculty have grown up since then. The perceptions of younger faculty about the Church and the theological enterprise are sometimes at odds with those of older faculty who were adults during the Council. Generational differences, which sometimes mean ideological differences, threaten faculty unity at some schools, and at others the lack of a shared purpose renders the programs less effective. Newly aware of the tensions they had not experienced previously, many older faculty members are eager to engage in dialogue with younger faculty to prevent deep divisions between them. If faculty are to demonstrate effective collaboration to students, such efforts to develop a common purpose are mandatory.

---

[4] The Wabash Center programs and the Keystone Conferences are dedicated to the improvement of teaching and learning, and the ATS and NCEA Seminary Department have both offered workshops.

d. Planning and evaluation across all aspects of institutional life are critical, especially in relation to personnel and students as well as technology and finances. In light of the myriad tensions and pressures that impinge on theologates at this time, administrators have a serious obligation to plan carefully for the future and to do so after thorough evaluation of current educational processes and outcomes. Maintaining a talented and appropriately educated staff, faculty, and administration will require more long-range planning than ever before. Research shows that fewer priests are being given permission to do graduate study in theology; thus it is becoming increasingly difficult for some schools to hire the proportion of priests they would like to have on their faculties. With the general shortage of priests, those who already have degrees are sometimes being recalled to parish or diocesan service outside the theologate.

Lay women and men with graduate degrees in theology are finding higher-paid and perhaps less demanding positions in colleges and universities where they are not expected to take on the additional responsibility of doing formation. Ten years ago schools could still depend on hiring religious priests who had been displaced from the many seminaries that had closed up through the 1970s, but those men have now reached retirement age. Together all these factors argue strongly for rectors/presidents and academic deans to establish a plan for staffing their schools that will carry them through the next ten to fifteen years.

The difficulty of recruiting a sufficient student body was mentioned earlier, but planning for enrolled students is also necessary. Evaluation of their formation needs, for example, older students, or those from other countries, will make it possible for faculty to be trained in areas in which they may not now have experience. Signs of the changing student bodies have already appeared: Older students expect adult pedagogy, students with little experience of Catholicism need to begin theology at a different level and curricula must be adjusted accordingly. Students representing backgrounds and ideological orientations that conflict with the majority of the Catholic population may require modified versions of human, spiritual, and pastoral formation if they are to minister effectively. No longer can faculty and administrators assume that the programs currently in place are reaching students; they must revise them in the face of new circumstances.

Finances and technology have also been mentioned before but, because they are so important to the future, careful planning by rectors/presidents in both areas is essential. During the past decade almost every theologate has either established or enhanced its development office. To ensure resources for the future, a few schools have been accumulating significant endowment funds, but many have barely begun. Long-term stability of theologates is more likely if an endowment is secured. Finally, planning for an investment in technological resources is indispensable for future viability along with relevant training for all personnel. Theologates must make continual progress and keep up with advances or they will soon find themselves outside the mainstream of modern education. Initial efforts have been promising, but much more remains to be done.

Concluding Reflections

Present and future ministers are struggling to discern how they can best serve the more than sixty million Catholics in the United States, whose backgrounds and convictions vary so markedly. The Church is in a period of enormous transition with heroic attempts being made to adapt to new conditions. Changes involving staff alone are telling: In the 1950s typically two or more priests ministered in medium-sized and small parishes, with many women religious serving in educational roles; in the 1990s one priest usually serves a large parish or multiple parishes in collaboration with numerous lay ministers. The cultural and social characteristics of Catholic congregations are more diverse and, as described by Scott Appleby in chapter 1, Catholic culture in the United States is dramatically different from what it was thirty years ago.

When theologates frame their vision and determine how to implement their mission, the above conditions must be taken into account. The present time of transition is painful for many, invigorating for some. The work of educating men and women for ministry is complicated by this unprecedented era in the history of the Church. Theologate faculty bear a significant part of the burden of instructing students in how to be authentic and credible witnesses to the Gospel under these demanding new circumstances. Administrators must devise structures and consolidate resources to ensure that the mission of theologates continues to be realized.

What thematic focus might serve as a guiding light on the brink of the twenty-first century? As I come to the end of this research, I believe that, above all, these times invite us to strive for greater charity and trust, and for a profound union of hearts and minds based on the Gospel. Significantly, Jesus concluded his discourse at the Last Supper by praying that "they all may be one" (John 17:21). Practically speaking what does that "oneness," that union, require of us as followers of Christ? In words attributed to St. Augustine, it means "in essentials, unity; in doubtful matters, liberty; and in all things, charity."

St. Ignatius's "Presupposition" at the beginning of the *Spiritual Exercises* (no. 22) further interprets the requirement: ". . . it is necessary to suppose that every good Christian is more ready to put a good interpretation on another's statement than to condemn it as false." In present times, Cardinal Bernardin's Catholic Common Ground Initiative echoes these themes by calling for openness, honesty, civility, and mutual respect in a dialogue seeking to reduce the polarization that exists in the Church. Attaining oneness of heart and mind calls for humility and for openness to revise one's opinions and not canonize them beforehand as necessarily the only orthodox interpretation.

The fruits of charity and trust leading to unity are obvious. In situations where this spirit is present, institutions are flourishing and the achievements of their graduates are noteworthy. In situations where dissension threatens, institutions are hindered and the work of those associated with them is impaired. Reviewing the major accomplishments of the past decade, we see how an atmosphere of charity and trust is strengthened by competent administrators and participative board members, by racially and ethnically heterogeneous students and personnel who are learning to communicate more gracefully with one another, and by faculty who have broadened their horizons by teaching students from a range of backgrounds and by interacting with representatives of different religious traditions.

To suggest that greater unity is called for seems unnecessary to some and crucial to others in ministry. The former group would argue that polarization is not a factor in the Catholic Church, or at least that its effects are grossly exaggerated. They would assume the presence of unity—usually based on their own beliefs and values—and see little point in worrying about trying to achieve it. The latter group would point to the radically divergent ideological perspectives found among current students preparing for ministry—lay and ordained—that belie the former view. When graduates are assigned or undertake a position in a parish or other pastoral setting, they bring with them their own beliefs and practices, expectations and goals, which may or may not correspond to those already present in the environment. If accommodation is not sought out of respect for the community, discord will be exacerbated. If achieving charity and trust is the overriding goal, new staff will be prepared to adapt to the life of the community as it has evolved, and harmony will prevail.

Theologates should do everything in their power to ease polarization in the Church and in no way should they further it. The critical concerns that must be addressed in order to avert dissension and build solidarity set the agenda for the future. Curricula must address multicultural issues, encourage ecumenical and interfaith dialogue, and teach by example and content the practice of collaboration. Students with an aptitude for ministry must be led through carefully constructed human and spiritual formation programs to embrace people of all backgrounds and beliefs, to extend their ministry into the public realm, and to serve the poor and disenfranchised.

Faculty development programs must focus on ways to promote trust among their own ranks and to narrow the gap between seminarians and faculty on matters that will affect future ministry. Finally, planning and evaluation across the institution must take into consideration the ultimate reason for the existence of theologates: to bring about the reign of God by enacting the message of Jesus throughout the world.

As I conclude this study I am aware of how much is demanded of those who staff theologates. They are asked to respond to the tensions that arise daily, to toil with uncertainty about whether the outcomes they seek will be realized, and to persevere in their work whether they are repudiated or honored. Nothing less than entering into the passion of Christ is called for—a passion that embraces both suffering and a burning love of God. Without suffering burning love cannot endure and without burning love the suffering is unbearable. The faculty, administrators, and other staff of theologates have stayed the course and their love and fidelity are sure to continue to yield good fruit.

Appendix A:
Theologate Ownership and Operation

■   ■   ■   ■   ■   ■   ■   ■   ■

A. Theologates Owned and Conducted by One or More (Arch)diocese(s)

St. John's Seminary, California
[Owned and conducted by the Archdiocese of Los Angeles]

St. Vincent de Paul Regional Seminary, Florida
[Owned and conducted by the Archdiocese of Miami, Dioceses of Palm Beach, St. Petersburg, Venice, and St. Augustine]

University of Saint Mary of the Lake, Mundelein Seminary, Illinois
[Owned and conducted by the Archdiocese of Chicago]

Notre Dame Seminary, Louisiana
[Owned and conducted by the Archdiocese of New Orleans]

St. John's Seminary School of Theology, Massachusetts
[Owned and conducted by the Archdiocese of Boston]

Pope John XXIII National Seminary, Massachusetts
[Owned and conducted by the Archdiocese of Boston]

Sacred Heart Major Seminary, Michigan
[Owned and conducted by the Archdiocese of Detroit]

The Saint Paul Seminary, Minnesota (Seminary is part of the School of Divinity of the University of St. Thomas)
[Owned and conducted by the Archdiocese of St. Paul and Minneapolis]

Kenrick-Glennon Seminary, Missouri
[Owned and conducted by the Archdiocese of St. Louis]

Immaculate Conception Seminary School of Theology, New Jersey
[Owned and conducted by the Archdiocese of Newark]

Christ the King Seminary, New York
[Owned and conducted by the Diocese of Buffalo]

St. Joseph's Seminary (Dunwoodie), New York
[Owned and conducted by the Archdiocese of New York]

Seminary of the Immaculate Conception, New York
[Owned and conducted by the Diocese of Rockville Centre]

Athenaeum of Ohio, Mount St. Mary's Seminary of the West, Ohio
[Owned and conducted by the Archdiocese of Cincinnati]

Saint Mary Seminary and Graduate School of Theology, Ohio
[Owned and conducted by the Diocese of Cleveland]

Saint Charles Borromeo Seminary (Overbrook), Pennsylvania
[Owned and conducted by the Archdiocese of Philadelphia]

St. Mary's Seminary, Texas (Students attend St. Thomas University)
[Owned and conducted by the Diocese of Galveston-Houston]

Saint Francis Seminary, Wisconsin
[Owned and conducted by the Archdiocese of Milwaukee]

B. Theologates Owned and Conducted by Other than (Arch)diocese(s)

Mount Saint Mary's Seminary, Maryland
[Owned by a corporation of clerical and lay trustees; conducted by diocesan priests]

SS. Cyril and Methodius Seminary, Michigan
[Owned by a corporation; conducted by diocesan priests]

Pontifical College Josephinum School of Theology, Ohio
[Owned by a corporation; conducted by diocesan priests]

The Catholic University of America School of Religious Studies, Washington, D.C.
[Owned by the bishops of the United States]
   (Diocesan seminarians come mainly from Theological College operated by the Sulpicians; religious order seminarians come from other houses of formation)

The American College Catholic University of Louvain, Belgium
[Owned by United States Bishops and conducted by diocesan priests
from dioceses in the United States and Canada]
(Students attend the Catholic University of Louvain)

The Pontifical North American College, Rome
[Owned by United States Bishops and conducted by diocesan priests;
academic programs conducted by the Jesuits at the Gregorian University or the Dominicans at St. Thomas Aquinas University]

C. *Theologates Owned by (Arch)dioceses or Religious Orders and Conducted by Religious Orders for Diocesan Students*

Saint Patrick's Seminary, California
[Owned by the Archdiocese of San Francisco and conducted by the
Society of St. Sulpice]

Holy Apostles Seminary, Connecticut (M.S.S.A.)
[Owned and conducted by Missionaries of Holy Apostles]

Saint Meinrad School of Theology, Indiana (O.S.B.)
[Owned and conducted by Benedictine Monks of St. Meinrad
Archabbey]

St. Mary's Seminary & University, Maryland (S.S.)
[Owned and conducted by the Society of St. Sulpice]

Saint John's School of Theology, Seminary, Minnesota (O.S.B.)
[Owned and conducted by the Benedictines of St. John's Abbey]
   (Priesthood students from St. Cloud Diocesan Seminary and from
   St. John's Abbey)

Mount Angel Seminary, Oregon (O.S.B.)
[Owned and conducted by Benedictine Monks of Mount Angel]

Saint Vincent Seminary, Pennsylvania (O.S.B.)
[Owned and conducted by Benedictine Monks of St. Vincent
Archabbey]

Oblate School of Theology, Texas (O.M.I.)
[Owned and conducted by Missionary Oblates of Mary Immaculate]

Sacred Heart School of Theology, Wisconsin (S.C.J.)
[Owned and conducted by the Congregation of the Priests of the
Sacred Heart]

D. Theologates Owned and Conducted by Religious Orders for Religious Order Students

The Dominican School of Philosophy & Theology, California (O.P.)

Franciscan School of Theology, California (O.F.M.)

The Jesuit School of Theology at Berkeley, California (S.J.)

Dominican House of Studies, Washington, D.C. (O.P.)

Washington Theological Union, Washington, D.C. (many religious orders)

Catholic Theological Union, Illinois (many religious orders)

Moreau Seminary, Indiana (C.S.C.)
   (Students attend University of Notre Dame)

Weston Jesuit School of Theology, Massachusetts (S.J.)

Aquinas Institute of Theology, Missouri (O.P.)
   (Students take some courses at St. Louis University)

E. University-based Master of Divinity Programs for Lay Students

The Institute of Pastoral Studies at Loyola University, Chicago, Illinois

The Institute of Catholic Theological Studies at Seattle University, Seattle, Washington

Bibliography

■　　■　　　■　　　■　　　■　　　■　　　■　　　■　　　■

The 1997 Catholic Almanac. Huntington, Ind.: Our Sunday Visitor, 1997.

Abdul-Rahman, Mary. "Career Paths and Hiring Practices of Chief Academic Officers in Theological Schools." *Monographs on Academic Leadership* vol. 3. St. Paul: University of St. Thomas, 1996.

Appleby, R. Scott. "Crunch Time for American Catholicism." *Christian Century* 113 (April 3, 1996) 370–76.

____. "One Church, Many Cultures." *Church* 14, no. 2 (Summer 1998) 5–9.

____. "Present to the People of God: The Transformation of the Roman Catholic Parish Priesthood." In *Transforming Parish Ministry: The Changing Roles of Catholic Clergy, Laity, and Women Religious.* Jay P. Dolan, R. Scott Appleby, Patricia Byrne, and Debra Campbell. New York: Crossroad, 1989.

Ashley, Benedict M., O.P. "The Loss of Theological Unity: Pluralism, Thomism and Catholic Morality." In *Being Right: Conservative Catholics in America.* Eds. Mary Jo Weaver and R. Scott Appleby. Bloomington, Ind.: Indiana University Press, 1995.

Barna, George. *Baby Busters: The Disillusioned Generation.* Chicago: Northfield, 1994.

Baum, Cardinal William. "The State of U.S. Free-Standing Seminaries." *Origins* 16 (15 October 1986) 315.

Beaudoin, Thomas. *Virtual Faith: The Irreverent Spiritual Quest of Generation X Catholics.* San Francisco: Jossey-Bass, 1998.

Bellah, Robert et al. *Habits of the Heart: Individualism and Commitment in American Life.* Berkeley: University of California Press, 1985.

249

Bianchi, Eugene C. and Rosemary Radford Ruether, eds. *A Democratic Catholic Church: The Reconstruction of Roman Catholicism.* New York: Crossroad, 1992.

Blanchette, Melvin, S.S. "On Screening Seminarians through Behavioral Assessment and Psychological Testing." *Seminary Journal* 3 (Spring 1997).

Catalog. Cambridge, Mass.: Weston Jesuit School of Theology, 1997–1998.

Catalog. Columbus, OH: Pontifical College Josephinum, School of Theology, 1996–1998.

Catalog. Mundelein, Ill.: University of Saint Mary of the Lake, Mundelein Seminary, 1996–1997.

Catalog. San Antonio, Tex.: Oblate School of Theology, 1997–1999.

Catalog. St. Louis, Mo.: Kenrick-Glennon Seminary, 1996–1997.

Catalog. Weston, Mass.: Pope John XXIII National Seminary, 1995–1997.

Corrigan, John E. "Catechetics for Christian Living." *Worship* 39 (May 1965).

Cozzens, Donald B., ed. *The Spirituality of the Diocesan Priest.* Collegeville: The Liturgical Press, 1997.

D'Antonio, William V. et al. *Laity American and Catholic: Transforming the Church.* Kansas City, Mo.: Sheed and Ward, 1996.

Davidson, James D., Dean R. Hoge, and Ruth A. Wallace. *Laity: American and Catholic: Transforming the Church.* Kansas City, Mo.: Sheed and Ward, 1996.

Dolan, Jay P. *The American Catholic Experience.* New York: Doubleday, 1985.

Espín, Orlando. *The Faith of the People: Theological Reflections on Popular Catholicism.* Maryknoll, N.Y.: Orbis Books, 1997.

Finn, Virginia Sullivan. "Formation for Non-Ordained Ministry." *The Way* 56 (Summer 1986) 45.

Flannery, Austin P., O.P. ed. "Dogmatic Constitution on the Church." In *Documents of Vatican II.* Grand Rapids, Mich.: William B. Eerdmans, 1975.

____. *Vatican II.* Northport, N.Y.: Costello, 1996.

Harrington, Daniel. "How Can I Find God? Another Look." *America* 177, no. 5 (August 30, 1997) 11.

Hemrick, Eugene R. and Dean R. Hoge. *A Survey of Priests Ordained Five to Nine Years.* Washington, D.C.: National Catholic Education Association, Seminary Department, 1991.

_____. *Seminary Life and Visions of the Priesthood: A National Survey of Seminarians.* Washington, D.C.: National Catholic Educational Association, Seminary Department, 1987.

Hemrick, Eugene F. and James J. Walsh. *Seminarians in the Nineties: A National Study of Seminarians in Theology.* Washington, D.C.: National Catholic Educational Association, Seminary Department, 1993.

Hemrick, Eugene F. and Robert Wister. *Readiness for Theological Studies: A Study of Faculty Perceptions on the Readiness of Seminarians.* Washington, D.C.: National Catholic Educational Association, Seminary Department, 1993.

Hennessy, Paul K., ed. *A Concert of Charisms: Ordained Ministry in Religious Life.* New York: Paulist Press, 1997.

Hollinger, David A. *Post-Ethnic America: Beyond Multiculturalism.* New York: BasicBooks, 1995.

Holtz, Geoffrey T. *Welcome to the Jungle: The Why Behind Generation X.* New York: St. Martin's Griffin, 1995.

Immaculate Conception Seminary Academic Bulletin. South Orange, N.J.: Seton Hall School of Theology, 1991–1993.

John Paul II. "Pastores dabo vobis: Post-Synodal Apostolic Exhortation on the Formation of Priests in the Circumstances of the Present Day." *Origins* 21 (16 April 1992).

Krenik, Thomas W. "Formation for Celibate Chastity: A Resource Book." St. Paul: The Saint Paul Seminary School of Divinity of the University of St. Thomas, August 1996.

Laghi, Cardinal Pio. "Horizons and Limitations of the Catechism in Education." *Origins* 26 (24 April 1997).

Lee, Bernard J. *The Future Church of 140 B.C.E.: A Hidden Revolution.* New York: Crossroad, 1995.

Ludwig, Robert. *Reconstructing Catholicism for a New Generation.* New York: Crossroad, 1995.

McCarter, Neely Dixon. *The President As Educator: A Study of the Seminary Presidency.* Atlanta: Scholars Press, 1996.

McDonough, William C. *The Church in the Modern World: Re-reading* Gaudium et spes *After Thirty Years.* Ed. Anthony J. Cernera. Fairfield, Conn.: Sacred Heart University Press, 1997.

McLean, Jeanne P. "Leading From the Center: The Role of Chief Academic Officer." *Monographs on Academic Leadership* vol. 1. St. Paul: University of St. Thomas, 1996.

____. "Professional Development for Chief Academic Officers: A Call to Action." *Monographs on Academic Leadership* vol. 4. St. Paul: University of St. Thomas, 1996.

Nelson, Rob, and John Cowan. *Revolution X: A Survival Guide for Our Generation.* New York: Penguin Press, 1994.

Niebuhr, H. Richard. *Christ and Culture.* New York: Harper & Row, 1951.

Oates, Mary J. *The Catholic Philanthropic Tradition in America.* Bloomington, Ind.: Indiana University Press, 1995.

O'Malley, John W., S.J. "One Priesthood: Two Traditions." In *A Concert of Charisms: Ordained Ministry in Religious Life.* Ed. Paul K. Hennessy, C.F.C. New York: Paulist Press, 1997.

"Pastoring Prophetically in a Global Church." Unpublished paper. Berkeley: Jesuit School of Theology at Berkeley.

Porter, Jean. *The Recovery of Virtue.* Louisville: Westminster/John Knox, 1990.

Potvin, Raymond. *Seminarians of the Eighties: A National Survey.* Washington, D.C.: National Catholic Educational Association, Seminary Department, 1985.

Program of Priestly Formation. 4th ed. National Conference of Catholic Bishops, 1993.

Ristau, Karen M. "Challenges of Academic Administration: Rewards and Stresses in the Role of the Chief Academic Officer." *Monographs on Academic Leadership* vol. 2. St. Paul: University of St. Thomas, 1996.

Roof, Wade Clark and Lyn Gesch. "Boomers and the Culture of Choice." In *Work, Family and Religion in Contemporary Society.* Eds. Nancy Tatom Ammerman and Wade Clark Roof. New York and London: Routledge, 1995.

Rorty, Richard. *Objectivity, Relativism, and Truth: Philosophical Papers.* vol. 1. Cambridge: Cambridge University Press, 1991.

Ryan, Mary Perkins. *Are Parochial Schools the Answer? Catholic Education in the Light of the Council.* New York: Holt, Rinehart and Winston, 1964.

Schuth, Katarina. *Reason for the Hope: The Futures of Roman Catholic Theologates.* Wilmington: Michael Glazier, Inc., 1989.

_____. "Theological Education in Seminaries." In *Theological Education in the Catholic Tradition*. Eds. Patrick W. Carey and Earl C. Muller, S.J. New York: Crossroad, 1997.

Schwartz, Robert M. "Servant of the Servants of God: A Pastor's Spirituality." In *The Spirituality of the Diocesan Priest*. Ed. Donald B. Cozzens. Collegeville: The Liturgical Press, 1997.

Senior, Donald. "Scripture and Homiletics: What the Bible Can Teach the Preacher." *Worship* 65 (1991) 394.

Thiel, John E. *Nonfoundationalism*. Minneapolis: Fortress Press, 1994.

Weaver, Mary Jo and R. Scott Appleby, eds. *Being Right: Conservative Catholics in America*. Bloomington, Ind.: Indiana University Press, 1995.

_____. *What's Left: Liberal Catholics in America*. Forthcoming.

Wister, Robert, ed. *Priests: Identity and Ministry*. Wilmington: Michael Glazier, Inc., 1990.

Wister, Robert. "The Study of the Seminary Presidency in Catholic Theological Seminaries." *Theological Education* XXXII, Supplement I (1995).

Witherup, Ronald D. "The 'Intellectual' Formation of Priests." *The Priest* (August 1993) 49–51.

Index

Academic Deans, 105–109
Academic programs, 153–192
(*see also* Intellectual formation)
Accreditation, 61
Accomplishments, 231–235
Administration, 99–111, 232–233
    academic deans, 105–109
    other administrators, 109–111
    rectors/presidents, 99–105
    relationship with faculty, 105
    turnover, 102, 108
Admission, 35–36, 51, 65, 238
    policies, 34, 80
    requirements, 27–28, 33, 34
    screening, 27–28, 34
Advisers—*see* Formation, directors
Advisory boards—*see* Boards
African-American Catholics, 3, 12–13, 18–19, 201–202, 234
Asian-American Catholics, 3, 12–13, 18–19, 208, 212, 234
Assimilation, 18–19, 202
Association of Theological Schools, 61, 95, 104, 116, 233, 240
Authority, 45–46, 49–50, 208

Baum, Cardinal William, 25–26, 34
Benedictines, 61
Bible—*see* Sacred Scripture
Bishops, 24, 29 (*see also* Ordinaries)
Boards, 94–98
    education and role, 98
    membership, 96–98
    structure, 95–96 (*see also* Governance)

Candidates—*see* Students
Canon law, 80, 185
Catechetics—*see* Religious education
Catholic Common Ground Initiative, 45, 92, 216, 243
Catholicism, 3–7
    American, 1, 19–23
    knowledge of, 43–44
    "virtual," 16–17
Celibacy, 31, 138–139, 148
Center for Applied Research in the Apostolate (CARA), xviii, 58
Church
    in the United States, 1–23
    ministry, 207–223
    understanding mission, 61–63

Church history—*see* Historical studies

Clinical Pastoral Education (CPE), 200

Code of Canon Law—*see* Canon law

Collaboration, 32, 61, 63, 190, 220–223, 237–238

Collaborative model, 95, 127–131

Concerns, future, 235–242

Conference of Major Superiors of Men, 141

Confraternity of Christian Doctrine (CCD), 5, 8

Continuing education/formation, 28, 33, 34, 191–92

Critical method—*see* Historical and critical methods

Culture, 37, 42, 63–64, 169–171, 189, 209–212

Culture wars, 8–10, 11

Curriculum, 153–192
  positive features, 187–189
  problems, 189–192
  requirements, 155–157, 159, 163–164, 167–168, 173–174, 177–178, 182, 190–91

Degrees
  Master of Arts (M.A.), 157
  Master of Divinity (M.Div.), 155
  of academic deans, 107
  of faculty, 112–113
  of rectors/presidents, 101

Development, financial, 242

Diversity, 1–3, 31, 46–47, 66–67, 92–94, 212–216

Dogmatic Theology—*see* Systematic theology

Dominicans, 61

Ecclesiology, 7, 28, 166–168

Ecumenism, 32, 190, 208, 236–237

Education, academic—*see* Curriculum, Intellectual formation, Programs
  Field—*see* Field Education, Supervised ministry

Enrollment, 58–59, 238–240

Ethics—*see* Moral theology

Ethnic and cultural diversity of Church membership, 19, 208, 212–214

Eucharist, 145, 177–179

Evaluation
  of programs, 241–242
  of students, 148, 195–197, 204

Evangelization, 208, 212, 216–217

Faculty, 111–123
  as role models, 91–92, 116, 127
  attitudes, 116
  composition, 111–112
  development, 240
  education, 112–113
  hiring and retention, 113–115
  morale, 112–116
  relationship with students, 120–121
  role, 115–116
  scholarship, 115
  turnover, 113–115
  vocational status, 112–113

Field education, 192–206
  development, 192–193, 203–206
  directors, 197–198
  goals of, 193–197
  outcomes, 202–203
  structure and content, 198–202

Formation programs, 124–206
  academic/intellectual, 153–192
  changes, 124–126, 233–235
  contexts, 127–131
  directors, 131–133, 136–137, 145

evolution and development, 124–127
goals, 126–127
human, 133–139
implications of student backgrounds, 89–91
pastoral, 32
spiritual, 32, 131–153
Franciscans, 61
Freestanding model, 95

Gaudium et Spes, 61, 171
Generation X, 6, 12–14, 17
Generational differences, 3–8, 12
Governance, 94–98, 232–233 (*see also* Boards)

Hemrick, Eugene F., 74, 87
Hispanic-American Catholics, 3, 12–13, 18–19, 212, 234
Historical and critical methods, 158–159, 163–165
Historical Studies, 162–165
Homiletics, 183–185
Hope, xv–xvi, 214
Human formation, xx, 30, 35, 131–139
personnel, 131–133
programs, 133–139

Identity—*see* Priesthood, identity
Immigrants, 212–213
Integration, 61, 63
Intellectual formation, 32, 153–192 (*see also* Academic)
Interfaith relations, 32 (*see also* Ecumenism)

Jesuits, 61
Justice, 31, 49, 218–219

Lay
admission, 238–239
background, 84–85
formation, 126, 239–240

participation in theologates, 56–57, 141–143
scholarships, 239
students, 71–73, 215–216
transition to ministry, 192
Liturgy
celebration of, 144–145, 178–179
study of, 176–180
Lumen Gentium, 2, 168

Magisterium, 26, 34, 154, 158, 166, 169, 173
Mass—*see* Eucharist
Methodology of the study, xvi–xix
Ministry, 207–223
Mission of theologates, 26, 28, 54–66
changes, 36–39, 63–66
present status, 59–63
purpose, 54–56
values, 56–57, 61–66
Models, education, 63–64, 127–131 (*see also* Theologates, types)
Moral theology, 171–176
Multicultural society; multiracial society, 207–212 (*see also* Ethnic and cultural diversity)
Multicultural, 12–13, 18, 27, 46, 63–64, 180, 236
theological, 8–11, 14–18, 23, 28, 66
tolerance of, 44–45

National Catholic Education Association (NCEA), 27, 34, 100, 104, 133, 233, 240
National Conference of Catholic Bishops (NCCB), 27, 55, 97 (*see also The Program of Priestly Formation*)
New Age religion, 7

Optatam Totius, 24, 61, 142, 181

Ordinaries, 26–29 (*see also* Bishops and Religious superiors)

Parish, 23, 35–53
  expectations, 41–51
  implications for seminary education, 51–53
  leadership, 36, 41–42, 49–50
  membership, 42–43
  participation, 38–41
Pastoral
  care and counseling, 185–186 (*see also* Field Education)
  leadership, 41–42, 49–50, 221
  pastoral studies, 180–187
  theology—*see* Theology, pastoral
Pastores dabo vobis (PDV), xix, 24, 29–30, 55, 60, 63, 79, 86, 124, 134, 139, 141, 154, 158, 166, 167, 171, 177, 181, 224, 233
Peace, 31
Personnel—*see* Administration, Faculty
Planning, 241–242
Polarization, 66, 244
Prayer, 143–147
Preaching, 183–185, 219
Pre-theology, 33, 109, 156–157, 190, 234–235
Presbyterorum Ordinis, 61
Presidents/rectors—*see* Rectors/presidents
Priesthood
  definition, 26
  identity, 28–29, 31–32, 34, 223–230
  orders, 34–35
  pastoral expectations, 36–38, 47–51
  role, 35–36, 41, 226–227
  spirituality, 140–142
Program of Priestly Formation (PPF), xix, 24–35, 55, 60, 112, 125, 134, 145, 148, 150, 153, 154, 156, 158, 166, 167–168,

171, 176, 181–183, 185–186, 190, 221, 228, 237
Programs—*see* Formation programs

Rectors/presidents, 99–105
  appointment of, 102
  education, 101
  role of, 32, 100, 102–104
  title, 100
Religious superiors
  life, 32–33
  orders, 229
Religious education
  curriculum, 186, 190
  need for, 212–213, 216, 217–218
Respect for life, 31

Sacred Congregation for Catholic Education, 25–26
Sacred Scripture, 157–162
Scholarships, 239
Screening process—*see* Admission
Second Vatican Council, 2, 4, 7, 9–10, 210–211
Seminarians—*see* Students
Seminaries, 24–35
  national developments, 26–35
  Vatican influences, 25–26
Seminary education/formation
  implications of background, 89–94
  parish relationships, 51–53
Sexuality, 90–91 (*see also* Celibacy)
Site visits, xvii
Spiritual, advisers, 132–133
  direction, 147–149
  directors, 32
  formation, xx, 32, 33, 139–143
Spiritual formation, 149–153
Spirituality, 149–153
  content, 143–149
  diocesan, 140–141

intensives, 149–153
lay, 141–142
Sponsorship, 245–248
Students, 66–94
    age, 241
    composition, 58–59, 88–89
    cultural considerations, 88–89
    human profiles, 85–88
    intellectual profiles, 79–85
    lay, 71–73, 215–216 (*see also*
        Lay)
    numbers, 58–59
    qualities of, 85–88
    religious background, 74–79,
        189–190
    seminarians, 68–71
Sulpicians, 61, 133
Supervised Ministry—*see* Field
    Education
Systematic theology, 166–171

Teaching, methods, 121, 188
    (*see also* Faculty)
Technology, 235, 242
Theologates, 245–248
    definition, xvii
    numbers, 56
    purpose of, 56, 59–60

types, 127–131
Theological reflection, 196
Theology
    historical, 162–165
    liturgical, 176–180
    moral, 171–176
    pastoral, 180–187
    systematic, 166–171
Third Plenary Council of Balti-
    more, xiii
Training—*see* Curriculum, For-
    mation programs
Transition, 34

Union model, 113
Unitatis Redintegratio, 168
University relationship, 95

Vatican visitations of seminaries,
    24–26
Vision, 207
Vocation directors, xviii

Wabash Center, 188, 240
Women
    on faculties, 189
    relationships with, 214, 222
    religious, 196